KNOW

Turning *the* Christian Life

BE

Right Side Up

DO

LARRY ALAN THOMPSON

WESTBOW
PRESS®
A DIVISION OF THOMAS NELSON
& ZONDERVAN

The Holy Bible, New International Version®, NIV® Copyright © 1973, 1978, 1984, 2011 by Biblica, Inc.® Used by permission. All rights reserved worldwide.

Scripture taken from the King James Version of the Bible.

Scripture quotations taken from the New American Standard Bible®, Copyright © 1960, 1962, 1963, 1968, 1971, 1972, 1973, 1975, 1977, 1995 by The Lockman Foundation. Used by permission. (www.Lockman.org)

Scripture taken from the Holman Christian Standard Bible ® Copyright © 2003, 2002, 2000, 1999 by Holman Bible Publishers. All rights reserved.

WestBow Press books may be ordered through booksellers or by contacting:

WestBow Press
A Division of Thomas Nelson & Zondervan
1663 Liberty Drive
Bloomington, IN 47403
www.westbowpress.com
1 (866) 928-1240

ISBN: 978-1-5127-3567-3 (sc)
ISBN: 978-1-5127-3568-0 (hc)
ISBN: 978-1-5127-3566-6 (e)

Library of Congress Control Number: 2016905255

Print information available on the last page.

WestBow Press rev. date: 05/12/2016

CONTENTS

PROLOGUE

In the beginning, God created the world right side up.

Ever since, man has lived mostly upside down. God made man and woman to *know* Him, to *be* in His image. Satan immediately twisted the truth, deceiving them into believing that life is a doubtful list of *dos* and *don'ts*.

Next, God chose Israel to *know* Him in a special way, to *be* His children. Yet they repeatedly neglected their relationship with the Father and got lost in a dry desert of laws and obligations.

Then God started fresh with the church. A few centuries later, Christ was no longer the Head. Instead, the rules ruled.

Christians through the ages? Same old story. Take God's right-side-up world. Flip the truth upside down. It's nothing new.

Consider the Pharisee and the tax collector (@Luke 18:9–14). The Pharisee was focused on what he *did* and what others *didn't do*. He prayed, "God, I thank You that I'm not like other people—greedy, unrighteous, adulterers, or even like this tax collector. I fast twice a week; I give a tenth of everything I get" @Luke 18:11. He was focused on himself. He was focused on *doing*.

The tax collector? He was focused on his relationship with God. "But the tax collector, standing far off, would not even raise his eyes to heaven but kept striking his chest and saying, 'God, turn Your wrath from me—a sinner!'" @Luke 18:13.

The Pharisee began with *do* and never made it to God.

The sinner began with a desire to *know* God, to connect with Him. He saw who he was in God's eyes, and in the end, went home justified.

"Everyone who exalts himself will be humbled, but the one who humbles himself will be exalted" @Luke 18:14.

In the upside-down world, you exalt yourself.

In the right-side-up world, you exalt God and humble yourself. Then you will *be* justified.

In the upside-down world, you begin with *do*. You begin with you.

In the right-side-up world, you begin with *know*. You begin with God.

Are you living upside down? Are you weary from the frustration, futility, and failure of always *doing* but never doing enough?

Then hang on, and get ready to let your world roll right side up. Get ready to *know* Him like never before, to *be* who you truly are in Christ, and *do* more than you ever thought possible through Him.

Know. Be. Do.

BOOK ONE

Chapter 1

MY JOURNEY

The last day of school.

As a 12-year old boy coming home from Glendover Elementary School, my mind was racing faster than my skinny legs could churn. Once at home inside my room, I got down to business. I looked around at the walls of my bedroom. One wall lined with hot-rod cars I had drawn. Another lined with neat shelves holding dozens of model cars I had built. In a corner was my most prized possession: a copy of the Official Revell Master Modeler's Club quarterly magazine for members only. One issue contained a drawing of a car I had submitted and they had published. And there below the drawing was my name—in print! A real magazine with my creation and my byline. I had done it! I drew it. I sent it. And they liked it. I fed on the sense of accomplishment, of doing something that was published, that would last for a long time. It was a feeling that later sparked a career in ad copy and design.

With the whole summer before me, my mind began to think through the possibilities. I thought how I didn't want to get to the end of summer and have nothing to show for it, so I took out a piece of paper and began a list. A to-do list. "Goals for the Summer." I carefully thought through all the things that I had been wanting to do—the cars to draw, the books to read, the things to build, the places to go, the things to learn more about—all the things I wanted to be able to say, "I did it!" by the end of summer.

Looking back on it now, I wonder how I ever became such a nerdy kid. I could have been outside playing already. I could have flat been doin' nothin', because it's summertime, and that's OK. But even at such a wide-eyed age, I had this drive inside me to *do* things. To accomplish. To publish. To finish. I was a *doer*.

One of my favorite things to do was assemble model cars. To this day, I still remember with remarkable clarity a rare and relished compliment my father gave me in the presence of my mother. "That Larry is good at following instructions." See, you had to follow instructions carefully in order to assemble a model car. Each kit came with a detailed set of step-by-step instructions, and you had to follow each one exactly, in precise order. If you tried to skip ahead to something more fun, the motor might not fit in the engine compartment or you might get glue on your fresh paint job. Oh, the *horror*! You had to do it right. And when it was finished, the best part was sitting back and admiring what you *did*.

As I got older, I never outgrew making to-do lists. In fact, I got better at doing it. I made multiple lists. Books to read. Things to learn more about. Home projects to complete. Work projects to accomplish. Personal goals. Spiritual goals. I needed a list of all my lists!

Accomplishing things on my to-do lists made me feel good. Validated. Productive. Accomplished. Nothing matched the feeling of completing a task and—the grand finale!—*crossing the item off the to-do list*. Oh, what bliss! Another item checked off! Sometimes, when I did something that wasn't on my to-do list, I would add it after the fact, just so I could cross it off and relish the sense of accomplishment that only came from achieving something on my official to-do list. Done!

JUST DO IT

It's the American way—although really, it's basic human nature. We're a people of doers. We build. We write. We plant. We drive. We compute. We entertain. We design. We explore. We manufacture. We practice medicine. We get degrees. We work, and we play—hard. We just do it.

We measure success by our accomplishments. What you do determines where you get to live, how nice your cars are, what school you graduate from, what status goes on your Facebook page.

When you meet someone, especially if you're a man, what's the first question that comes out of your mouth? "What do you *do*?" We want to quickly size up someone based on his or her occupation. We are defined by what we do.

The modern church is no different. When we're shopping around for a church, the first thing we want to look at is the church's long list of "ministries," meaning things that church members can do together or for others. We even have "Activities Ministries." If you want to be a growing Christian, you better remember "Three to Thrive," that is, attend all three services each week—Sunday morning, Sunday evening, and Wednesday evening.

I grew up in one of those churches. Since it was all I had ever known, I didn't realize it at the time, but the focus was clearly on *doing*. Like the world around us, we measured success as a Christian in terms of what you *did*—and perhaps even more importantly, what you *didn't do*. We had an approved list of activities: attending services, dressing a certain way, wearing your hair a certain way, saying certain things a certain way, carrying the right version of the Bible, and saying "amen" at the right time during the sermon. But what really got people excited was the list of things we didn't do: go to certain movies (or better yet, any movies), dance, drink, wear long hair (if you're male) or short hair (if you're female). It was the ol' "Don't drink, cuss, smoke, or chew—or go with girls who do." Of course, in our church in the middle of Kentucky tobacco country, we made exceptions if the deacons wanted to go out and light up their "burnt offerings."

So by the time I finally figured out that faith is not something that you muster up within (that is, that's it's not something you "do") and genuinely accepted Christ as Lord and Savior at age 19, my concept of Christianity was pretty well warped and bent toward one word: *Do*. I was saved by grace through faith, but it took me several years to figure out that "the just shall *live* by faith" @Galatians 3:11. I understood that we are *saved* by faith, but it took some time for me to get it, that we *lived*, we *walked* the

Christian life the same way we *received* it—by faith. That journey and what I learned on it is the subject of this book, and looking back at it now, I feel a bit like Christian from *The Pilgrim's Progress*, stumbling through life and making discoveries along the way. Each time I scaled a new summit, I discovered that this new peak was simply the vantage point that revealed an even higher summit, an even clearer perspective of God. As I trekked forward on this guided tour with Christ, He showed me that *do* is not the starting point in the Christian life, and it's not the destination. It's not the focal point. It's not the defining characteristic. And it's not the cause. It's the effect.

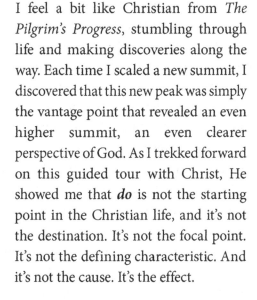

> **Do is not the starting point in the Christian life, and it's not the destination. It's not the focal point. It's not the defining characteristic. And it's not the cause. It's the effect.**

STILL ANOTHER TO-DO LIST

Like the boy who ran home on the last day of school and made a to-do list for the dawning summer break, the first thing I did as a brand-new, 19-year old Christian was make a to-do list of sins that I needed to *stop doing.* I had resolved to stop doing some of these things in the past—which usually lasted a day or so. But now I was a new creation in Christ. "If anyone is in Christ, he is a new creation; old things have passed away, and look, new things have come" @2 Corinthians 5:17.

Jesus Christ—He was certainly a *doer.* He made a voyage to Earth, had an amazing ministry filled with miracles and powerful preaching and teaching, allowed Himself to be crucified, and then arose from the grave. Now, it is finished. He *did* it.

What's more, I had a powerful new Helper on my side. The Holy Spirit. Now there's a doer. The Bible even calls Him a "Helper." "But the Helper, the Holy Spirit, whom the Father will send in my name, he will teach you all things and bring to your remembrance all that I have said to you" @John 14:26.

Of course, I also had a new Father, the Father of all Doers, God the Father, the One Who created the Heavens and the Earth, along with the other two Persons of the Trinity. The One Who *gave*, gave His Son and gives us life. The One Who will call His children home one day. The One Who will judge.

So, I was in pretty good company when it comes to getting things done. And I began working my way down the list. Stop smoking pot. Check. Stop drinking. Check. Stop looking at women. OK, still working on that one. Start reading my Bible daily. Check. Start having a daily quiet time. Check. Start sharing my faith. Check.

Before you know it, I was fitting in pretty well down at the church where I had learned that the key to the Christian life could be summed up in one word:

Do.

After all, you had the Ten Commandments—the ultimate To-Do List—and a whole bevy of commands throughout the Old and New Testaments, enough to keep me busy for eternity. All I needed to do was focus on the to-do list and not forget to enlist the help of the Holy Trinity.

I think I've got this figured out.

I HAVE A CONFESSION.

Hi, my name is Larry, and I am a recovering legalist.

It didn't take me long to figure out that I didn't have this figured out. Along the way, I began to become aware of this concept of "legalism." It turns out it's nothing really new or unique to the church. In fact, the Apostle Paul wrote a whole book about it to another church that suffered from the same malady, the Galatians.

Legalism focuses on the externals, the behaviors, the things others can observe about you. It's one ditch on the side of the road. The ditch on the other side of the road is "libertinism." This one is also focused on outward behaviors, but whereas Legalists know what they believe and tend to be mad about it, Libertines revel in God's lavish grace, and they are delighted about it. Legalists make lists of to-dos and not-to-dos. Libertines can't think of much that shouldn't be on the to-do list in the first place—it's all good.

So the goal of the Christian life, I surmised, was to keep it between the lines. Of course, with my background, I walked as close as I could to the edge of the Legalism ditch. In fact, I formulated my philosophy into a pithy slogan which I shared with my legalistic friends.

"Legalism and love have the same behavior but different motives."

Actually, there's a lot of truth in that, and I was beginning to think more and more about motives. "If I speak human or angelic languages but do not have love, I am a sounding gong or a clanging cymbal" @1 Corinthians 13:1. That Scripture kept ringing in my ear. I was beginning to understand that there was something deeper than merely the external *doing*. The inner man was emerging in my Christian consciousness. I was beginning to discover that there was another dimension to the Christian life behind *do*, and that was...

Be.

When I was saved I *became* a new creation. I wasn't the same person I was before. The old Larry was dead. "I have been crucified with Christ; and it is no longer I who live, but Christ lives in me; and the *life* which I now live in the flesh I live by faith in the Son of God, who loved me and gave Himself up for me" @Galatians 2:20. They should have made me an honorary member of the First Church of Galatians, because Paul has to keep reminding this ol' legalist of the same thing: I am all-new.

As this began to sink in, *doing* seemed to become easier, more natural—or maybe I should say, more supernatural—because I was focused on *being* who I am in Christ, and letting Christ *be* Who He is in me. All the self-effort I put into mustering up the unction to do what I should looked like a little kid trying to act like a grown up compared with the Strongman I was and am in Christ. So I felt like I'd cracked the code. Focus on *be*, and *do* will take care of itself. Cool!

I even invented a little shorthand motto for my new discovery:

Be = Do

> **Do without Be is hypocrisy.**
> **Be without Do is complacency.**
> **But when Be = Do, that's integrity.**

It's actually a pretty good definition of integrity. In the life of a person of true integrity, Be = Do. If the two don't align, there's no integrity.

Do without Be is hypocrisy.

Be without Do is complacency.

But when Be = Do, that's integrity.

So I focused on *being* who I am in Christ. I read an excellent book entitled *The Search for Significance* by Robert McGee that really helped me see myself as God sees me:

"I am deeply loved by God. I am completely forgiven and am fully pleasing to God. I am totally accepted by God. I am a new creation, complete in Christ."

Remarkably, this new self-concept full of Christ-esteem fueled a drive for obedience that legalism could never muster. I was growing and learning to love the Christian life all the more.

I look back at my years of focusing on *do* as my Christian childhood. It was a time of learning to obey. When I became more aware of who I am in Christ, I grew up some, and began to focus not just on "what" but also on "why." "Be" was progress, but I was essentially a Christian adolescent. And just when I thought I knew it all, God showed me that Be wasn't the final destination. There was one more door to go through, one more room to abide in, the inner sanctum, the "Holy of Holies"…

Know.

Knowing God. If God lives in me, and Who I am is defined by Who He is, then I can never fully *be* who God wants me to be until I understand more about Who He is. The Great I AM. I AM changes who I am. His being gives life and light to my being. Focusing on *knowing* Him informs who I am which in turn inspires what I do.

So I had a new focus. Knowing God. Know God, and Be takes care of itself. Be who you are in God, and Do takes care of itself.

Know. Be. Do.

It all made sense now. But I hadn't arrived spiritually. I had really just begun.

Chapter 2

KNOW

"Hello, Man. My name is God. Allow Me to introduce Myself..."

Excellent. What then would you expect God to tell you about Himself right off the bat?

"I love you"?

"I will comfort you"?

"I will never leave you"?

"I will redeem you from your sin"?

I would expect a PR-polished, politically correct, put-on-your-best-Facebook-front introduction.

But God...well, He's complicated.

To Adam, He says, "You are free, *but*..." Turns out the "but" came back to bite him.

To Job, whose story is recorded in the Bible's oldest book, God thundered, "I'll ask the questions around here. You just listen." Job had a devil of a time figuring God out, but he finally shut up and listened.

To Moses, He said, "Tell 'em I AM sent you." Enough said.

To Saul/Paul, God demanded, "Why fight me? Now get up and get going." I'm one Gentile who's glad Paul got the message—and delivered.

Turns out, it pays to listen to God. And what He says, well, it's not always what you might expect.

Let's just get that out on the table. Yes, God *is* complicated. Yes, sometimes He's hard to understand. Yes, He doesn't always tell us what we want to hear. And yes, we have a lot of questions about what He says.

But don't forget this is God we're talking about here. The One Who speaks one word and a new galaxy comes into existence. The One Who has an answer for every question—and usually a question for every one of our answers. He is the universe's most awesome, powerful, smart, creative, rich, loving, any-and-all-positive-superlatives-you-want-to-add Being.

The most amazing part? He *wants you to know Him.* Don't let that go by too quickly. Pause for a moment right now and just ponder that thought. God, the CEO of the universe, wants you to *know* Him. I couldn't get 60 seconds with Bill Gates, Warren Buffet, or the President of the United States, but the One Who owns everything they have and everything else, too, wants me to know Him.

Perhaps even more remarkably, He already knows all about me—and yet He *still* wants me to know Him. He's *dying* for us to get to know Him. In fact, God the Son *did* die so that we could know Him. But I'm getting ahead of the story.

In the beginning, was the Word. A word is something designed to communicate from a sender to a receiver. God wanted us to get the message about Him, So sent His Word—both in the flesh and in writing.

THE AUTOBIOGRAPHY OF GOD

God wanted so much to make sure that we got to know Him, He wrote a book about Himself.

The Bible.

Penned by men, inspired by God the Spirit, the Bible is literally the Autobiography of God. It's not just history, it's *His story.* It's a story that's rolled out precisely the way He knew that man needed to receive it. It gives us everything we need to know about Him and nothing we don't. *Nothing we*

> Trying to communicate an infinite God to a finite mind is already like trying to put *War and Peace* into a 140-character Tweet.

don't. That's no small point. Because trying to communicate an infinite God to a finite mind is already like trying to put *War and Peace* into a 140-character Tweet. He knows exactly how much we can absorb about Him. And that's exactly what He wrote.

His Autobiography is the primary way to know Him, but it's not the only way. From the beginning, God wanted man to know about Him. He created a universe with heavens that shout His glory.

> *The heavens declare the glory of God, and the sky proclaims the work of His hands. @Psalm 19:1*

He walked and talked with Adam in the Garden. He made covenants with Noah and Abraham. He engraved His expectations with His own finger on tablets containing the Ten Commandments. He created a whole nation whose history would speak volumes about Him. He rose up prophets who would act as His spokesmen. Then He Himself became a man, the Divine Communication. The Word. "In the beginning was the Word... The Word became flesh and took up residence among us. We observed His glory" @John 1:1, 14.

God wanted man to know Him so much He planned a full-on multimedia campaign. He broadcast it through the heavens. He printed it on paper. He spoke it at seminars. He created His own world wide web, Paul and his broad band of fellow missionaries—from the first century until today. And if that wasn't enough, He transmitted from Heaven to Earth the ultimate Medium, the God-Man Jesus Christ, Who wrote the message in blood. Indeed, God went out of His way to communicate Himself so that man could *know* Him.

Making sure that everyone had a channel to respond to, God used five "media" to reveal Himself, a Romans Road of Revelation:

Creation.

> *Since what can be known about God is evident among them, because God has shown it to them. For His invisible attributes, that is, His eternal power and divine nature, have been clearly seen since*

the creation of the world, being understood through what He has made. As a result, people are without excuse. @Romans 1:19–20

Man's heart.

So, when Gentiles, who do not have the law, instinctively do what the law demands, they are a law to themselves even though they do not have the law. They show that the work of the law is written on their hearts. Their consciences confirm this. Their competing thoughts will either accuse or excuse them. @Romans 2:14–15

Word.

But now, apart from the law, God's righteousness has been revealed—attested by the Law and the Prophets—that is, God's righteousness through faith in Jesus Christ, to all who believe, since there is no distinction. @Romans 3:21–22

History.

They are Israelites, and to them belong the adoption, the glory, the covenants, the giving of the law, the temple service, and the promises. The ancestors are theirs, and from them, by physical descent, came the Messiah, who is God over all, praised forever. Amen. @Romans 9:4–5

Jesus.

Now to Him who has power to strengthen you according to my gospel and the proclamation about Jesus Christ, according to the revelation of the mystery kept silent for long ages but now revealed and made known through the prophetic Scriptures, according to the command of the eternal God to advance the obedience of faith among all nations. @Romans 16:25–26

Yes, God thought of everything when it came to revealing Himself. Even the very language He chose for the New Testament itself says much about the fact that He wanted *every*one to get the message. He chose the Greek language, the most universal language of the day. It's a language that excels in precision and clarity. And God didn't write it in classical Greek, but in Koine Greek, the common street language of the day. He wanted not just the intellectual elite, but *every*one to know. Then God made sure it lasted through all the centuries and was translated into hundreds of languages. It's the most widely distributed, widely read, widely studied book of the ages—all so we could *know* Him.

Contrast the God Who created man with the gods that man created. Through the ages, man- made gods have tended to be aloof, distant, indifferent, unconcerned with man. They're hard to get to know. They have little desire to have a relationship with mere mortals. How different the one true God is! He not only walks and talks with man. He became a Man. He did it all so we could truly *know* Him.

WHY MAN?

Why is it that every newly married couple seems to get a dog right off the bat? I suppose it's like training-wheels for starting a family later. But all too soon, the responsibility they bit off turns out to be more than they can chew, and the dog seems to be doing more than his share of chewing— furniture, shoes, curtains. By about the third call to the carpet cleaners, they're wondering what they were thinking.

Sometimes I wonder if God didn't get that feeling in the Garden of Eden. He created a perfect environment. He created two perfect people. And before He knew it, they were chewing something they weren't supposed to.

Of course, God in His foreknowledge wasn't taken by surprise at this development, but we have to wonder what the Holy Trinity was thinking when they decided to make man.

Let's be clear about one thing right up front. The creation of the world wasn't out of need or weakness in the fellowship of the Trinity. God didn't *need* to make man because God doesn't need *any*thing. The Holy Trinity is self-sufficient and fully satisfied. Within Itself, the Trinity enjoys all the love and community it needs. Being worshipped and glorified and loved doesn't add one iota of value to Its Persons. God the Father, God the Son, and God the Spirit weren't bored one day and decided to create a pet—mankind. In fact, the Bible doesn't tell us exactly *what* prompted God to create man. It simply says that we were created because it was God's will.

> *You have created all things, and because of Your will they exist and were created.* *@Revelation 4:11*

If an all-powerful, all-knowing Being decides something is His will, that's mind-blowing enough for me.

The Bible does say that God takes pleasure in us.

> *For the LORD takes pleasure in His people.* *@Psalm 149:4*

Now there's a refreshing thought. We can make God smile!

The Bible does tell us that we were created in His image, and that means many of the things that bring God pleasure bring us pleasure. Loving. Serving. Sharing. Likewise, many of the things that bring us pleasure—in their purest form—bring God pleasure. Fellowship. Friendship. Companionship. Man was created out of an overflow of love in the Holy Trinity.

To sum up: Smile, God loves you. Love, and God smiles at you.

The Holy Trinity—God the Father, God the Son, and God the Spirit—know and enjoy one another to an infinite degree. They know what each other are thinking. They finish one another's sentences. They never disagree. They always coexist in complete love, peace, and joy. They're the original BFFs—Best Friends Forever.

Man, being created in God's image, has this same yearning for intimate fellowship with God and with one another. Like the Holy Trinity Itself, we have in our DNA an innate desire to be one with God and with one another.

> *I am in them and You are in Me.*
> *May they be made completely one,*
> *so the world may know You have sent Me*

and have loved them as You have loved Me.
@John 17:23

What a picture of oneness! This remarkable verse is a portion of a prayer that Jesus offered to His Father on our behalf. Get a mental picture of this. God the Father is in Jesus. And Jesus is in us. And all of us are in unity. All wrapped in the same love that God loved His own Son.

One. Love.

When our daughters were young, I used to take them on Daddy-Daughter camping trips. One time we went to one of Kentucky's natural rock bridges, an amazing 30-foot high rock arch carved right out of the top of a mountain ridge. To get on top, you had to climb a ladder made of logs. My daughter was too young to climb the ladder on her own, so I picked her up and told her to wrap her arms around my neck and hold on tight, because my arms would be occupied climbing the ladder. She did exactly as instructed, wrapping her arms and legs around me so tightly I could barely breathe. As we started up the ladder, she got scared, her grip got tighter, and she began repeating over and over, "I love you, Daddy. I love you, Daddy. I love you, Daddy." She never stopped saying it, all the way up the ladder. Finally, we made it to the top. And she relaxed her grip as her feet touched down on the solid rock bridge. We had done it—together. We were one unit as we climbed the ladder, unified and wrapped in love.

One. Love.

CREATED TO KNOW

So here we are. God and man. Now what?

I'm pretty sure it's not just a case of God needing a gardener. He's got quite the green thumb. And I'm quite certain it's not all about us. He is God. And we are not. Period. But we're here. God. Us. What now?

This is eternal life:
that they may know You, the only true God,
and the One You have sent—Jesus Christ.
@John 17:3

To *know* Him.

This is life.

This is eternal life. This is abundant life here on earth. This is the purpose for which we are created. To *know* God—Father, Son, and Spirit.

Now everybody knows that *know* has different levels. I know *about* the President. I know a *lot* about him. I know him as my President. But I don't really *know* him. I don't know him as a friend. He doesn't know me.

I once served at a 30,000-member church, and some viewed the Pastor as a bit of a celebrity. He said people sometimes asked to get together with him because "they wanted to get to know him better." He said, however, in reality, they already knew him quite well. For 30 years, he had poured out his heart to them three times a week from the pulpit. The pastor said what they really meant is that they wanted *him* to get to know *them*. He wanted to know all his members, but he was only one man with a flock of 30,000.

God knows each one of His creatures. All seven billion on the planet. Plus the billions that came before. Now that's a mega flock!

Furthermore, He knows everything about us. He knows more about us than we know ourselves.

Even the hairs of your head have all been counted. @Matthew 10:30

He knows our thoughts and our subconscious thoughts. He knows our motives and our deceptions. He knows our past, our present, our future. God knows.

But what He wants above all else is for us to get to know Him.

Be still, and know that I am God. @Psalm 46:10

WHAT DOES *KNOW* MEAN?

Relax, I'm not giving a lecture on Greek here, but I mentioned before that Greek has advantages over English in its precision and clarity. An example is the word *know.* Greek has two words for the concept of *know.* One is *eido.* That's the common word for *know* in the sense of awareness or perceiving. The other word for *know* is *ginosko.* This word has the idea of coming to know through personal experience. It involves a relationship between the person knowing and the person known.

John, the disciple whom Jesus loved, is the *know* author of the New Testament. *Ginosko* know is used 246 times in the New Testament—96 of them by John. That's 40 percent of the *knows* in the New Testament, even though he wrote only about 18 percent of it. He used the word about twice as often as the average New Testament writer. He *knows* a thing or two about *knowing*.

A good example is the following passage in his first letter. He uses *know* seven times in six verses:

> I have written these things to you who believe in the name of the Son of God, so that you may **know** that you have eternal life.

> Now this is the confidence we have before Him: Whenever we ask anything according to His will, He hears us. And if we **know** that He hears whatever we ask, we **know** that we have what we have asked Him for….

> We **know** that everyone who has been born of God does not sin, but the One who is born of God keeps him, and the evil one does not touch him.

> We **know** that we are of God, and the whole world is under the sway of the evil one.

> And we **know** that the Son of God has come and has given us understanding so that we may **KNOW** the true One. We are in the true One—that is, in His Son Jesus Christ. He is the true God and eternal life.

> @1 John 5:13–15, 18–20

The first six times we see *know* in this passage, it's the *eido* kind of *know*, your run-of-the-mill *knowing*, as in awareness. The final time, however, in verse 20...

> *so that we may* **KNOW** *the true One*

...John uses *ginosko*. In English, it's still translated *know*, so it's hard for us to see. But to the original readers, it was quite plain here that John was shifting gears from knowing things *about* God to truly *knowing* Him.

Personally.

Relationally.

Intimately.

This type of *ginosko* knowing is the same word that is used when Mary said to the angel,

> *"How can this be, since I do not* **know** *a man?" @Luke 1:34*

It's the same *ginosko* knowing that the Lord will use one day at judgment,

> *On that day many will say to Me, "Lord, Lord, didn't we prophesy in Your name, drive out demons in Your name, and do many miracles in Your name?: Then I will announce to them, "I never* **knew** *you! Depart from Me, you lawbreakers!" @Matthew 7:22–23*

It's the same *ginosko* knowing that Jesus described,

> *My sheep hear My voice, I* **know** *them, and they follow Me. @John 10:27*

Like a husband and wife *know* each other. Like a master and a servant *know* each other. Like a sheep and a shepherd *know* each other. That's the kind of *know* that that God desires between us and Him. Bonding with Him at the highest level.

One church I served used to present a passion play every Easter. A large musical production, the presentation used live animals including baby lambs. One year, a particular baby lamb had a "starring" role in the presentation, themed *His Sacrifice, My Substitute.* The lamb became part of the cast as it rehearsed night after night with the actors and musicians. When the production was over, the lamb returned to the farm different, distant. The farmer made a discovery, however. Whenever he needed to get the lamb's attention, he played the theme song from the passion play. Immediately, the lamb would perk up and begin to follow the music. The lamb knew the tune and made the connection with his master.

My wife does that with me when we get separated in a large store. She has a particular note that she whistles as she walks around, and if I'm within earshot, I immediately recognize it. I'm sure she gets some strange looks from other shoppers, but it brings us together. They know (*eido*) she's whistling, but only I know (*ginosko*) what she means.

KNOWING GOD—OUR HIGHEST CALLING

I've always had a drive inside me to distill things down to their simplest form. The irreducible essence. It's a game I play to help me remember and focus on the most important things. In journalism and advertising school this was ingrained in us—take the complex and make it simple. David Ogilvy, the "Father of Advertising," wrote in a memo of 10 tips to his employees, "Never write more than two pages on any subject." Consequently, it's actually a real challenge for me to write a full-length book.

So as I related in the first chapter, I began this distilling process when I became a Christian. I thought I had it with the word *do*. And then *be* superseded *do*. And now I see that *know* is the highest calling of the Christian. To *know* God.

Billy Graham put it this way:

> Have you ever wondered why God put you on earth, what is the purpose and meaning of life? It is to know Him, and to know His love.

But wait a minute, you may say. Isn't *love* our highest calling?

Now these three remain: faith, hope, and love. But the greatest of these is love. @1 Corinthians 13:13

But how can you love someone—or love others *because* of someone—that you do not *know*?

How can you have faith in someone that you do not *know*?

How can you have hope in someone that you do not *know*?

To the degree that you *know* someone, you can love more deeply. You can believe in more faithfully. You can hope in more earnestly.

But, you may say, isn't praising and worshipping our ultimate objective?

Again, I say, how can you praise and worship someone that you do not *know*?

But, you may protest, what about evangelism and discipleship? Isn't that our primary assignment?

How can you tell others about someone that you do not *know* yourself?

But, you may say, what about bringing Him glory? Surely that is the chief end of man. After all, it's right there in the Westminster Shorter Catechism:

Man's chief end is to glorify God, and to enjoy him forever.

Indeed, glorifying God and enjoying Him forever is our purpose, the reason we were created. But again, how can you bring glory to and enjoy someone that you do not *know*?

Knowing God supersedes everything else because it is the supreme *cause.* Everything else—being, doing, loving, believing, hoping, praising, worshipping, evangelizing, glorifying, enjoying—is an *effect.*

Knowing God is priority one. Out of it flows all the rest of the Christian life.

The one who does not love does not know God, because God is love. @1 John 4:8

Are you not loving? It's because you don't *know* God.

> Knowing God supersedes everything else because it is the supreme cause. Everything else—being, doing, loving, believing, hoping, praising, worshipping, evangelizing, glorifying, enjoying—is an *effect*.

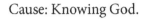

Cause: Knowing God.

Effect: Love.

The more you know Him, the more you will love. The more you know Him, the more you will praise Him. The more you know Him, the more you will tell others about Him. The more you know Him, the more you will glorify and enjoy Him.

Note Paul's inspiring charge to the Philippians:

*My goal is to **know** (ginosko) Him and the power of His resurrection and the fellowship of His sufferings, being conformed to His death, assuming that I will somehow reach the resurrection from among the dead. @Philippians 3:10–11*

To *know* Him is power. It is fellowship. It is eternal life.

BUT I ALREADY KNOW GOD

At this point you may be thinking, "I already know God. I'm a believer. But I don't feel like I'm living out the Christian life to the fullest. I sin. I fail. I feel defeated. I act like a lukewarm Christian most of the time. I'm not getting this."

I can relate. For years, I struggled with trying to muster up the faith to resist temptation. To do great things for Christ. To live "the victorious Christian life." To live up to standards of the Bible heroes—and the Christian "self-help" books. In fact, often one of the most discouraging exercises I inflicted on myself was reading Christian discipleship books. They were always well-intentioned, and I'm sure I often missed their point. But the picture of the biblical Christian that they painted seemed unattainable. After reading them, I felt like the puny 7th grader who was the first to be cut from my junior high school basketball team. I just wasn't close to measuring up.

That's when I began to understand that I was focusing on the measuring stick instead of the Measurer. I was beginning with *do* instead of with *know*.

My wife is a wonderful Christian woman who is extremely gifted in discipling women and providing biblical guidance. God sends her a steady stream of ladies with various hurts, habits, and hang-ups. She meets with them for Bible study, and a few months later, an amazingly high percentage of them get back on their feet, hit their stride in their spiritual walk, and go on with life recovered and revived. How does she do it?

> I began to understand that I was focusing on the measuring stick instead of the Measurer. I was beginning with *do* instead of with *know*.

Some might be suffering from eating disorders. Some are having marriage problems. Some are overcoming the pain of divorce. Some just feel they are at a dry place in their Christian journey. You might think she would pull out verses that address their situation or go through a Christian book about their particular problem. But that's not how she approaches the problem at all.

She takes them through a study of the names of God.

That's it. No magic bullet verses. No pop psychology books wrapped with Christian self-help packaging. Just a simple, straightforward study of God using His names and titles to learn about His attributes and benefits.

*"My goal is to **know** Him and the power..." @Philippians 3:10*

Get up close and personal with God and everything becomes clearer. Once, a man was browsing through an art gallery when he came across a curious abstract painting. It was distorted, almost grotesque, yet intriguing. He stared at it, tilting his head and squinting his eyes, trying to make sense of the shapes. Finally, a man approached him, and said, "Get closer to it." So he moved closer. "Now get lower." So, he bent over, never taking his eyes off the painting, yet still, it didn't look right. "Get closer, lower." He moved in some more and crouched down. "Closer, lower," the stranger urged. Now he was on his knees right next to the wall, looking straight up at the painting. Suddenly, a glowing amazement broke across his face as his mouth opened, "The Cross!" Viewed from the right position and at the right perspective—closer and lower—the "abstract" painting revealed an amazing rendering of the Cross.

Come to the foot of the Cross.

> *So that you may know and believe Me and understand that I am He. @Isaiah 43:10*

Get to *ginosko* know Him as you grow in understanding and trust. Get up close and personal with Him. As you get closer and lower, your relationship will get warmer and deeper. It's at the foot of the Cross that your perspective on life comes into focus. It's under His care that you'll live secure and satisfied. It's by His side that you'll discover who He wants you to *be* and what He wants you to *do*. It all starts with *knowing* Him. And that's really All you need to know.

Chapter 3

BE

When our children's choir sings, it sounds and—even more importantly—*looks* heavenly. Like Heaven itself, a wide variety of races are represented. Our church family itself is fairly diverse. But our children's choir is a veritable rainbow of nationalities. "Red and yellow, black and white, they are precious in His sight." The reason for the diversity is because so many families in our congregation have adopted internationally. It's not uncommon in our church to see a family with two parents, a couple of biological children, and several African or Hispanic children.

The parents go to great expense and great lengths to rescue these children through adoption. One set of parents was forced to wait nine months in the host country waiting on the signature of one stubborn government official. Another couple literally snatched a child from the heinous crime of abortion by agreeing on the spot to adopt the child if the mother would carry her to full term.

What a poignant picture of what God has done for His children.

> So you have not received a spirit that makes you fearful slaves. Instead, you received God's Spirit when he **adopted** you as his own children. Now we call him, "Abba, Father." For his Spirit joins with our spirit to affirm that we are God's children. @Romans 8:14–16

Like these parents, God went to great lengths to come to us—leaving all the glories of Heaven to journey to earth, a humbling experience that makes going from America to a Third World nation look like a luxury vacation (John 6:38; Philippians 2:5-8). He spent—not nine months—but about 33 years waiting for stubborn government officials to sign our release papers, His death certificate. He rescued us from slavery and absolute death. He adopted us as sons and daughters. And then to top it all off, He even made us joint-heirs with His Son.

> *So you are no longer a slave but a son, and if a son, then an heir through God. @Galatians 4:7*

Praise Abba, Father!

As these newly adopted children of our church are assimilated into their new culture and new family, amazing changes begin to take place— sometimes slowly at first. At times, they're wide-eyed and wondering. At times, scared and still shy about fully trusting. They have so much to learn about their new life. Food is suddenly plentiful. Clothes are clean and bright. Faces are cheerful and smiling. Affection is plentiful and genuine. It's not always all roses and no thorns. But their old story has ended. A new story has begun. They have a new home. A new family. And a new family name. They are joint-heirs with their new siblings. They have a new identity. An old history. And a new future. Who they were is no longer who they will *be*.

ADOPTED BUT STILL ADAPTING

God adopted me when I was 19 years old. I had lived in the orphanage of sin for quite a while by that time. I had my security blanket and had learned how to get comfortable and where to find temporary happiness. I had my habits and pet sins that were not welcome in my new home. I had a history—that needed to become history.

I was wide-eyed and wondering about my new home, my new family. But I was scared sometimes and still shy about fully trusting. "Food" seemed to be abundant. But would it always be? I had new clothes, but sometimes my old ones seemed more comfortable. I was surrounded by cheerful faces, but not everyone was so rosy. I had a new family name. Christian. And a new future—but sometimes it seemed very far away. I wasn't quite sure what I should be doing and whether or not I could even do it. Everyone else seemed to be doing it, however, so I focused on *doing* the same things they were. They had a lot to say about what and how I should be *doing* it.

As I shared in the first chapter, my initial conception of the Christian life was summed up in that one word: *Do*. My perception of God was one of a taskmaster. And my self-perception was one of order-taker. I had plenty of ammunition from the Bible for this narrow view, starting with the Ten Commandments and going right on through the New Testament with verses like:

*You are My friends if you **do** what I **command** you. @John 15:14*

*We have confidence in the Lord about you, that you are **doing** and will **do** what we command. @2 Thessalonians 3:4*

*Whoever does not **do** what is right is not of God. @1 John 3:10*

My performance, however, was spotty. I excelled in some areas. In others, I was a dismal failure. Sometimes I would string together a series of successes. Other times, I would go through a dry desert. My Christian life was a roller coaster that soared or tanked along with my obedience report card. I wasn't making straight As, and I didn't feel good about my life, my future, nor my God.

Satan changes His tactics once you become a believer. Before you're saved, Satan lies to us by telling us we're good enough to earn God's favor on our own. After you're saved, Satan lies to us by telling us we will never be good enough to earn God's favor. It's kind of like marriage. Before two people get married, Satan does everything he can to get them in bed together. After they get married, he does everything he can to keep them apart. I was buying the lies.

THE LIGHT COMES ON

I had been a pretty good student in school. My intelligence was average, but I overachieved by working harder. My to-do lists served me well. I was organized, self-disciplined, and driven. And I was applying those qualities to my Christian walk. But the more I learned about God, the more I understood how little I knew—and how far short I was falling. I realized that the Christian life isn't difficult; it is impossible.

I believe the light began coming on for me as I became a father. I still remember the first day I brought our daughter home from the hospital. I carefully cradled her into the car seat and then drove home about 10 miles per hour, as if I were carrying a fragile crystal vase in the backseat that could tip over and shatter. Indeed, she was precious cargo.

I had not even realized that I possessed this reservoir of love which I had never explored until I held the "bone of my bone and my flesh of my flesh" in my arms. She shared my home, my name, my DNA, and yes, even my brown eyes. She was a Thompson—and always would be. No matter what she did. Period.

On the way home from the hospital that day, I did something that I've always wished I could reverse. I blinked. And when I opened my eyes, my daughter was standing in front of me with a strange boy by her side, wanting to know what time she had to be home from their date.

"Ten o'clock sharp," I said. "And not one minute afterwards." I meant it. "And remember who you are and Whose you are."

She was a Thompson. And she was a child of God.

KNOWING WHOSE WE ARE
INFORMS WHO WE ARE

Giving her the curfew command settled the specific matter of what time to be home (she missed it once and only once). But reminding her she was a Thompson was designed to cover all the many other decisions that she might be faced with on that date. She had lived with me for 16 years, and she knew how Thompsons think and behave. More importantly, she was God's child, and she understood much of what that entailed as well. Who she was and Whose she was defined her as a person. It informed her of her standing with both her Fathers. And it inspired her to live out the kind of life that was appropriate for their child.

We had a second daughter within a few years, and as they grew up, I was growing up in my Christian walk, too. I was beginning to grasp the meaning of unconditional love. I knew that my daughters would always be my daughters by virtue of their unconditional right of birth—not because they were making straight As at school. I began to apply that relationship to my own relationship with God.

I was beginning to understand that when I focused on Whose I was, it brought such value and purpose to my life that I didn't have to work as hard to *do* what I should be doing. It was more natural. It flowed out of my identity, my name, my relationship with my Heavenly Father.

Notice this prayer *from* God the Son *to* God the Father *for* us:

> *May they all **be one**,*
> *as You, Father, are in Me and I am in You.*
> *May they also **be one** in Us,*
> *so the world may believe You sent Me.*
> *I have given them the glory You have given Me.*
> *May they **be one** as We are one.*
> *I am in them and You are in Me.*
> *May they **be** made completely **one**.*
> *@John 17:21–23*

Notice how many times the words **be one** are in these three verses: *four* times. Once you are adopted into God's family, you are one with Him. You have an all-new identity. Your net worth just went way up. You're worth a King's ransom because you literally *are* the child of a King.

> You're worth a King's ransom because you literally *are* the child of a King.

The pity is so many Christians go through life defeated because they can't seem to do what they know they should be doing. They're focused on the *do* instead of the *be*—being who they *are* in Christ.

During the Great Depression, Ira Yates bought a ranch in a hardscrabble corner of West Texas. His sheep operation barely provided food and clothes for his family, let alone paid the mortgage. Surviving on government subsidies, he was gravely concerned that he would lose his ranch. The family lived in poverty as the situation got more and more grim. One day, an oil company came to explore his land for oil. They drilled a wildcat well and hit a gusher. Other wells were dug and began producing more oil than they could even store or transport. Three years later, production hit 41 million barrels, including one well that set the world record of more than 200,000 barrels in one day. Mr. Yates had owned it all along. The day he bought the land he got the oil and mineral rights as well. He had been living like a pauper, yet was rich as a king.

If you're God's child, you're sitting on a rich oil field. Why live an impoverished Christian life, content to subsist on husks fit for pigs, like the prodigal son? You are the son or daughter of the King. *Be* who you are! Why settle for a life that's *beneath* who you are in Christ?

Be the one who is so valued a King let His own Son pay the death penalty for you.

Be the one who has so much potential that God said you would do even greater works than His Son.

> *The one who believes in Me will also do the works that I do. And he will do even greater works than these. @John 14:12*

Be the one who has a Father and Big Brother clearing the path for you.

Be the one who has a future and a plan crafted by the One Who fashioned the universe.

Be the one who has a direct hotline to the CEO of the universe.

Be the one who is loved, valued, accepted, and empowered by God Almighty Himself.

Be one with Him.

Be who you are in Christ.

YOU ARE WHAT YOU WEAR

There's something about putting on a sharp business suit that makes you feel professional, buttoned-down, in control, smarter. Likewise, if I'm lying around in pajamas I feel a little lazy and unproductive—even at 12:00 noon. Nothing about me or who I am has changed. But the clothes bring on an awareness of qualities—or flaws—within myself.

Rather, clothe yourselves with the Lord Jesus Christ, and do not think about how to gratify the desires of the flesh. @Romans 13:14

How do you put on the Lord Jesus Christ? The sense of the original word for "clothe" is to "sink into." A form of the word was used to describe the sun setting, sinking into the earth. To put on Christ, we have to let *The Son* sink into, set on us. He immerses Himself in us, and we glow with Him. He is in us and on us. We are on Him and in Him. The two become one. We *be* Him. That's not good grammar, but it's great theology.

> **He is in us and on us. We are on Him and in Him. The two become one. We be Him. That's not good grammar, but it's great theology.**

When we take Him off, we're naked. We're in the flesh, gratifying the desires of the flesh. We're aware of our nakedness, just like Adam and Eve in the garden after they sinned. The moment they ate the forbidden fruit, "the eyes of both of them were opened, and they knew they were naked" @Genesis 3:7. They tried to clothe themselves with fig leaves, but that didn't cover it. Blood had to be shed as God made clothing made out of skins so that their flesh could be covered.

I walk around naked, er, in the flesh quite a bit, I'm ashamed to say. I find myself operating for long periods of time in the "power" of my own strength—in reality, more like the *weakness* of my own strength. Then the light goes on, I'm aware of my nakedness, and I put on Christ. Like putting on a sharp suit, I suddenly feel empowered, clean, ready for whatever's next. Suddenly, my awareness shifts, and I once again begin to live out my true identity. It's like Clark Kent ducking into a phone booth to don his Superman outfit. I am truly putting on *the* Superman—the Lord Jesus Christ.

I become one with Him. I become who I truly am. I am who I am.

WHO AM I?

If you want to truly *be* who you are in Christ, you need a good understanding of *who you truly are*—in God's eyes. Not your own self-image. It's probably warped. Pride. Failures. Disappointments. Delusions. Misperceptions. Deceptions. Satan's lies. And just plain old ignorance.

Nor should you rely on culture to tell you who you *are*. Advertisers, social media, society…they'll gladly tell you who you are and who you should be. You'll get a great *quantity* of input, but not much *quality*.

God's truth will clear away all this distortion.

When I was a boy, theme parks were called amusement parks, and what passed for amusement was not million dollar thrill rides. It was things like carnival mirrors. A few of these are still around in the fun houses at county fairs. They're mirrors with various curved sections that distort parts of your body. One might make your head look enormous. Another might make you look skinny. (I'd love to have one of those in my home!) Another might make you look wavy. Now we have apps on our phones to do this. Many believers have a self-image that's just as distorted.

Some have the big head. Pride has swelled their head bigger than a carnival mirror. Others think their future is defined by their failed past, and they just don't believe they will ever be any better. Most don't view themselves as children of a King—princes and princesses. Nearly all would be pleasantly surprised if they could genuinely see themselves through God's eyes. You may have heard of "beer goggles" that make drunken men think women look better than they really are. God wears "Jesus goggles." He sees us through the blood of Christ, so that we look just as clean and acceptable as His own Son. Don't just dismiss that thought as Christian-book hyperbole. It's 100% true!

He made the One who did not know sin to be sin for us, so that we might become the righteousness of God in Him. @2 Corinthians 5:21

For you have died, and your life is hidden with Christ in God. When Christ who is your life appears, then you also will appear with him in glory. @Colossians 3:3–4

Therefore, brothers, since we have confidence to enter the holy places by the blood of Jesus, by the new and living way that he opened for us through the curtain, that is, through his flesh, and since we have a great priest over the house of God, let us draw near with a true heart in full assurance of faith, with our hearts sprinkled clean from an evil conscience and our bodies washed with pure water. @Hebrews 10:19–22

So put your Jesus goggles on and take a look at yourself—but not in the carnival mirror. Read through those verses again and see yourself as God sees you:

1. Sin erased.
2. Righteousness put on.
3. Old self dead.
4. Side-by-side with Christ in glory.
5. Fit to enter the holy places.
6. True heart.
7. Full faith.
8. Clean heart.
9. Pure conscience.
10. Washed spotless.

Wow! That paints a picture that's way different than what I see in my carnival-mirror mind. It's vastly different than the feedback I get on my behavior from people around me. Yet God said it! I remember an old bumper sticker: "God said it. I believe it. That settles it!" You can cut the middle part out. It doesn't matter if you believe it or not. If God said it, that settles it.

Believe it!

Be it!

Focused on *doing*, and well aware of how short I was falling, I had a hard time swallowing this truth at first. Then I was asked to lead a study using the book *The Search for Significance* by Robert S. McGee. Here are key statements of the book:

> *I am completely forgiven by and fully pleasing to God. I no longer have to fear failure.*
>
> *I am totally accepted by God. I no longer have to fear rejection.*
>
> *I am deeply loved by God. I no longer have to fear punishment or punish others.*
>
> *I have been made brand-new, complete in Christ. I no longer need to experience the pain of shame.*

Each statement is a true response to a false belief.

> *The Performance Trap*
> *Approval Addict*
> *The Blame Game*
> *Shame*

Just concentrate on who you are in Christ and then *do* what's natural because what's natural is actually *super*natural because it will be Christ doing it through you.

The false beliefs are the carnival mirrors. The truth is how God sees you through Jesus goggles. Forgetting our self-image and focusing on our God-image is incredibly freeing. It takes all the pressure off of *doing*. No more performing, impressing, blaming, shaming. Just concentrate on who you *are* in Christ and then *do* what's natural because what's natural is actually *super*natural because it will be Christ doing it through you.

"The me I see is the me I'll be," our beloved pastor, the late Adrian Rogers, used to say. He wasn't quoting pop psychology. He was paraphrasing Proverbs 23:7: "For as he thinks within himself, so he is."

The Proverb cites a negative example, but the believer who abides in an awareness of who he is in Christ frees himself to be that one he sees in his inner man.

You will know the truth, and the truth will set you free. @John 8:32

Know truth. Know God. *Be* who you are in Him.

WHY DOESN'T MY EXPERIENCE MATCH UP WITH GOD'S TRUTH?

If you're like me, you may be thinking, "I've heard all that before. But the fact is I don't act like a new creation in Christ. I keep failing over and over. I thought the old self was supposed to be dead, but a lot of the time, it seems like the old self is alive and kicking."

What are we to do with this?...

For we know that our old self was crucified with Him in order that sin's dominion over the body may be abolished, so that we may no longer be enslaved to sin. @Romans 6:6

If my old self has been crucified, executed, dead and gone, why is it that so much of the time I feel like I'm in a contest with Paul to see who really is the chief of sinners? And I may just have him beat.

Here's what's going on.

Satan is the master deceiver. He's a counterfeiter. He's a liar. He's a con artist. He doesn't have any original material of his own. He merely takes the good things that God creates and perverts them. Inverts them. Subverts them.

Take sex for example. God created it, and it is good. Very good. Satan perverts it. He does everything he can to bring people together sexually before marriage, and then to keep them apart afterwards.

Take food. God created it, and it is good. Almost as good as sex, as my wife says. Satan cooks up a way to make it make it bad. He promotes gluttony. He turns good ingredients into strong drink. And I'm pretty sure he's behind the consumption of spinach and other greens.

One more example before we see how he confuses the crucified flesh.... Money. Money is the fruit of hard work, and work is a gift from God.

> *God has also given riches and wealth to every man, and He has allowed him to enjoy them, take his reward, and rejoice in his labor. This is a gift of God. @Ecclesiastes 5:19*

But the *love* of money is the root—the hidden, hard to "root out" part—of evil. So Satan cons us into always wanting more. How much is enough? Just a little bit more. We spend our lives chasing the elusive dollar, only to find that the devil pays in counterfeit money.

Satan is a pro at deceiving us.

> *There is no truth in him. When he tells a lie, he speaks from his own nature, because he is a liar and the father of liars. @John 8:44*

He takes one of God's truths, distorts it, discounts it, dismisses it, or denies it. He's got no material of his own, only perversions of what God has made.

What has God made? If you're a believer, He made a new you. A brand spanking new creation (2 Corinthians 5:17) that is good. Very good. Completely forgiven. Fully pleasing. Totally accepted. Deeply loved. Brand-new, complete person in Christ.

Your old self? Dead. Crucified with Christ.

So, back to our problem...why do we still act like the old, dead person?

Satan, lacking his own material, loving to pervert God's creation, and lying every step of the way, stages a false resurrection of our old self, comes to us disguised as our old self, and invites us to put it on.

Remember our verse from above:

> *Rather, clothe yourselves with the Lord Jesus Christ, and do not think about how to gratify the desires of the flesh. @Romans 13:14*

Satan can't resurrect anything. But he can counterfeit it. And he is the master of disguise.

Satan disguises himself as an angel of light. @2 Corinthians 11:14

So get the picture. Here you are, a child of God, *being* who you are in Christ. Pleasing. Loved. Brand new. Capable of doing anything that Christ can do through you. And there is Satan, dressed up like the old you. It seems so real, it's easy to forget that the old you is dead, never to be resurrected. Now you have a choice.

Clothe yourself with the Lord Jesus Christ. Or put on Satan's "old self" disguise.

That's the choice you face at every point of temptation. *Be* who you truly are. Or be fooled by a fake old self.

Believe God's truth. Or swallow Satan's lie.

It's such a black and white choice when we see through God's eyes. And that is why knowing Him is the key and the starting point—the crux of this book. But the deception is subtle, and many of us fall for it time after time. Satan's counterfeits are often difficult to detect. And where our old, dead self ends and our new, living self begins isn't always obvious. The Bible says Satan comes in sheep's clothing, but inwardly are ravenous wolves (Matthew 7:15). That's why God encourages us to...

Put on the full armor of God so that you can stand against the tactics of the Devil. @Ephesians 6:11

Keep that armor on. It's not easy to put one of Satan's "old self" costumes over a full suit of armor.

The key to recognizing the difference between our new self and our old self disguise is to know the difference between God's truth and Satan's lies. Don't focus on recognizing the lie. That's tricky. Just get to *know* God and His truth so well that anything false seems foreign.

When bank tellers are trained to identify counterfeit bills, they are given real currency to handle, to examine, to touch and feel. They become so familiar with the real thing that when a counterfeit bill crosses their hands, they can detect it immediately.

That's the key to identifying God's truth vs. Satan's lies. Get to know God and His truth currency so well that any lies Satan tries to pass you feel foreign.

That way, when Satan offers you the falsely resurrected, old-self suit, you can immediately tag it as a fake. You can wrap yourself in Christ and His pure truth, knowing that you are...

Forgiven by and pleasing to God.

Accepted and deeply loved by God.

A brand-new, complete creation in Christ.

Free from the fear of failure or rejection.

Free from the fear of punishment and the need to punish others.

Free from the pain of shame.

You are in Christ.

Be it.

Don't worry about "Just do it."

Just *be it.*

HIS WORTH = OUR WORTH

Early in my career as an ad copywriter, I was contacted by an ad agency who was interested in recruiting me. They flew me and my wife to their city, the first time we had ever been on a plane. They picked us up at the airport, and put us up in a luxury hotel. We had dinner at an elegant restaurant with one of the principals of the firm. He drove a beautiful black Jaguar and had just bought another brand new one as a gift for his attractive girlfriend. He was loaded. As we admired his car, he insisted that we take it the next day so that we could drive around and get acquainted with the city. As a young man in my 20s, I had never been made to feel so wanted by someone so important and wealthy. He made me a job offer that I couldn't refuse, and needless to say, I took the job. He made me feel like I was the best copywriter since David Ogilvy, and I was ready to do anything for that man.

In reality, I was still the same guy who had been pecking out a living at my old job, but because of the worth of my new boss, I felt elevated. I was ready to write award-winning advertising, and start saving for *my* new Jag. I felt like a million bucks because my boss who liked me was worth a million bucks.

I'm sure by now you're making the connection. If you could only see how much Christ is worth, you could see how much *you* are worth. It goes back to *knowing* God. If you could truly get a glimpse into His unfathomable net worth. His extravagant grace. His audacious love. His lavish forgiveness. His exquisite character. His exorbitant long-suffering. His infinite wisdom. His impeccable holiness. His effulgent power. His... my copywriter's thesaurus is running out of adjectives...unspeakable glory.

Then, with His value in mind, if you could only see, oh, how he loves you. How He was willing to suffer for you. How He calls you His friend, His child, His workmanship, His chosen, His heir. How He even says He is jealous for you. Then you would see who you *are* in His eyes. To the extent that you *know* and grasp this, you will *be* who you *are* in Christ, and then *doing* will be a light burden, an easy yoke (Matthew 11:30).

Know Him. *Be* His.

Chapter 4

DO

If you did man-on-the-street interviews with average people and asked them this question, "What is Christianity all about?" you would be likely to get a lot of answers like this:

"Helping your fellow man."

"Going to church.

"Obeying the Ten Commandments."

"Following the Golden Rule."

"Praying to God."

The average church member would probably give you a lot of the same answers. People tend to define Christianity in terms of the externals, the things you *do*.

As I mentioned before, that was me. A legalist, now in rehab. The one whose first act of my Christian life was to compile a to-do list and start checking off each action item.

Action. That was my concept of the essence of Christianity. Just call me Martha. You remember her. She was the one whining to Jesus because her sister Mary was lounging around doing nonproductive things like sitting at Jesus feet and listening to His every word.

"Lord, don't You care that my sister has left me to serve alone? So tell her to give me a hand." @Luke 10:40

Jesus told her to stop being worried and upset and focus on the one thing that matters most: getting to *know* Jesus.

Doing stuff for Jesus is the first priority for most Christians. But it's the *last* thing you should do. I mean that literally. The very last thing. *Doing* shouldn't be the first thing. *Knowing* God comes first. Then *being* who you are in Christ. Then *do* as the Spirit empowers you.

I believe some people are wired to be Marthas—task-oriented. Others are wired to be Marys—people-oriented. Some like to be in the kitchen. Some like to be in the living room. That's OK. God uses our unique personalities. If we were all Marthas, our churches might have clean hallways but dirty hearts. If we were all Marys, we might preach the Light of the World but the church may be too dark for anyone to see.

Being aware of how you're wired can help you avoid blowing a fuse when the other type of person isn't doing what you think they should. And it will help you keep first things first and yet not neglect the full counsel of what God intended for you.

GOD'S ORDER

God built a natural order into things that is really quite supernatural. There's a structure and a symmetry to life that is godly, holy, and orderly.

> *Everything must be done decently and in order. @1 Corinthians 14:40*

Take marriage. God's order is love, marriage, sex. Culture seems to prefer sex, sex, sex, and then maybe marriage and perhaps love.

Finances. God's order is work, pay, enjoy. In today's buy-now, pay-later economy, we're taught to enjoy, enjoy, then pay, pay, pay, pay; work only if you have to.

Here's one more: listen, think, speak. For far too many people, it's speak, speak, think, speak some more. Forget about listening.

When it comes to Christianity, there's also an order: know, be, do. For many, including me when I first became a believer, it's do, do, do. *Know* is something we might do on Sunday mornings. And *be* is something we only fake.

Putting *do* before *know* and *be* does not produce good results. The Apostle Peter was a pro at this. Boasting about how loyal he was, ready to go to prison. Only to deny Christ within 24 hours. Then there he is again, impetuously cutting off the servant's ear, and getting scolded by Jesus for his impulsive violence. Later, he's at it again, suggesting they build three shelters—one for Jesus, one for Moses, and one for Elijah. He just didn't get it.

Peter's not alone in Scripture. David wanted to build a temple, but God said no. Then there's the census that he took which God didn't order.

History is full of overzealous quests and conquests in which mankind focused on doing things for God, when God's Kingdom would have been better served had they done their due diligence to *know* Him better and *be* who He wanted them to be. It's quite possible that things *done* in the name of Christianity have done more damage than things left *undone*.

CONFUSION OF CAUSE AND EFFECT

When we put *do* before *know* and *be*, we not only get the cart before the horse, we confuse the cause and the effect of the Christian life. Examine this verse closely:

> *This is how we are sure that we have come to know Him: by keeping His commands.* @1 John 2:3

What's the cause here? Knowing Him.

What are the effects? 1. We are sure we are His (*being*). 2. We keep His commands (*doing*).

Confusing the cause and effect of the Christian life can have devastating consequences. When we fail to acknowledge that our Source is God, we attempt to do things in our own strength. We fail to give Him credit and steal His glory.

Confusing cause and effect can even prevent people from experiencing salvation. Paul warned us of this when he said, "For you are saved by grace through faith, and this is not from yourselves; it is God's gift—not from works, so that no one can boast" @Ephesians 2:8–9.

Cause: God's grace. Effect: Salvation.

James makes the same point, only from the opposite point of view. He wrote:

> *What good is it, my brothers, if someone says he has faith but does not have works? Can his faith save him?...But someone will say, "You have faith, and I have works." Show me your faith without works, and I will show you faith from my works...Are you willing to learn that faith without works is useless? ...You see that a man is justified by works and not by faith alone.... For just as the body without the spirit is dead, so also faith without works is dead.* @James 2:14–26

On the surface, it almost appears that Paul and James disagree about which is the cause and which is the effect of salvation. But they are describing two sides of the same coin. In both cases, they point to grace and faith as the cause, and works as the effect.

Paul describes the side that God sees: Faith alone saves.

James describes the side that man sees: *True* faith is never alone; it's always accompanied by works.

Both uphold the full **truth**: Faith = Salvation + Works

Paul is guarding against this **error**: Faith + Works = Salvation

James is guarding against this **error**: Faith = Salvation - Works

Yes, true faith is never alone. It produces works. But works are the fruit, not the root. The product, not the prerequisite.

Now, don't hear me minimizing the importance of obedience and doing good works. To the contrary, I want to maximize good works by stressing the proper order: *know* first, *then* be, *then* do. The purpose of this book is not to under*mine* the value and necessity of

> The purpose of this book is not to under*mine* the value and necessity of *doing* for God (works), but it's to under*line* the preeminence of living in Him (*knowing*) and Him in you (*being*).

doing for God (works), but it's to under*line* the preeminence of living in Him (*knowing*) and Him in you (*being*).

TRIMETRY

I love the beautiful symmetry, or to invent a new word, trimetry, in God's Word and creation. God Himself is a Holy Trinity: God the Father, God the Son, and God the Spirit. The Godhead is coequal, coeternal, and cohesive.

Man, created in God's image, is a tripart being:

- Spirit
- Heart or soul (mind, will, and emotions)
- Body.

The rest of creation is divided into three parts: animals (which have heart and body, but no spirit), plants (which have body only, no heart or spirit), and minerals (which have no life at all). Man is the only creation with all three: spirit, soul, and body.

There are three heavens: the first heaven, the home of birds and weather. The second heaven, the area of space, planets, and galaxies. And the third Heaven, the abode of God.

The time-space continuum in which we exist is tripart: Time consists of past, present, and future. Space consists of length, width, and depth.

Even man-made creations often mimic the three-part motif of creation, such as the classic tripart skyscraper design or the three branches of government: executive, legislative, and judicial. Indeed, God's DNA is stamped everywhere we look.

Returning to man's tripart nature, each part of man is a center for one of the three aspects: *know, be, do*. Of course, there is overlap, just as the three Persons of the Holy Trinity are each interactive. Each aspect—*know, be, do*—has a center, Divine Leadership, and a focus.

ASPECT	KNOW	BE	DO
Tripart Center	Spirit *Spiritual*	Soul *Mental*	Body *Physical*
Divine Leadership	God the Father *God the Father created us so that we could relate to Him.*	God the Spirit *God the Holy Spirit guides our spirit with regard to who we are.*	God the Son *God the Son (Jesus) set the supreme example for all our actions.*
Focus	Eternal Acknowledge His attributes— awareness of His presence	Internal Abide in His ability— acceptance of our position	External Act on His authority— appropriation of His power

OUT OF BALANCE

So let's take a look at a picture of how we're supposed to look. *Know* is the foundation, the biggest and most important part. *Be* builds on that knowledge and connects *know* with *do*. And *do* is the point, the smallest, yet often the most visible part.

Let's look at you from God's perspective, top down, when everything is as it should be.

Sometimes, however, things in our life get out of alignment.

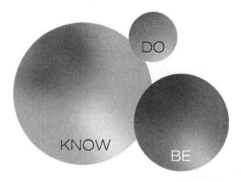

Do without *be* or *know* is **hypocrisy.** This is the Pharisee syndrome, legalism at its worst.

Be without *do* or *know* is **complacency.** If you sit back resting on your co-heir status without letting new life flow in or service flow out, you will stagnate. You will sit, soak, and sour.

Know without *be* or *do* is blasphemy. Because when we *know* God and yet fail to *be* what we should *be,* and *do* what we should *do*…we insult God.

But when *know*, *be*, and *do* line up—that's **integrity!**

The reason it's so important to understand how we are made is because the three parts must act in concert—like strings, wind instruments, and percussion—in order to live harmoniously with God and others. If one area of your life grows disproportionately large, your life will get out a balance, like an orchestra where the brass is too loud or you can't hear the woodwinds. The Conductor helps keep each section balanced and in harmony.

Part of what my business does is creating websites for various organizations. Often, when I begin a new website project, the client already has ideas about how they want the homepage to look, right down to colors and spinning logos. It's my job to lead them to take a step back and consider foundational issues, such as the purpose for the website, objectives and goals, and the target audience. The next step is to create a site map that outlines the content, and serves as a blueprint for building the site. Only then, can we begin to make informed decisions with regard to design—layout, colors, images, and fonts.

Many Christians live their lives the same way. They are focused on the externals, the *do*, the "fun" part that everyone sees. It's like they're focused on what colors will be on their homepage before they've ever really understood the purpose for their site. Take a step back, and invest the necessary time it takes to understand your "Source," your purpose, your assets, the map God is drawing up for your life. Don't jump ahead to *doing* until you're fully familiar with *knowing* and *being*.

Here are some questions to ask yourself to see if you're overly focused on *do*:

Is your obedience motivated by love for God or how it looks to man?

Are you more interesting in getting to know God or earning brownie points to win His favor?

When doing ministry, are you merely reacting to needs or proactively seeking God's will for your life?

Do you spend more time cultivating a relationship with God or crafting a godly PR image on social media?

Do you feel better about yourself when you consider how much God loves you or when you've done something really nice for someone?

Do you behave the same when only God is looking as when all eyes are on you?

Are you more focused on the fruit (*do*) than on the root (*know*)?

GOD DOESN'T NEED YOU

Ever notice how we project our own human thoughts on God? We forget that He is self-sufficient and sovereign. We think He suffers from the same limited resources and weaknesses that we do. Sometimes we think and act like if we don't do something for God, He's going to be left in a lurch, panicking, ready to call an emergency session of the Holy Trinity. Get this:

He doesn't need you to *do* anything for Him.

> *The God who made the world and everything in it—He is Lord of heaven and earth and does not live in shrines made by hands. Neither is He served by human hands, as though He needed anything, since He Himself gives everyone life and breath and all things. @Acts 17:24–25*

Even more remarkable, though: He *wants* you to *do* many things for Him.

Let that sink in. God—Who can speak a word and pop a galaxy into existence—wants you to do stuff for Him. It's been His pattern since the beginning of time. He put Adam and Eve in the garden to tend it. Work. It was a gift from God, even before sin even entered the picture and made it more difficult.

He used men—a diverse group of men—to help write the Bible.

He gave us the Great Commission—the Great Co-Mission, evangelizing the world together as partners. He provided the authority and the power—the air cover, if you will—and we are the ground troops, boots on the ground.

He didn't need to involve us in the Great Commission. He could have written the Gospel across the sky every morning. (Come to think of it, He did!) He could have written John 3:16 on the back of every man's hand. But He *chose* to let us be partners. He gave us responsibilities. What a privilege to be part of His enterprise! We're full partners in God & Son.

> He *chose* to let us be partners. He gave us responsibilities. What a privilege to be part of His enterprise! We're full partners in God & Son.

He gave us a number of commands, things He wants us to do. Not *for* Him, but *with* Him. But notice this: God never begins with the imperative (*do*). He always begins with the principles (*know and be*). The Book of Romans is a classic example. On the macro level, it's 11 chapters of *principles* followed by five chapters of *imperatives*, beginning with…

> *Therefore, brothers, by the mercies of God, I urge you to present your bodies as a living sacrifice, holy and pleasing to God; this is your spiritual worship. @Romans 12:1*

Even at the micro level, such as Romans 6, you see the pattern of *principles*…

> *What should we say then? Should we continue in sin so that grace may multiply? Absolutely not! How can we who died to sin still live in it? @Romans 6:1–2*

…Followed by *imperatives*,

> *Therefore do not let sin reign in your mortal body, so that you obey its desires. @Romans 6:12*

Follow this pattern in your own life. Fill yourself with principles for Who God is (*know*) and Whose you are (*be*). Then *do* will flow naturally, supernaturally from the overflow. You won't have to muster the strength to *do* things for Him. You won't have to question your motives. You won't have to worry about doing the wrong things, or even the right things at the wrong time or for the wrong reason.

Never start with *do*. Start with *know*.

Acknowledge His attributes—awareness of His presence (*know*).

Abide in His ability—acceptance of your position in Him (*be*).

Act on His authority—appropriation of His power (*do*).

FITS LIKE A GLOVE

Being a Christian is a lot like a glove. A glove just lays there on the table until you put your hand in it. It does nothing on its own. In fact, it would be a little creepy if a glove suddenly took on life of its own and started running around the house, flipping switches and grabbing people by the arm. No, a glove does nothing until you put your hand in it. Then it comes to life. Then it can pick up a shovel or open a door. It does the will of its master, you. It doesn't tell *you* what to do. It doesn't make suggestions about how you should be doing something. Its job is to remain soft and supple. A stiff glove that resists the movements of your hands is a glove that is asking to be whipped around a little, until it better yields to your hand's will.

We're nothing until God fills us, like a hand in the glove. His commands are not meant to be carried out in our own strength. Let's go back, for example, to the Great Commission. "Go, make disciples" (Matthew 28:19) is the imperative. But we're in such a hurry to get to the "Great Go" that we forget about the "Great God." Back up, to the forgotten verse of the Great Commission—verse 18: "Then Jesus came near and said to them, 'All authority has been given to Me in heaven and on earth.'" Authority. Power. Dominion. Control. Right. Weight. The hand in the glove. Just look at all we can learn about God from this verse. And then the kicker in verse 20, "And remember, I am with you always." Always remember *know* before attempting *do*.

> *For it is God who is working in you, enabling you both to desire and to work out His good purpose. @Philippians 2:13*

Think about something you did "for" God. How did it turn out? Did you feel like God was the hand in the glove and you were simply being a soft, supple glove for Him to do it through you? Or did you feel stiff and noncompliant? Or maybe like the creepy little glove running around on its own doing its own thing in its own power? Next time, before you *do* anything for God, back up. Focus on *know*. What does *He* want to *do through* you? Then focus on *be*. Who are you in Christ? Once, you've done this, you'll find that *do* is an easy burden and a light yoke. Because He supplies the authority and power. He'll *do* it *through* you.

We make the Christian life way too complicated. All we have to do is follow His lead. Reflect Him.

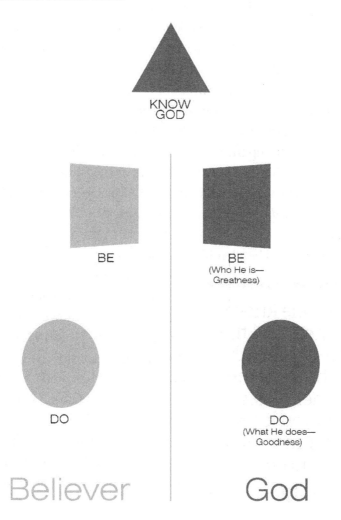

KNOW
GOD

BE

BE
(Who He is—
Greatness)

DO

DO
(What He does—
Goodness)

Believer   God

Know God. Then *be* a reflection of Who He is—His greatness. And *do* what He does—His goodness. Just mirror Him. Note, however, it all begins with *know.* You can't be like Someone you're not intimately in relationship with. You can't do what Someone wants to do through you unless you're aware of His presence and power.

IT'S NOT *WHAT* YOU KNOW
IT'S *WHO* YOU KNOW

Many a frustrated job seeker has been heard to say, "I have the know-how to *do* the job!" only to find the job went to someone with the "know-*who*," like the boyfriend of the bosses' daughter.

When it comes to *doing* the job in the Christian life, "know-*Who*" works in our favor. It really helps to know the bosses' Father. Even Christ Himself practiced this pattern. Listen as He gives the pharisaical Jews a strong dose of truth (@John 8):

"You *know* neither Me nor My Father," Jesus answered. "If you knew Me, you would also *know* My Father." (verse 19)

"When you lift up the Son of Man, then you will *know* that I am He, and that I do nothing on My own. But just as the Father taught Me, I say these things. The One who sent Me is with Me. He has not left Me alone, because I always *do* what pleases Him." (verses 28–29)

"You've never *known* Him, but I *know* Him. If I were to say I don't *know* Him, I would be a liar like you. But I do *know* Him, and I keep His word." (verse 55)

> Everyone knows a father: God the Father of truth or the devil the father of lies. *Who* you know determines what you *do.*

Notice the strong connection Jesus makes between knowing the Father and doing what pleases Him, keeping His Word. Read this entire chapter, and you'll see the corollary truth, too. Everyone knows a father: God the Father of truth or the devil the father of lies. *Who* you *know* determines what you *do.*

Do is the easiest thing to fake. The Pharisees made a living at that. But while we can *do* without truly knowing God, but we can't truly *know* Him without *doing*.

> *This is how we are sure that we have come to know Him: by keeping His commands.* @I John 2:3

Again, notice the cause and effect. Cause: Knowing Him. Effect: Keeping His commands. Don't get these reversed and think that keeping His commands is the way to God. Holiness isn't the way to God. God is the way to holiness. Remember the right order: Know. Be. Do. Knowing Him is the key to being in Him, and being in Him is the door to doing.

It's that simple. I didn't say easy. But simple.

ACTIVITY DOES NOT EQUAL ACTION

One of the most depressing books I've ever read was a book about how to be an effective Christian leader. The book contained a circle graph that showed how the leader should divide up his 24-hour day. It was so full of spiritual activities, it made me tired just reading it. There was no time allotted for watching basketball. For lingering around the dinner table. For watching a sunrise. For reading a novel. For writing a letter to an old friend. For discovering how jet engines work. For just sitting around wondering why God made so many different species of animals and so many planets we'll never probably even see, let alone visit.

Most of us lead frazzled, stressed, and distressed lives trying to do too much—and that includes doing too much for God, too much *for* Him and not enough *through* Him.

I saw a TV show about a Hindu man who believed a divine voice told him to roll to Pakistan. Literally, lie down and roll 1,500 miles across India. He brings new meaning to the term "holy roller." He ended up getting stopped at the border and didn't make it to his destination.

Too many of us are spending our lives rolling along doing things for God. Sometimes God never asked us to do it in the first place. Sometimes we're doing it in our own strength. Maybe we're doing the right thing in the wrong way or for the wrong motive. Maybe we're doing the wrong thing for the right motive. Maybe we're doing the right thing at the wrong time. I could go on and on with the pitfalls.

We don't start with us and see what we can offer God. We start with God and what He offers us.

When we know Him so intimately and we abiding in Him and who we are in Christ, *doing* just flows. It's not a chore. As Adrian Rogers puts it, "Duty turns to delight and mandates become melodies."

Maybe He'll tell you to roll across the country. More likely He'll tell you to slow down and spend some more time with Him.

We have two wonderful daughters. When they were teenagers, they were busy doing anything and everything. School. Church. Hobbies. Boys. It was non-stop activity. But I will always remember one night during their busiest teenage years, when they pulled out an old family photo album. They started looking through it and asking me questions about my life, about seasons in my life that were unknown to them. Where I went to college my first year. How I landed my first real job. What my dad did for a living. Why we moved to this city or took that job. They were soaking it up.

There were plenty of things around the house that night that needed doing. But I didn't need them to *do* anything for me. Truth be told, I could do it myself easier. Or I had enough money that I could pay someone else to do it. I didn't want them to *do* anything except just *be* my daughters. All I wanted that evening was to just milk every moment of that time when my girls wanted to *know* me better.

How long has it been since you've taken an evening or a morning off, and didn't *do* a thing for God? Just sat down next to Him, talked to Him, and let Him talk to you. It's a refreshing time. It will change the way you think about Him (*know*). It will change the way you see yourself (*be*). And it will turn doing things for Him from duty to delight.

BOOK TWO

Chapter 5

GOD—ILLUMINATION

God kept a pretty nice scrapbook for us to get to know Him. Check out the old newspaper clippings about the creation of the world. Look at that snapshot of Noah's Ark. Here are a few greeting cards that David sent Him. There's a collection of white papers from the prophets. Here's a series of reports about His Son. And check out the in-depth feature story about the origins of the church. Here's a pile of letters written to some churches. And finally a panoramic photograph of the end of history. Very interesting stuff.

You could spend a lifetime looking through all the material, asking God questions about it, and getting to know Him. Many lifetimes have been fruitfully spent doing just that. And many books have been written recording observations.

This isn't a book about knowing God *per se.* J. I. Packer already wrote that book, *Knowing God*, and I'm not attempting to improve on it. I read his book in preparation for writing my book, and I started underlining key thoughts. But I stopped underlining, because I was just underlining the entire book!

This also isn't a systematic theology outlining the attributes of God. It isn't a devotional approach to knowing God. It isn't a memoir about how I got to know God.

In addition, this is not a book about knowing *man*, about understanding yourself. It's not a theology of who you are in Christ. And it's certainly not another Christian self-help book or God-as-therapist book about how to *do* better in the Christian walk.

The objective for this book is to help you connect the dots between *knowing* God, *being* a Christian, and *doing* what God wants to do through you. In life, you can't abstract these three aspects and major on any one of them. My goal with this book is to integrate all three aspects into one cohesive Christian lifeview—a grid for living out the Christian experience to the fullest. It starts with *knowing* God, which illuminates who we *are*, which in turn inspires what we *do*.

In this section, Book Two, we look at the grid from the top down—God: Illumination. In the next section, Book Three, we look at the grid from the bottom up—You: Inspiration. Book Two looks at the attributes of God. Book Three looks at the application for man.

In the next seven chapters, we'll sample seven different attributes of God, viewing them from the perspective of knowing the God of this attribute, being a Christian who reflects this attribute, and doing what the God of this attribute wants to do through you.

These are just seven attributes or grouped attributes among countless characteristics of God. But the grid we use to examine the attributes can be used in your own journey with God, as you get to know Him and yourself through interaction with His Word and His integration with your life.

HOW TO KNOW GOD THROUGH HIS ATTRIBUTES

Who is the one person in your life that you know better than anyone else on the face of the earth? Maybe it's a long-time friend. Maybe it's a parent. Maybe it's your boss. Maybe it's a mentor.

For me, it's my wife, Tina. After more than three decades of going through the great adventure of life together, I know her better than I know any other human being. I'm the world's foremost expert on Tina; no one else comes close to knowing as much about her as I do. I've also been linked romantically to her.

I can pick up on almost imperceptible body language to know how she's really feeling inside. I know that a half smile, where one side of her mouth goes up, but the other stays down means she's trying to put on a positive front, but the down side of her mouth belies her true feelings. I know that she expresses what she really wants by phrasing it as a question, instead of a declarative statement. So when she says, "Do you want to get the red chair?" She means, "I want to get the red chair." I know when to bring up something critical and when not to (although I don't always heed what I know). I know when she needs encouragement, and when to just stay out of her way. I *know* Tina.

I've been on the trail with God for the exact same number of days that I've known Tina. I became a believer at age 19. On the night it happened, I went forward at church to talk to the preacher, and a new girl from Ohio came forward to join the church. I tell people I met my Master and my mate the same evening.

When I'm talking about *knowing* God, I'm talking about *knowing* Him to an even greater degree than that person you best know on earth. I'm talking about *knowing* at such deep levels—and ever deepening levels—that you unite with Him. Let's unpack this further.

INTIMACY: THE INTERSECTION OF GOD AND MAN

Knowing God involves not just the interaction between God and man, but the intersection between God and man. Because we were made in the image of God, we have a huge advantage in getting to know God. Other created beings lack this advantage. Angels, for example, share some attributes with God, but they are not made in His image, therefore they can never *know* God to the same degree which we can. If science could someday train and educate an animal to approach human levels of

> Knowing God involves not just the interaction between God and man, but the intersection between God and man.

intelligence, the animal could not know God fully because it lacks a spirit. If technology could someday create artificial intelligence that surpassed man in nearly every area, that machine still could not know God as we can *know* Him.

Man shares God's image, so he is uniquely crafted to interface with God in a way that no other created thing can. It's like God has a special connector, and only humans have a port that it fits.

Furthermore, only the believer can plug in to God and receive all the data available from God. That's because the non-believer is operating with a dead spirit, to take the computer metaphor one step (probably one too many) further, a dead motherboard, or should we say, Fatherboard.

And you were dead in your trespasses and sins. @Ephesians 2:1

So while the non-believer can connect on the physical and mental levels with God, he cannot connect on the spiritual level until God the Spirit brings the non-believer's spirit to life:

And when you were dead in trespasses and in the uncircumcision of your flesh, He made you alive with Him and forgave us all our trespasses. @Colossians 2:13

For just as the body without the spirit is dead, so also faith without works is dead. @James 2:26

And if the Spirit of Him who raised Jesus from the dead lives in you, then He who raised Christ from the dead will also bring your mortal bodies to life through His Spirit who lives in you. @Romans 8:11

The non-believer can know a lot *about* God, on the physical and mental levels, in the same way they know a lot about a celebrity, without truly knowing God. It is not until God first reaches down with His hand of grace and gives a person the ability to reach up and take His hand with the hand of faith, that the connection is made.

For you are saved by grace through faith, and this is not from yourselves; it is God's gift—not from works, so that no one can boast. @Ephesians 2:8–9

At the point this occurs, the rebirth takes place. A person becomes a believer, his spirit is "quickened," made alive by God's Spirit. This is the first step of knowing God. It is the point at which God accepts the sinner because of Christ's atonement. And the sinner accepts God's acceptance of him.

It is at this point in which God begins to intersect with man. It is the beginning of truly knowing God. Intimately. Like a husband *knows* a wife. In fact, in a very real, yet non-sexual way, the way that a man and woman become one flesh is precisely the way God and a person become united and intimately related. We are the bride of Christ. The Bible uses the word *ginosko* to describe how a husband *knows* his wife (Luke 1:34), for how Jesus *knows* the Father, and for how we *know* God. In all cases, there is an infinite union and an intimate unity.

ACKNOWLEDGE HIS ATTRIBUTES— AWARENESS OF HIS PRESENCE (*KNOW*).

ACKNOWLEDGING HIS ATTRIBUTES SYSTEMATICALLY

A student of noted zoologist and Harvard professor Jean Agassiz tells the story of how his distinguished mentor taught him the art of close observation. "Take this fish," the professor said, "and look at it; by and by I will ask what you have seen."

In 10 minutes the student had seen all that he could see, and began to get restless, but since the professor was nowhere to be found, he halfheartedly went back to studying the fish some more. He turned it over and around, looked at it in the face, from behind, sideways, and so on. The morning passed, and still no professor. During the afternoon, a thought struck him: He would draw the fish. With surprise he began to discover new features in the creature. Then the professor returned, and encouraged him with, "That is right. A pencil is one of the best eyes." But after hearing the student's brief description of what he had observed, the professor said, "You have not looked very carefully, why?" He continued, earnestly, "Look again, look again."

The student was flabbergasted. Still more of that fish! So he diligently focused on the task until at the end of the day, the professor enquired, "Do you see it yet?"

"No," the student replied. "I am certain I do not, but I see how little I saw before."

"That is the next best," the professor said.

For three long days, the professor put the fish before the student for observation, forbidding him to look at anything else. "Look, look, look," was the professors repeated injunction.

The lesson sunk in for that student, the brilliant American entomologist Samuel H. Scudder (1837–1911). Years later, Dr. Scudder wrote:

> *This was the best entomological lesson I ever had—a lesson, whose influence has extended to the details of every subsequent study.... Agassiz's training in the method of observing facts and their orderly arrangement was ever accompanied by the urgent exhortation not to be content with them.*
>
> *"Facts are stupid things," he would say, "until brought into connection with some general law."*

Many of us think we can get to know God in about 10 minutes a day or during an hour each Sunday. We take a cursory glance at Him, observe a few surface attributes, and think we've learned about all there is to know. But the more we look, the more we see. And the more we see, the more certain we are of "how little I saw before."

The way to know God's attributes is to study them systematically. That means spending time looking at Him and to Him. It means studying Him with a pencil in hand. "A pencil is one of the best eyes." One of the best disciplines I learned as a young student of God was to keep a Daily Spiritual Diary. Each day I would read a passage, systematically working my way through the entire Bible one book at a time—over and over.

Each day I made entries into my Spiritual Diary, carefully recording five observations:

- God's message to me today
- A promise from God
- A command to keep
- A timeless principle
- How does this apply to my life?

This daily exercise got me into the lifelong habit to "Look, look, look" at God. Later, in Chapter 20, we'll discuss in much more depth the Know Be Do Bible Study method. But for now, heed Professor's Agassiz's advice. When you think you've seen it all. "Look again, look again." You'll see more. And more.

This is what the LORD *says:*

> *The wise man must not boast in his wisdom;*
> *the strong man must not boast in his strength;*
> *the wealthy man must not boast in his wealth.*
> *But the one who boasts should boast in this,*
> *that he understands and knows Me—*
> *that I am Yahweh, showing faithful love,*
> *justice, and righteousness on the earth,*
> *for I delight in these things.*
> *This is the* LORD*'s declaration.*
> *@Jeremiah 9:23–24*

ACKNOWLEDGING HIS ATTRIBUTES EXPERIENTIALLY

Far and away the most reliable, comprehensive, and inspirational way to get to know God is through His Word, the Bible. In fact, most errors in Christian doctrine result from putting priority of our *experience* over and above the Word of God. So Christian existentialism is not what I'm talking about here. What I am talking about is having an awareness of where God intersects our lives. *Sola Scriptura*, indeed. The Bible contains everything we need to know to *know* God.

Since we are made in the image of God, however, we can learn things about ourselves by knowing God, and we can learn things about God (as long as Scripture corroborates what we learn) by knowing ourselves. The key is *awareness*. So many people go through life with little awareness of how active God is in their lives, how their history is His story. Their story becomes part of His story.

Slow down and see how God is working in your life for His glory and for your good. You'll learn much about yourself and about Him.

I was downtown in a large city once when I encountered a couple of men wearing masks. One knocked me out, and the other pulled a knife and left an 8-inch scar that I still sport across my abdomen. I woke up a good deal poorer.

But I was never so thankful. You see, the first man was an anesthesiologist, and the other was a surgeon performing an emergency appendectomy.

Sometimes God causes a little pain in order to make things better in the long run. God's attributes at work: grace, foreknowledge, mercy, love, wisdom. These are attributes we read about all the time in the Bible, but one personal experience with them leaves a mark that lasts a lifetime.

My first job out of seminary was at a missions education agency for men and boys. But just months after taking the position, the denominational leadership announced a plan to consolidate my agency with a larger organization. My job would almost certainly be a casualty of the merger. We were baffled why God would do this. Was this our reward for three long, faithful years of seminary? We were more than a little miffed at God, and downright angry at one of the denominational leaders who seemed to be railroading this through.

We were at the meeting when the vote was taken. We sat there stunned, surrounded by oblivious thousands in the large arena who had just voted for me to lose my job. My wife and I cried.

Less than a month later, God provided a position at a church that turned out to be one of the biggest blessings of our lives. And the denominational leader who put an end to my job? He became a close friend and one of the greatest mentors in my life.

When Dr. God pulls out His scalpel, we shouldn't hide. We should shout "Hallelujah!" But that's a part of getting to *know* God that you really have to learn by experience.

ABIDE IN HIS ABILITY—ACCEPTANCE OF YOUR POSITION IN HIM (*BE*)

We've looked at some examples of how we get to know God through His attributes. Through His Word. And through His working in our lives. We'll go much deeper into that in the following seven chapters.

It's tempting to jump right on to *do*. After all, that's the exciting part. Where the rubber hits the road. We've seen God provide the example. Now let's try our hand at it, right?

Not so fast. You can't skip steps in the Christian life. If you skip, you stumble. David is the classic case.

Pity the poor persecuted young David, falsely accused by Cush the Benjamite and being chased all over creation by Saul the wacko. Listen as poor David pours out his heart to God in Psalm 7, sometimes called the "Song of the Slandered Saint," calling for God to deliver and vindicate him:

> See, the wicked one is pregnant with evil,
> conceives trouble, and gives birth to deceit.
> He dug a pit and hollowed it out
> but fell into the hole he had made.
> His trouble comes back on his own head,
> and his violence falls on the top of his head.
> @Psalm 7:14–16

Whoa, stop the music! David bemoans those bullies Cush and Saul here in Psalm 7. But it sure sounds like something that could have been written about *David*—approximately eight months after his little escapade with Bathsheba. Ironic words, Dave. Pregnant with evil. Conceives trouble. Dug a pit, but fell into the hole he had made. Trouble and violence comes back on his own head.

David's failure? *Knowing* without *being*. That leads to *not doing*.

Sure David knew attributes about God. His power, His strength, His deliverance. He had read about them in the book of Moses. He had even experienced them first-hand in victories over Goliath and other warriors. But knowing doesn't always equate to doing. You can't skip a step. You can't skip *being*. Being is integrity: Be = Do. *Being* takes the eternal attributes of God and makes them internal.

I wonder if David reread Psalm 7 later in life. Those words may have stung. I've done it myself, so I don't want to pile on David. I myself have quoted a Scripture to someone, only to need it quoted back to me a few days later. It's a dangerous pitfall for every Christian. How can you make sure you don't pull a David?

Know has to become *be* before *be* can become *do*.

Be is the pivotal connector between *knowing* God and *doing* what He wills. Pull out that hinge pin, and everything begins to collapse.

So how can you make sure His attributes turn into your ability? How can you *be* what God wants?

BEING BY ABIDING

Let's assume for now that you've got the *knowing* God part down. You've acknowledged His attributes through your study of His Word and through your experience with His work in your life. You're intimately aware of His presence. Now you're ready to *be* so you can *do*. You've failed at this before. So what's going to be different this time?

Your *position*.

> *I am the vine; you are the branches. Whoever abides in me and I in him, he it is that bears much fruit, for apart from me you can do nothing. @John 15:5*

Note your position in this chain of vine-branch-fruit. You're not the vine. You're not the fruit. You're the branch. *Be* the branch. Let the Divine be the

> Note your position in this chain of vine-branch-fruit. You're not the vine. You're not the fruit. You're the branch. *Be* the branch. Let the Divine be the Vine (*know*).

Vine (*know*). You be the branch (*be*). Then, the fruit (*do*) will take care of itself. It will happen naturally—supernaturally.

Your abode is to abide.

Abide in His ability.

Live in a constant state of awareness that you are connected to Him ("Whoever abides in me") and that He flows through you ("and I in him").

Again, exceedingly simple, yet not easy.

I have an electric razor I use every morning. It's rechargeable, and it's always in one of three states. Plugged in and fully powered. Unplugged and lacking full power. Or dead. I keep it plugged in most of the time because when it's unplugged, it loses power quickly. In no time, it's dead.

We have a lot of rechargeable Christians running around, half dead or fully dead. They plug in for an hour or two on Sunday morning and expect to perform well all week long. Maybe they get a recharge on Wednesday night, if they're really committed. But apart from Him, they "can do nothing."

Why not stay plugged in constantly? The power is free! Abiding in Him. Being who you *are* in Him and letting Him *be* in you. It's not enough to merely *know* He's the power source. You need to stay close enough to be plugged in. *Being* in a constant state of prayer and communion with Him. I believe that's what the Bible means by "pray without ceasing" @1 Thessalonians 5:17.

You'll remember that I said the difference between failing and successfully *doing* is your *position*. By that I mean not only as a branch in between the vine and the fruit, but also your position as in your standing and acceptance by God. Remembering that you are fully embraced by God will keep you energized, flowing with His Spirit. Don't discount yourself when God is flowing through you. Listen again to this amazing statement by Jesus just a few verses before His vine and branches lesson:

> *I assure you: The one who believes in Me will also do the works that I do. And he will do even greater works than these, because I am going to the Father. @John 14:12*

You will do even greater works than Jesus? How can that be?

Because in reality, God the Father, God the Son, and God the Spirit are doing the works *through* you. If only you will simply *be*—abiding in your position in Him. "Not I, but Christ" @Galatians 2:20.

Don't ask how. Don't ask why. Ask *Who*.

Him. Through you.

Just *be* it.

ACT ON HIS AUTHORITY— APPROPRIATION OF HIS POWER (DO)

Then, finally, just *do* it.

Have you ever looked at a grape vine carefully? The vine, the main trunk of the plant, stands straight, solid, and singular. From it radiates a plethora of branches of all lengths, shapes, and sizes. Some are larger, not nearly as large as the vine, but obviously mature. Some are smaller. Some are brand new and still quite green. Yet as long as they are connected to the vine, they are the same in essence as the vine. Then there's the fruit. Full dependent on the vine, yet growing on the branches.

The branches don't muster up the unction to produce the fruit. All they have to do is *be*, abiding and connected to the vine.

Our focus too often is on the *do*—producing fruit. But if we simply focus on *knowing* the vine—connecting intimately with its power—and then be in our position of letting His Spirit sap flow through us, then the fruit will come. After all, it's the fruit of the *Spirit*, not the fruit of the Christian (Galatians 5:22).

The Know-Be-Do pattern is stamped all throughout Scripture. We've already looked at Philippians 3:10–11, but let's look at the rest of the passage:

> *My goal is to <u>know</u> Him and the power of His resurrection and the fellowship of His sufferings, <u>being</u> conformed to His death, assuming that I will somehow reach the resurrection from among the dead.*
>
> *Not that I have already reached the goal or am already fully mature, but I make every effort to take hold of it because I also have been*

taken hold of by Christ Jesus. Brothers, I do not consider myself to have taken hold of it. But one thing I <u>do</u>: Forgetting what is behind and reaching forward to what is ahead, I pursue as my goal the prize promised by God's heavenly call in Christ Jesus. Therefore, all who are mature should think this way. And if you think differently about anything, God will reveal this also to you. In any case, we should live up to whatever truth we have attained. Join in imitating me, brothers, and observe those who live according to the example you have in us. @Philippians 3:10–17

Note how Paul begins with knowing God, moves on to being in the right position, and concludes with a description of what he is *doing*.

The Know-Be-Do theme is woven into every biblical writer's teaching. Here's an example from Peter:

His divine power has given us everything required for life and godliness through the knowledge of Him (know) who called us by His own glory and goodness. By these He has given us very great and precious promises, so that through them you may share in the divine nature, (be) escaping the corruption that is in the world because of evil desires (do). @2 Peter 1:3–4

I like what Adrian Rogers says about this passage in his book *Kingdom Authority*:

One of these days, we're going to wake up and understand what God has already given his children and stop asking him for what we already have. Living victoriously isn't your responsibility; it is rather your response to God's ability.

We already have his authority to *do* great works. We have the power. We have the position. All we need to do is appropriate it. To know. To be. To do.

Are you familiar with an Invisible Fence? It's an electronic system for dog owners that keeps your pet in your yard—and out of your plant beds—with no real fence. An electric wire is buried underground around the perimeter of the yard and plant beds. The dog wears a special electronic collar that gives him a small, safe shock anytime the dog tries to cross the buried line. The dog soon learns his limits, and eventually, the collar can even be turned off, and the dog will not cross the boundaries.

Many of us go through life like dogs collared behind an invisible fence. Satan controls the collar. Every time we try to reach forward, pursue the prize, and *do* something for God, he gives a little shock—except it's not so safe. The shock may be, "You'll fail again." Or "You're not worthy." Maybe "You'll be rejected." He has quite a repertoire of lies and deceptions. Eventually, we learn our "boundaries" and don't even bother to go beyond our small "comfort" zone.

God calls, and we go right up to the boundary, but then we stop, afraid of the shock. We never even get to attempt to do what God can do through us. How do we break this cycle?

Know. Be. Do.

Know attributes of God, acknowledging His presence.

Be aware of your position in Christ, abiding in His ability.

Do actions on His authority, appropriating His power.

The success you find may *really* shock you.

THE LIKENESS OF GOD

I believe one of the most under-valued, under-preached, under-studied—yet least understood—concepts in the Bible is that we are made in the image of God.

> I believe one of the most under-valued, under-preached, under-studied— yet least understood— concepts in the Bible is that we are made in the image of God.

In many ways, it's the foundational concept behind Know Be Do. We have hope that we can be reflections of His greatness and goodness only because we were created in His image. We are echoes of His original Words.

What blows my mind about being made in His image first of all is how valuable it makes me feel. A person like me?…a creation that shares attributes with Almighty God? But secondly, as honored as it makes me feel, I'm immediately humbled to an even greater degree. My sin and weakness is ever before me, and that image scarcely looks anything like Holy God. If I bear the image of God, I feel I'm like a kindergartner's rendering of the Sistine Chapel.

But how the concept makes me *feel* has little to do with its reality. You. Me. Billy Graham. Hitler. We are all made in the image of God. I was reminded of this one day by a good friend who rebuked me for railing against our U.S. President. "Remember, that he is an image-bearer, just like you."

Some may argue that only Adam and Eve were made in the image of God, but that's not what the Bible teaches. Here's what it says in Genesis 9:6, well after sin entered the picture:

> *Whoever sheds man's blood, his blood will be shed by man, for God made man in His image.*

One of the reasons behind justice and morality is that we are made in the God's image and any assault against man is an affront to God. It's part of what sets us apart from the animals.

Of course, sin has badly distorted the perfect image which God originally created, like a pebble cast in water distorts the reflection on its surface. The silversmith heats the silver intensely in a crucible and skims off the dross, removing the impurities. When he can perfectly see his reflection in the surface of the silver, he knows the silver is pure. Yet even in our impure state, we are still cast in God's likeness.

> *We praise our Lord and Father with it (our tongue), and we curse men who are made in God's likeness with it. @James 3:9*

MADE IN THE IMAGE, BUT NOT A CLONE OF GOD

No matter how pure we become, however, we will never be God because He has certain unique attributes that man will never share. We are made in the image, the likeness of God; we're not a clone. God possesses certain incommunicable traits that are not shared with man, such as His omnipotence (all powerful), omniscience (all knowing), and omnipresence (the ability to be all places simultaneously). But He also has many communicable traits which He does share with man. We already discussed the triune nature of both God and man. He shares many more. Compassion. Power. Wisdom. Communication. Creativity. Justice. Holiness. To a lesser degree, all of these and more are reflected in man's nature, and that is focus of this and the rest of the chapters in Book Two.

The idea in this set of chapters is to take an attribute of God and look at it through the Know-Be-Do grid. Sometimes we'll look at a group of related attributes, as the next chapter does with God's kindness (His grace, mercy, forgiveness, longsuffering, and compassion). We'll take a three-pronged approach:

1. We'll get to *know* God through this character trait.
2. We'll learn who we, as image bearers, are to *be* in light of this trait.
3. We'll discover what we *do* as image bearers and reflectors of this trait.

I think back to the best boss I ever had. What was it that made him such a great boss? Why did I enjoy working for him so much, and how did he manage to get more out of me than any other boss I'd ever had? He did three things. 1) He started me off with a meeting with the head of the organization, who gave me the 30,000-foot vision for who they were and where they were headed. Then he encouraged me to have meetings with all the department heads to get the same information at their level. These meetings helped me get to **know** the organization and its goals. 2) He empowered me by giving me the full authority and the responsibility of my position. I was the man. He was behind me, supporting me, but I was the one entrusted—and accountable—for **being** everything the job required. 3) He let me **do** it. He *expected* me to *do* it. He didn't second guess or micro-manage or get in the way. He gave me all the resources I needed to do the job, but didn't do it for me, and he didn't force me to do it. A great boss makes all the difference in the world.

God is the World's Greatest Boss. The more we *know* about Him, the more we discover about who we *are* in Him, and the more we can *do* through Him. Let's get busy.

Chapter 6

GOD'S KINDNESS

The cloudless Kentucky sky was powder blue, the sun was scorching hot, and the three feet of fresh water in our new above-ground pool in the backyard was cool and beckoning. The only thing standing between my energetic little 6-year body and that sparkling water was the bologna sandwich my mom said I had to eat before I could get back in. She was out in the backyard hanging up freshly laundered white towels on the clothesline as I wolfed down the sandwich and shot toward the back door, headed for the pool.

Then I did something my father had told me a million times not to do. Instead of pressing on the door frame to push open the rickety old storm door, I pushed my hand right on its glass window pane. The glass gave way, and my small hand shot right through as shards of glass splintered everywhere. Blood from my skinny wrist landed on the concrete stoop of our back porch.

The crash startled my mom, and she whipped around, clothespins in her mouth and a white towel still in her hand, beholding the gruesome sight of what had just happened. She ran over with the towel and quickly wrapped my wrist in it. The thirsty white towel soaked up the bright red blood as she led me through the house and out the front door toward the car. Halfway down the driveway, I looked up at her and asked a question, what seems now like quite a peculiar question, but to my 6-year-old mind, it was something I needed to know above anything else at the moment.

"Mommy, do you still love me?"

Compassion and bewilderment flitted across her face. "Yes, honey, I still love you…"

I don't really remember what else she said because once I heard the words, "Yes, I still love you," nothing else mattered.

In my small mind, I asked the question because I had broken a glass window, ruined one of her good towels, and was causing a major catastrophe. I wasn't sure if she still loved me after all that. How little I understood about love. The value of windows and towels were the furthest thing from her mind right then. All she wanted was for her little boy to be alright.

A few stitches later, I was just fine, but I had learned three important lessons that day. 1. Never press on the glass to open a door. 2. Dad knows what he's talking about. 3. Mom will love me no matter what I do.

Despite that lesson, and many others since, I still often suffer from small-minded thinking and an inability to grasp unconditional love when it comes to my Heavenly Father. How many times have I broken windows, ruined towels, or cut myself to shreds and then looked up at my Heavenly Father and doubtfully asked, "Do you still love me?"

"How could you love me…after I did that? Again? And again? And again? And again?…"

How little I still understand about God's love. He's not concerned about breaking glass and ruining towels. He's concerned about us being alright. Like my earthly father, when God says, "Don't do that," He's really saying, "Don't hurt yourself."

> When God says, "Don't do that," He's really saying, "Don't hurt yourself."

We expect His wrath. And as His children, we get His mercy. Yes, we may get some discipline, as I did from my father after the dust settled over that broken window pane. But we always get His love.

"Thou shalt not…" means "Don't hurt yourself."

"Thou shalt…" means "Help yourself to some happiness."

And yet Satan, the world, and sin have really done a number on me. I believe the lie. I believe sin can satisfy. And even more sadly, I believe that God doesn't love me when I sin.

All my life, I've felt like I was such a disappointment to God.

How could He love me, when I keep going around breaking windows and ruining towels? Never learning from my mistakes, I keep pressing my hand through that glass pane over and over. And then doubting the Father's love for me. Over. And over. And over. And over…

Eventually, I have the courage to look up at His face and ask, "Do you still love me?"

The answer always comes back, "Yes, of course, I still love you."

After all, He bled first.

ZAPPING US

Which of these scenarios do you most associate with God?

You do something bad and get zapped.

You do something good and get kindness.

You do something bad and get kindness.

You do something good and get zapped.

Growing up in a legalistic environment, the order I just listed them in was the order I believed was true. Mostly, I thought at that time, God was just itching to zap you the moment you messed up.

But as I grew to *know* God better, I made a couple of discoveries: 1) God's love is unconditional; 2) Zapping and kindness are both good expressions of His love.

God in His infinite wisdom knows exactly when to use zapping (discipline for His children; punishment for everyone else) and when to use kindness (grace and mercy) to maximize His glory and our good. We'll look at His discipline more in later chapters. But the focus of this chapter is God's softer side, a set of attributes that make up His kindness, including:

- Grace (giving us good things we don't deserve)
- Mercy (withholding punishment we do deserve)
- Compassion (empathetic suffering alongside our suffering)

We're not going to do a word study on this, but the Bible gives us a long list of words that describe God's kindness: goodness, reconciliation, forgiveness, longsuffering, benevolence, lovingkindness.

Notice I didn't include love. Love may involve kindness or zapping.

Now that I know God a little better, I would reorder my statements from above as follows:

You do something bad and get kindness.

You do something good and get kindness.

You do something bad and get zapped.

You do something good and get zapped.

The overwhelming majority of the time, I am experiencing God's kindness. In fact, 99 percent of the time, I'm not even cognizant of God's goodness to me. I didn't once have to think about my heart beating during the past hour. I didn't once have to look around and wonder where I would get my next lung full of air. I made zero effort to keep the atoms in my body from flying apart and exploding. I didn't lift a finger to stop myself from floating off the face of the earth. So much of God's kindnesses are "automatic." I cringe at myself for my constant lack of gratitude, like the nine lepers who never returned to thank the Lord.

BENEFITS VS. ENTITLEMENTS

The key to *knowing* more of God's kindness is to intentionally focus on his benefits instead of our entitlements. Once we do this, we are freed to *be* kind and *do* kind acts.

One of the first Bible verses my daughter learned was "Be kind to one another." She used to quote it with a little sassiness in her voice to her younger sister when they were fussing. I think her theology was better than her motive, but the full verse is still a classic one-verse synopsis of Know Be Do applied to God's kindness.

> And be kind and compassionate (be) to one another, forgiving one another (do), just as God also forgave you in Christ (know).
> @Ephesians 4:32

You might remember the story (@Matthew 18:21–35) Jesus told about the king who had pity on a servant who owed him the equivalent of millions of dollars—more than he could ever repay. The king cancels his debt, free and clear. Yet the servant turns around and demands immediate repayment of a small debt *he* is owed, just a few hundred bucks, and when his debtor can't pay, has him thrown in jail. Slimeball.

The parable was in response to Peter's question about how many times we should forgive. "Seven?" Peter suggested generously, since the rabbis required only three.

Pause it here…alert: we're getting ready to *know* something about God…

Seven times 70. 490. Or you could go ahead and say, there's no limit.

Limitless forgiveness! Oh, the lavish extravagance of His mercy and grace!

OK, so this we *know* about God, His mercy is infinite. Next step…in light of this, what should we *be*?

Be kind and compassionate. *Be* it. Make that the habit of your mind, will, and emotions. Be constantly aware of the unpayable debt for which God forgave you. Let that awareness shape your attitude towards others, so that when the offense comes—and it will come—you are kind-hearted.

You're visiting friends, the Joneses, marveling at their new home, the *Better Homes & Garden* cover home in the neighborhood you wish you could afford, and your wife looks over at you and says, "Hon, you're just going to *have* to get a second job!"

Ouch. That hurt. You're going to pay for that one—I'm throwing you in jail. Solitary confinement for the next three days.

Or….*knowing* how God has forgiven you of offenses millions of times worse than that, you *be* the humble forgiven debtor that you are, and cancel the debt instantly (*do*), quipping with a sincere smile, "Or maybe we can just move in with the Joneses! Got a spare bedroom?"

Know. Be. Do.

It's so simple. But not easy.

The key is appropriating *His* power over and against your own power.

Our power makes us think of our entitlements. His power reminds us of His benefits.

True mercy is voluntarily yielding rather than wielding power you possess.

POWER UP, POWER DOWN

The book of Genesis is a steady Hit-and-Miss Parade of powerful characters who get their chance to shine, but fall short of God's plan. Adam…blames God. Cain…kills his brother. Noah…gets drunk and naked. Abraham…gets ahead of God. Isaac…disregards God's covenant plan. Jacob…deceives. Finally, we get to Joseph, a character so important and so similar to Christ that the entire last quarter of the book is devoted to his story. God really wants us to get this.

The plot has plenty of ups and downs, twists and turns, but the climax comes at the end of the book after Joseph has been promoted all the way to the top as Pharaoh's right-hand man. He is approached by his famished brothers, the same group that poked fun at him and sold him into slavery. They need food, and Joseph has plenty. He has the resources to save their lives or the power to really make them pay. This is his chance; let them twist in the wind. Let 'em starve. Send them to prison. Need food, huh? Well, revenge is best served cold, and Joseph has the opportunity to set the table with a bountiful feast of retribution.

His response? He weeps. Then he makes a remarkable statement that embodies every element of a Know-Be-Do understanding of God's mercy, grace, and compassion:

> *But Joseph said to them, "Don't be afraid. Am I in the place of God? You planned evil against me; God planned it for good to bring about the present result—the survival of many people. Therefore don't be afraid. I will take care of you and your little ones." And he comforted them and spoke kindly to them. @Genesis 50:19–22*

Now *that's* kindness. Let's look at how he got there. Notice Joseph's acknowledgement of God, his awareness of God's presence (*know*): "Am I in the place of God?" He acknowledged that God alone is the Supreme Judge. With the same rhetorical question, Joseph also accepts his own position within God's Kingdom: he is a servant of God the King, subject to His authority and recipient of His mercy (*be*). What's more, Joseph realizes he is in the position of being worship leader in this very teachable moment. So he sings the praises of God's gracious sovereignty. He shares an insight about God, noting that when man makes evil plans, God rules and overrules by bringing glory to Himself and good to humankind. Finally, Joseph takes care of *do*: "I will take care of you." He comforted and "spoke kindly."

Kindness. It's all about appropriating *His* power over and against your own power.

WHY ARE WE SUCH BAD ADVERTISEMENTS FOR CHRISTIANITY?

In his book *What's So Amazing About Grace?*, Phillip Yancy opens with a sad story of a prostitute who came to a counselor for help. "At last I asked if she had ever thought of going to a church for help. I will never forget the look of pure, naive shock that crossed her face. 'Church!' she cried. 'Why would I ever go there? I was already feeling terrible about myself. They'd just make me feel worse!'"

Why are we such bad commercials for God?

In the eyes of non-believers, they see the Christian and assume our God is the mirror image of us. If we are all anger and condemnation, then that is how they perceive God. That's because they don't see God directly or fully, they see only us. So if we are warped, then they perceive God as distorted. If that's who we are, they reason, they don't want any part of us or Him.

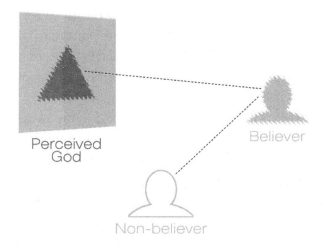

Perceived
God

Believer

Non-believer

It should be the other way around—us reflecting *Him*. We want them to see the perfect God, so we should be a reflection of *Him*. God is the reality. His Word is the light, illuminating Who He is and revealing who we are. We are mirrors, reflecting His glory.

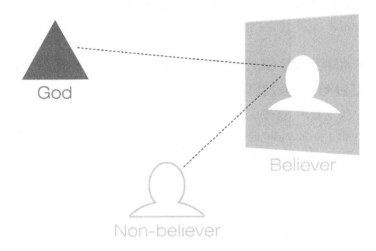

If we stay out of the light, we might look good to ourselves and to others. But the reflection will be dim, and the defects will be hidden. We must stay in the light in order to be the best and brightest reflection of God that we can *be*.

Staying in the light, studying God's Word, is how we see Him and get to *know* Him. The more perfectly we see Him, the more accurately we see ourselves. When we see Him for all He is, we see our flaws, but we also see our value and potential, for we are a reflection of Him—with the opportunity to be a winsome advertisement for Him.

I've worked in the ad agency world for years, and the one thing you can say for most ads is that they make the product sound *better* than it really is. Most Christians are the opposite. Their pitch for God turns off most "buyers" quicker than a McDonald's commercial

> One thing you can say for most ads is that they make the product sound *better* than it really is. Most Christians are the opposite.

on Animal Planet. And yet we have the ultimate "product" to advertise! Why are we such bad ads?

In a nutshell…

First, we don't truly *know* God intimately.

Second, we fail to see ourselves as we truly *are*—both the assets and the liabilities.

Third, because we're not *knowing* and *being*, we're not inspired to *do* what we should do.

Let's break this down even further, starting at the very beginning.

God *is*. God is a being. He has *being* just as we have *being*. The goal is for our being to be a perfect reflection of His being. That won't happen in full until we get to Heaven. But in the meantime, the way we sync up His being and our being is by getting to *know* Him. As we get a more and more complete picture of Who He is, we can see who we *are*, where we resemble Him and where we don't. As we begin to accentuate the similarities and eliminate the dissimilarities, we can begin to *do* what He wills through us.

Take God's kindness, for example, and let's begin with *know*. Can you say you truly and intimately *know* the extent of God's grace to us? Grasping it begins with a recognition of how sinful we are, just like how large our debt truly is. Most people I know consider themselves to be pretty good people. But look at God's standard of perfection. Think about all the times you do the right thing for the wrong motive. The evil thoughts you have that nobody knows but you. All the good things you should do but you fail to do. The more you *know* about God's holiness, the more you see how far short you fall. From this humbled position, we can begin to *be* who we really are. Forgiven wretches. From there, it's a whole lot easier to reach out with mercy, grace, and compassion to our fellow man and *do* kindness.

When I first began to draw, I was given a book containing various simple illustrations with instructions for how to copy them. I just copied the strokes that the original artist made. I wasn't an artist yet, so it was very mechanical, or legalistic, if you will.

Next I graduated to drawing the live object in front of me. I had to study the object, to see how the light reflected off some parts and left shadows on other parts. I had to take an image snapshot in my mind, internalize it, so that I could remember it as I looked down at my pad.

Next I introduced color. I learned to see the true color of the object so that I could replicate it as I mixed paints. Gradually, I began exploring various media: pastels, watercolors, oils, digital. All the while, I was using the same principles I learned at the beginning: *Study* the object. See how the light reflects off of it. Imprint its image into your own mind so that you *become* it. And then *let it flow* out onto your work.

Know. Be. Do. Let the Master help you create a Masterpiece of grace.

UNIQUE SELLING PROPOSITION

Returning to the advertising analogy, one of the main things I learned in Advertising Principles 101 is the concept of the Unique Selling Proposition or USP. The USP is the exclusive benefit that your product offers that none other has. It's what sets your product or service apart from the crowd, makes it different, distinctive, better. The challenge is to identify your product's USP and make it the core of your sales appeal, your message.

I believe the USP for the Christian is grace. There are a lot of characteristics that make the Christian unique (shall I say peculiar?). But for my money, the one that stands out the brightest against a dark world is this attribute of God's grace. Grace is the Christian's USP.

Jesus had a way of finding the darkest backgrounds He could so that His grace would shine most brilliantly. Sinners, prostitutes, tax collectors, Samaritan "dogs", serial divorcees, women caught in adultery, lepers, cheats, thieves, drunkards, idolaters, murderers, the poor, the outcast, the lonely, the unclean. He caught a lot of flak from the religious leaders for hanging out with such a seedy crowd.

The contrast between *knowing* God's grace and *not* knowing it is never clearer than in the story of Jesus at Simon the Pharisee's house (@Luke 7:36–50). Jesus is anointed by a woman who wets His feet with her contrite tears, wipes them with her hair, kisses them, and pours perfume on them. Simon the Pharisee criticizes Jesus for allowing this, seeing "what kind of woman this is…a sinner," possibly a prostitute since only hookers wore long hair in that day.

Jesus gives Simon a little lesson on grace, pointing out that one who is forgiven loves much more than one who is forgiven little. "Your sins are forgiven," Jesus says to the woman. "Your faith has saved you. Go in peace."

Want to do more acts of grace? Get a handle on how much you've been forgiven. Get to *know* how holy God is—and how unholy you are. That knowledge will give you a true appreciation for how amazing God's grace in your life is. Then you can begin to understand "your sins are forgiven," you *are* holy in God's eyes, just as pleasing to God as His only Son. And then you can "go in peace," reflecting God's grace and doing acts of kindness.

Tony Campola tells a story about being in a late-night diner when a group of prostitutes came in. He overheard one of them, Agnes, say that tomorrow was her birthday. He suggested to the gruff owner that they throw a surprise birthday party for her the next night, and to his surprise, the owner not only agreed, but offered to bake a birthday cake. The owners got the word out, and the next night at 3:30 a.m., the restaurant was packed with prostitutes when Agnes walked in. "Happy birthday!" they all screamed. Agnes was stunned. She couldn't take her eyes off the cake, and finally asked if she could take it home, just a few blocks away, and come right back. When she left, the place was silent. Tony didn't know what else to do, so he said, "What do you say we pray?" When he finished, the owner said, "Hey, you never told me you were a preacher. What kind of church do you belong to?"

"I belong to a church that throws birthday parties for (prostitutes) at 3:30 in the morning."

"No you don't," replied the owner. "There's no church like that. If there was, I'd join it. I'd join a church like that!"

Kindness is the best advertisement for Jesus that I know. If we can only know it, be it, and do it, our churches would be full—full of prostitutes and other sinners like us. What a wonderful party it would be.

Chapter 7

GOD'S POWER

God scares me to death.

I don't make that remark flippantly. Or irreverently. Or as hyperbole.

I state it deliberately.

God literally scares me to the point of mortifying sin and self. And that's a good thing. Not a bad thing.

Fearing God is not a popular notion these days. You don't see a lot of best-selling books about it. Or seven-part sermon series. Or TV evangelist fear-fests.

We're afraid of fear.

People prefer thinking about God as a gentle Father. Or a Friend. Or a Savior. Or a Healer. Or a Prayer Granter. And certainly He is all those things.

But the same divine attributes that make Him such an amazing Father, Friend, Savior, and more are the very characteristics that make Him worthy of fear.

He is omnipotent. Omniscient. Omnipresent. Holy. Jealous. Infinite. Self-sufficient. Just. Sovereign. And yes, wrathful.

Scary.

After all, this is the God who struck a man dead for simply trying to keep the Ark of the Covenant from falling off a cart (@1 Chronicles 13)!

Of course, they were disobedient for putting the Ark on a cart in the first place. But the bottom line is: God is holy, God is powerful, and God is wrathful—a combination that certainly evokes fear.

> *"The fear of the LORD is the beginning of wisdom."*
> *@Proverbs 9:10*

Fear has all kinds of benefits. I just mentioned wisdom. The Bible also links the fear of the Lord with understanding, praise, instruction, avoiding being a fool, departing from evil, honor, humility, good counsel, might, stability, strength, treasure, and salvation.

Fear is a lot like the sensation of pain. Pain might be perceived as a negative. Until you realize that pain tells you to remove your hand from a hot stove. Tells you to go see a doctor when something's not right. Keeps you from doing something stupid like jumping off a tall building or grabbing a live wire. Were it not for pain, many of us might be dead.

Fear has helped me "depart from evil." God reminds me as He did Job: "And unto man he said, Behold, the fear of the LORD, that is wisdom; and to depart from evil is understanding" @Job 28:28.

I remember a time in my life when I had fallen into the grip of sin that had a particularly strong hold on me. I could feel it sapping my strength, leading me away from God, and enslaving my mind, will, emotions, and spirit. For about a month I was in a free fall. Then for about the next three months, God unleashed the longest string of bad things that I can recall ever happening to me. Rapid fire. Almost daily. It brought me to my knees. There was no doubt in my mind that God was taking me to the woodshed, getting my attention. Scaring me to *death*.

> *"For if you live according to the flesh, you are going to die. But if by the Spirit you put to death the deeds of the body, you will live."*
> *@Romans 8:13*

> *"Therefore, put to death whatever in you is worldly: sexual immorality, impurity, lust, evil desire, and greed, which is idolatry."*
> *@Colossians 3:5*

Many translations use the phrase "put to death." I like the King James here: "mortify." It captures the feeling of being scared to death, "mortified," which is precisely what the fear of the Lord should properly do.

The fear of the Lord should make us scared to death to sin. That's OK to say, all you who can't conceive of a wrathful God. Remember, that fear, like pain, can be a healthy thing, often, the most gracious thing He can do.

Growing up as a kid, I was scared of my Dad. He had a temper. And I didn't want to set it off. I did a few times. Like the time he told me to clean up my mess in the garage, and I let him know that I would get around to it when I was good and ready. I didn't exercise a lot of wisdom on that one. And he gave me a dose of understanding. And trust me, he mortified my rebellious attitude.

My heavenly Father gave me a lesson I won't forget. I won't forget the pain and fear I experienced. But I dropped that sin cold turkey, and don't plan on testing God on that one again.

THE FEAR FACTOR: GOD'S POWER

The force behind our fear of God is His power. Why do our knees get shaky when we're called in to the boss's office? It's because he has power that can dramatically change our position in life. With two words, "You're fired," your boss can instantly send you to the ranks of the unemployed, bring untold stress into your life, devastate your self-esteem, and damage your life for years. Of course, with two words, "You're promoted," he can equally send you into the stratosphere, enhance your standard of living, and impact your financial situation well into your retirement years. That's a lot of power.

The big difference between your boss at work and the Boss of the world is that we have His promise He always gives us good gifts:

> He did not even spare His own Son but offered Him up for us all; how will He not also with Him grant us everything? @Romans 8:32

> What man among you, if his son asks him for bread, will give him a stone? Or if he asks for a fish, will give him a snake? If you then, who

*are evil, know how to give good gifts to your children, how much
more will your Father in heaven give good things to those who ask
Him!* @Matthew 7:9–11

*Every generous act and every perfect gift is from above, coming
down from the Father of lights; with Him there is no variation or
shadow cast by turning.* @James 1:17

Good gifts. Always.

But…*God's* definition of *good*, not ours. He defines good as: 1)
Something that advances His Kingdom, not ours; 2) Something that
promotes our holiness, not our happiness. It might enhance our earthly
situation and our happiness, but that's not the purpose of His power.

And that's what puts the fear of God in me. And His peace. Because
it's not Him using His power *against* me that scares me. It's Him using
His power *through* me.

One of the most surprising verses in the Bible to me is Psalm 130:4: "But
there is forgiveness with You, That You may be feared." What? Forgiveness
leads to fear? Huh? When I think of forgiveness, I think of peace. Relief.
Cleansing. But fear? Not so much. But what I'm missing is that both His
justice and His grace are expressions of His might and power. They invoke
fear equally. The thought of Him withholding forgiveness is sheer horror.
And the thought of Him extending it is surely humbling.

POWER TOOLS

Fear is just the *beginning* of understanding God and His power. It's just
kindergarten. He wants us to graduate beyond that. Once you move
beyond fear, you become an admirer of His power, and finally to an
instrument of His power. Sometimes we're a power tool in the Master
Carpenter's hands. Sometimes we're the apprentice woodworkers in His
Carpentry Shop.

The first time I was around a large table saw in a woodworking shop,
I was scared of it. It was loud and fast and sharp. I knew a man who used
one and now has only nine fingers. But gradually I moved beyond fear to
admire what it could do, the fine furniture it could create. I learned how

it worked and what it was capable of. I began to harness its power, and eventually turned out some nice woodworking projects with it. I never lost my healthy fear of it, though, and so far, I still have 10 fingers.

Our goal is to move beyond a yeoman's fear of God's power. Let's go back to our purpose for looking at God's power in the first place. The whole point of this section of the book is to examine the communicable attributes of God, the qualities that have at least a partial counterpart in mankind. In this chapter—His power. We do this so that we can *know* Him more intimately, *be* a reflection of His image, and *do* what He does.

Know. Be. Do. So let's examine God's power in more depth.

God is omnipotent, so His power compared with ours is like a Fortune 500 CEO and a mail clerk. He speaks, and a universe is born. He gives the word, and a dead man rises. He owns all the world's banks. He knows what's going on with each and every one of the world population of sparrows (@Matthew 10:29).

That's a lot of megawatts, megahertz, megamillions, and megaeverything.

We might think we're well acquainted with how powerful God is, but do we truly *know* it intimately? Personally?

Let me put the question to you another way. It's a question someone posed to me which I have never forgotten: Have you ever been at the end of your rope with nowhere to turn and no one to turn to but God?

Think about that question for a moment.

I'm not asking if you've read about Moses with his back to the Red Sea. Or Daniel in the lion's den. Or Elijah in the battle of the gods. Or Paul in a shipwreck. It's good to know these stories of God's power on display. But reading about woodworking is one thing. Putting the principles to work in the woodshop is where understanding turns into *ginosko* knowing.

So, have you experienced God's power in your life when He was the only way out? Maybe it was a big problem. Perhaps a small one.

When our second daughter was born, she was very sick. Her twin had miscarried a couple of months before, and her blood had mixed with my wife's, causing life-threatening complications. She had to have a total blood transfusion at one week old, and her tiny life was hanging in the balance. I can still see her fragile, jaundiced body crouched in the incubator, clinging to life.

I felt so powerless to help. The doctors were doing everything they could. But we weren't sure it would be enough. I was trying to be strong for my family. But I remember going into the tiny, sterile bathroom at the hospital, and the tears just let go as I dropped to my knees, the toilet becoming my altar of prayer. I told God that I had nowhere else to turn, nowhere else I *wanted* to turn. He had all the power—the power to heal, the power to take life. I flung myself on His mercy seat. And cried until I could cry no more. When I stood up, I felt His power and peace. Already, He had given hope, and I believed that He would grant healing—or give grace to endure the worst.

In this case, God granted healing, and within a week, we were taking our precious new daughter home.

I *know* God's power intimately. I've seen Him work over and over—in our lives and those we love. He's still the same God Who both flooded the earth and parted the Red Sea. He is an awe-inspiring God. Equally worthy to be feared and to vanquish fears.

> He's still the same God Who both flooded the earth and parted the Red Sea.

Once you *know*, it's time to *be*.

POWER-PACKED PASSAGE

One of, if not *the*, greatest passage about God's power is found in the opening of Paul's letter to the Ephesians:

> *I pray that the eyes of your heart may be enlightened, so that you will know…what is the surpassing greatness of His power toward us who believe. These are in accordance with the working of the strength of His might which He brought about in Christ, when He raised Him from the dead and seated Him at His right hand in the heavenly places, far above all rule and authority and power and dominion, and every name that is named, not only in this age but also in the one to come. @Ephesians 1:18–22*

It begins with a picturesque description of *knowing*, "that the eyes of your heart may be enlightened, so that you will know..." Oh, what a prayer! "Enlighten the eyes of my heart, Lord!"

Then Paul pulls out the Greek thesaurus to use all the major power words of the New Testament in one power-packed passage:

"the surpassing greatness of His **power**" (*dunamis*, origin of *dynamite*)

"in accordance with the **working**" (*energia*, origin of *energy* and *ergonomics*)

"of the **strength**" (*kratous*, origin of *–cracy*, or *rule*, as in *democracy* [common people *rule*] and *theocracy* [God *rules*])

"of His **might**" (*ischus*)

"which He **brought about** (*energeo*) in Christ"

"far above all **rule** (*arche*) and **authority** (*exousia*) and **power** (*dunamis*) and **dominion** (*kuriotes*)"

That's a powerful line-up! Bottom line?

The same power that raised Christ from the dead is *yours* today.

Enlighten the eyes of your heart with *that* thought! The resurrection power of Christ resides in your life. The same bundle of dynamite that put death to death and blew Satan's plan to Kingdom come is burning inside you. Now that's something to *be*!

Be powerful.

Be energized.

Be strong and mighty.

Be authoritative.

All in Christ.

Forget *do* for now. Just let the *being* of that soak in. You *are* as powerful as the resurrection itself.

Wow.

I don't know about you, but when a cop appears in my rearview mirror, my heart snaps to attention. Then I look down at the speedometer. The cop doesn't have to *do* anything. His mere presence is enough to keep me in check. That's because he carries with him the full power and authority of the government. The officer can require me to pull over, present certain documents, answer questions, perform certain tests—in general, cooperate fully with him. I may be bigger, faster, smarter, or richer than he is personally. But none of that matters, because of who he *is*. Simply his *being*.

We possess the same kind of power, strength, and authority. There may be forces all around us that are bigger, faster, smarter, or richer than we are. There are big-name rulers, authorities, powers, dominions—both in time and in eternity. But with Christ as our head, He puts them under His feet, and fills us with the full faith and credit of the Son Himself.

Now, that probably won't get you out of a speeding ticket, but it will make Satan shudder in his steps. To *be* powerful, keep enlightening the eyes of your heart with an unceasing awareness of your God-given authority. Be the kind of person that when your feet hit the floor each morning, the devil says "Oh, blue blazes, he's up!"

ENERGY CRISIS

You may be wondering to yourself at this point, "Since God is so powerful, and I'm supposed to be powerful, too, why does my life often seem so powerless?"

Fair question. Simple answers.

1. You're focused on *doing* first, not *knowing* and *being*.
2. You're looking at power through the eyes of the world instead of the eyes of your heart.

Let's take the first point first. If this concept of Know Be Do is sinking in for the first time, it will take some time for it to transform your spirit, soul, and body. Perhaps your entire life, your focus has been on *doing*. That's what you've been taught. That's the gist of how most Christians think the Christian life should work. *Do*. Doing the 10 Commandments.

Doing the Sermon on the Mount. Doing the Great Commission. Doing tithing. Doing all things your church says a good member should do. That's not all bad. Doing is better than not doing. And obedience is always a good thing.

It's possible, however, to *do* things for God externally and yet internally live in rebellion and deception. King Saul learned this lesson (@1 Samuel 15). God told him to go and destroy a wicked nation that had attacked God's children. Saul was to spare no one and nothing, not even their livestock. But Saul didn't carry out the instructions fully. He spared some of the people and kept the best livestock for himself. He thought he could make up for it by sacrificing a few animals to the Lord. So the prophet Samuel confronted him: "To obey is better than sacrifice" @1 Samuel 15:22. Partial obedience is disobedience. And obedience for the wrong motive is disobedience.

If you're focused on *do* rather than *know* and *be*, you may be a lot like Saul. He thought God could be bought, but God doesn't bargain and barter with us. He's not a power broker. He *gives away* power to those who are rightly connected with Him. Saul was focused primarily on the *do* of what God had instructed. So he thought he could improve on God's plan. He thought he should save the things that had value—political value or financial value—and that would make him more powerful.

What if instead Saul had focused on the *know* and *be* of God's plan? Saul would have understood that he was being used by God to execute judgment on a sinful people who had murdered God's own children. He would have felt the Father's righteous indignation. He would have become what a godly king should *be*, an instrument in God's hand to restrain evil and lead the people. Focused merely on *do*, however, Saul did things his own way. He ended up dethroned and powerless.

We need to *know* God so intimately that we feel his heartbeat. Medical studies have discovered that the bond between a mother and her baby is a

> *Doing* no longer becomes a burdensome responsibility. But a response to His awesome ability.

powerful force. It's so powerful, in fact, that by simply looking and smiling at each other, moms and babies synchronize their heartbeats to within milliseconds of each other. This remarkable phenomenon is but an echo of the powerful connection between us and our heavenly Father. When we look to Him and smile at each other, our hearts are in sync, and we become one. His power flows into us. We become what we should *be* in Christ. And then *doing* is not something we must muster up within us. Or a plan we negotiate with the Father. *Doing* no longer becomes a burdensome responsibility. But a response to His awesome ability.

REPROGRAMING THOUGHT HABITS

Let's turn to the other reason you may feel so powerless: Perhaps you're looking at power through the eyes of the world instead of the eyes of your heart. Your mind has been trained to perceive power a certain way, but you're totally missing power that's surrounding you. Adrian Rogers gives an eye-opening illustration of this in his book, *The Incredible Power of Kingdom Authority.*

A friend told about an experiment he had seen in a film. A large walleye pike was taken alive and placed in a huge aquarium. Then, buckets of live minnows were dumped in. Mr. Pike thought he was in heaven. He began rapidly swallowing these minnows.

A short while later, the researchers played a trick on the fish. They placed a large glass cylinder of water into the tank, then filled it with minnows. Mr. Pike started for the minnows again, only to bump his snout against the invisible barrier. He tried again and again and again. Finally he gave up and settled on the bottom of his "heaven" that had gone awry.

The researchers then removed the cylinder, and the minnows swam freely in the tank. But Mr. Pike never made a move for one of them. They could swim right past his face, but he never moved. He was convinced that he would never have another minnow. He finally starved, surrounded by minnows.

In psychology, this is called classical conditioning. Life conditions us to accept failure. We end up settling for a powerless, sub-normal Christian life. We experience defeat in a certain area of life over and over and over and over and over until we give up.

Thought habits are powerful. They're habits just like any other habits, like putting on your seatbelt or putting on your right shoe first every time. They are ruts in your thinking that are hard to jump out of. But there is a way.

Reprogram your mind.

God made the mind with a marvelous feature: We can think only one thought at a time. Thoughts may come in rapid fire, but only one at a time. The way to change a thought is to replace it with a better thought. The way to change a thought habit is to replace it with a better thought habit over and over and over again until the new thought habit takes over. The Bible calls this "transforming by the renewing of your mind."

> Do not be conformed to this age, but be **transformed by the renewing of your mind**, so that you may discern what is the good, pleasing, and perfect will of God. @Romans 12:2

Don't *be* conformed. *Be* transformed.

Displace the negative from Satan with positives from God.

> Finally brothers, whatever is true, whatever is honorable, whatever is just, whatever is pure, whatever is lovely, whatever is commendable—if there is any moral excellence and if there is any praise—dwell on these things. @Philippians 4:8

Reprogram your *being*.

Yeah, you hit your snout on that glass wall about a hundred million times. Your snout is conformed to the shape of that glass cylinder by now. But God's power removes the glass. Go get some minnows! Start developing a new thought habit. How?

> We all, with unveiled faces, are looking as in a mirror at the glory of the Lord and are being **transform**ed into the same image from glory to glory; this is from the Lord who is the Spirit. @2 Corinthians 3:18

Did you catch the Know-Be there? Gaze at the glory of the Lord. *Know* Him. Looking at Him is like looking at yourself in the mirror, because what He *is*, you *are*. You *are* powerful through Him. You *are* righteous and pleasing to God through Him. All the glorious qualities you see in Him are reflected in you. Let that awareness transform your mind.

No more bumping into the invisible glass wall. It's gone. Reprogram your mind to see the new reality.

Jot down a list of ways that your life resembles Mr. Pike's. Maybe it's a relationship that you think is too far gone. Maybe it's a repetitive sin that keeps you walled in. Maybe it's a goal that seems too far away. Maybe it's a thought habit—anger, resentment, envy, negativity—that has captured your mind.

Know God's power. His power is a transformer that you can plug in to. Then you'll have access to power that will help you *be* and *do* all that He wills.

Yes, His power is a force to be feared. Let it scare you to death. In the process, His power will lead you to transformed life.

Chapter 8

GOD'S INTELLIGENCE

Jesus was always the smartest guy in the room.

I don't believe we often think of Him like that. We think of Him as gracious, kind, compassionate, miraculous, amazing, and wise perhaps.

But if Jesus walked in to a room full of Wall Street wizards, He could explain every intricacy of the efficient market hypothesis and why investors on average will do better with a low-cost index fund than with a group of hedge funds. He'd make Warren Buffet feel like a schoolboy.

If he walked into a lecture hall filled with physicists, He could give an in-depth analysis of string theory, and he could explain to the chiefs of staff at the world's leading medical research hospitals how He turned elemental atoms into living matter. I imagine their response would be similar to the teachers at the temple who listened to the 12-year-old Jesus: "All those who heard Him were astounded at His understanding and His answers" @Luke 2:46.

This guy is smart. He's one know-it-all Who truly knows it all. He's omniscient.

I make a point of this because I believe many people, even Christians, think of Jesus as an authority on spiritual things, but when it comes to other matters—science, business, psychology, technology—they think He's a little out of His wheelhouse. Why is it important to recognize Jesus as the world's foremost authority on...everything? Because He is Lord of everything.

Have you ever had a boss who knew less about your job than you? Not that uncommon. Or have you been in a training class or lecture and heard the so-called expert say something you knew wasn't accurate? It calls into question everything else he taught, doesn't it?

God knows everything about everything. And He's known it before there was anything.

God the Father, God the Son, and God the Spirit were all three involved in the world from the ground floor. All three Persons of the Godhead were active in creation. "Let *us* make man in *our* image..." @Genesis 1:26.

God the Father: "I made the earth, and created man on it. It was My hands that stretched out the heavens, and I commanded all their host" @Isaiah 45:12.

God the Son: "For everything was created by Him (Jesus), in heaven and on earth, the visible and the invisible, whether thrones or dominions or rulers or authorities—all things have been created through Him and for Him. He is before all things, and by Him all things hold together" @Colossians 1:16–17.

God the Spirit: "The Spirit of God has made me, and the breath of the Almighty gives me life" @Job 33:4.

After inventing the cosmos, They wrote the user's manual for it. The Bible. As the Visionaries, Architects, Engineers, Builders, and Executive Management for the universe, I think They were well-qualified to write the instruction book for it. And we'd be pretty smart if we read it.

KNOW THE BUILDER

I served on a building committee one time for a large church that was constructing a multi-million dollar addition to its campus. The man who had been chosen to chair the committee was a godly man, but he didn't have a lick of experience in building or contracting. I'll always remember how he began our first meeting, "When the pastor asked me to lead this group, I told him that I don't know a thing about building, but I do *know* the Builder." The project ended up a complete success.

In business, they say it's not *what* you know, it's *who* you know. That may not be fair when it comes to your career, but if you want to get ahead in your spiritual life, focus on *Who* you know. I'm talking about real *ginosko* knowing, an intimate communion with God on a moment-by-moment basis. I'd rather know God intimately than have an encyclopedic knowledge of systematic theology. Not that you can't have both. But knowing the heartbeat of God will get you through more of life's ups and downs than all the Christian self-therapy books ever written.

> **I'd rather know God intimately than have an encyclopedic knowledge of systematic theology.**

God is the source of all wisdom. "Wisdom and strength belong to God; counsel and understanding are His" @Job 12:13. This includes God the Son: "Christ is God's **power** and God's **wisdom**" @1 Corinthians 1:24. And God the Spirit: "And the spirit of the LORD shall rest upon him, the spirit of wisdom and understanding, the spirit of counsel and might, the spirit of knowledge and of the fear of the LORD" @Isaiah 11:2.

God's power and His wisdom are often linked, and that's why I put these two chapters back to back.

> *May the name of God be praised forever and ever, for **wisdom** and **power** belong to Him.* @Daniel 2:20

> *He made the earth by His power, established the world by His wisdom, and spread out the heavens by His understanding.* @Jeremiah 10:12

I'm thankful that God is both powerful *and* wise. One without the other would be a dangerous combination. Imagine a fool who is very powerful (think Hitler, or perhaps your last boss!). Or how about a wise man who is powerless? Not much influence there. But God is both powerful and wise. In fact, with just the three attributes we've looked at so far, His kind heart, His kingly power, and His keen wisdom, I'm thinking

He must have been the inspiration for the "man behind the curtain," the Wizard of Oz. He's certainly willing to hand out brains, heart, and courage to those who come to Him, and that brings me to my next point.

BE THE SMARTEST GUY IN THE ROOM

I must confess that I rather enjoy when someone well educated and exceptionally intelligent looks at me with one of those incredulous looks, as if to say, "You seriously believe that stuff?"

I sat next to one of these types on a long plane ride one time and had the opportunity to share my faith. After I explained the Gospel and how he could respond, he looked at me as if I was an absolute lunatic and said, "So I could do this right now, and boom, all my sins would be forgiven?" I'll have to admit, he made it sound both amazing and foolish at the same time, but that's precisely what it is.

> *For the message of the cross is foolishness to those who are perishing, but it is God's power to us who are being saved. @1 Corinthians 1:18*

The first two chapters of 1 Corinthians are rich with revelation about God's wisdom. Note how Paul continues with a series of questions and logic that would make Socrates proud—and perhaps frustrated:

> *Where is the philosopher? Where is the scholar? Where is the debater of this age? Hasn't God made the world's wisdom foolish? For since, in God's wisdom, the world did not know God through wisdom, God was pleased to save those who believe through the foolishness of the message preached. @1 Corinthians 1:20-25*

Now on to the part I really want you to focus on:

> *Brothers, consider your calling: Not many are wise from a human perspective, not many powerful, not many of noble birth. Instead, God has chosen what is foolish in the world to shame the wise, and God has chosen what is weak in the world to shame the strong. God has chosen what is insignificant and despised in the*

world—what is viewed as nothing—to bring to nothing what is viewed as something, so that no one can boast in His presence. But it is from Him that you are in Christ Jesus, who became God-given wisdom for us—our righteousness, sanctification, and redemption, in order that, as it is written: The one who boasts must boast in the Lord. @1 Corinthians 1:26–31

If you're a believer, this should really make you feel like the smartest guy in the room. Look at all the amazing things you learn about yourself in this passage.

1. You are a brother or sister to the Apostle Paul…*The* Apostle Paul!
2. You are called and chosen by God to do something quite remarkable: to outshine the worldly wise and strong.
3. You are *in* Christ Jesus, Who became God's wisdom for us, as well as our righteousness, sanctification, and redemption.
4. You are welcome to boast about all this in the Lord.

With these kinds of credentials, you should never be shy about representing the Christian worldview in the midst of all the philosophers, scholars, and debaters of this age. You are wise in Christ. *Be* who you are!

HOW TO GROW IN WISDOM

Now, as a believer, you are more wise than the most intelligent non-believer. But that doesn't mean you are as wise as you can be. Even Jesus grew in wisdom (@Luke 2:40, 52). That's a mind-blowing thought. God the Son *grew*—advanced, made progress—in *wisdom*. The fact that Jesus, God the Son, grew in wisdom shows that He willingly laid aside certain attributes of His divinity to become human and fulfill the Father's plan. If Jesus grew in wisdom, how much more can we grow?

In the New Testament, wisdom (*sophia*, origin of philo*sophy*, love of wisdom) is used in referring to both man and God. The generic meaning of the word is insight, skill, intelligence. But it goes way beyond knowledge. It's knowledge *applied*. It's knowledge informed by morality. I can't improve on J.I. Packer's definition: "Wisdom is the power to see, and the inclination to choose, the best and highest goal, together with the surest means of attaining it."

I like to think of wisdom as the intersection of knowing, being, and doing. It's where all three come together. Knowing God, His truth, and His ways. Being in Him and Him being in you. Then simply doing what is consistent with Who you know and who you are.

Jesus grew in wisdom the same way we do—by filling Himself with the Father's supreme truth. In Luke 2:40, it says He was being "filled" with wisdom. The Bible here uses the same word for "filled" as it does when it says that we are to be filled with the Spirit (@Ephesians 5:8). So how are we filled? When we open ourselves to God, He fills us. Jesus was a perfectly clean vessel, so He filled up quickly. By the time He was 12 He was teaching the teachers. When *we* get filled with the Spirit, we have to first empty ourselves—of self and of sin. When we're filled with *wisdom*, we have to empty ourselves of the world's foolishness and folly.

MADAM FOLLY AND LADY WISDOM

Allow me to introduce you to two ladies: Madam Folly and Lady Wisdom.

The first nine chapters of Proverbs personify Wisdom and Folly as two ladies roaming the city streets, calling out to you. This is all written by King Solomon, a man who had 700 wives and 300 hundred concubines, so he knew a thing or two about women—although his love life wasn't the wisest thing he ever did.

Madam Folly is loud and proud. Attractive and brazen. Alluring and deadly. She's the woman your mother warned you about.

Lady Wisdom actually has a lot in common with Folly. They both invite seekers to their prominent home on the highest point in the city. They both offer refreshment. But whereas Lady Wisdom's guests gain longevity, Madam Folly's guests end up in the grave.

If you're going to *be* wise, you need a good companion. The fact that Madam Folly and Lady Wisdom share so many outward similarities underlines the need to look beyond the surface. Satan is the master of disguises, and he masquerades as an angel of light. Beautiful. Attractive. Promising. But his promises turn out to be lies, and that is the crux of the matter. Truth vs. lies. Wisdom vs. folly.

To *be* wise, you need to develop discernment between what's goodly and what's godly. Appearances are deceptive, and the heart is deceitful above all things. You need to be so close to the Father—to *ginosko* know Him—that you see things through His eyes.

WHICH WAY IS UP?

What if you were living life upside down, and you didn't even *know*?

Imagine…you wake up one morning, open your sleepy eyes, and are jolted awake as you discover all the furniture is on the ceiling. In fact, your bed—with you in it—seems to be nailed to the ceiling. You clutch your bed, for fear of falling. As you look down and around your room, you see your curtains standing tall, straight up from the floor like they've been starched stiff. You look over at your phone, which appears to be glued to the nightstand, lest it fall. You cautiously swing one leg off the bed and touch your old floor, the new ceiling. You get up, walking on the ceiling, and look out the window. To your amazement, the sky is down, the ground is up, and all the houses are hanging upside down, just like you.

It all feels incredibly strange at first, but you begin to get used to it. Your orientation starts to shift, and the fact that you're walking on the "ceiling" doesn't seem so scary. After a few weeks, the "upside-down" sensation begins to subside, because the whole world seems to be upside down. Your senses adapt to it, and before long, you hardly notice that you're upside down because everything is relative, and down seems to be the new up. Before you know it, everything feels perfectly normal again. You practically forget about the way it used to be. Until one day, you walk in to work, and someone is standing on the ceiling.

How strange that person is, standing on the ceiling. He definitely sticks out from the crowd. It's hard to take what's he's saying seriously, because, well, he's upside down. One day, you hear him telling a coworker that he can walk on the ceiling, too. All he has to do is believe and jump off the floor, and he'll be walking on the ceiling, too. Everyone laughs, and your coworker shoots him one of those incredulous looks, as if to say, "You seriously believe that? So I could do that right now, and boom, all of a sudden I'm walking on the ceiling?"

How foolish.

How amazing.

Most of us have spent so much time living in the upside-down world, that we forget sometimes which way is up. I hear people say sometimes that Jesus turned the world upside down. Actually, He was born into the upside-down world. He came to turn it right side up.

That's why so much of the wisdom He taught sounded "upside down."

Love your enemies. (Say what?)

The first shall be last. (Huh?)

To find your life, lose it first. (Not following you here.)

Turn the other cheek. (Ouch.)

Humble yourself, and He will lift you up. (I'm looking out for #1.)

It's more blessed to give than to receive. (I'm not getting it.)

The servant is master. (Have you met my boss?)

Blessed are the poor and persecuted. (Count me out.)

To live, you must first die. (Are you drunk?)

> I hear people say sometimes that Jesus turned the world upside down. Actually, He was born into the upside-down world. He came to turn it right side up.

Little flashes of the true right-side up world keep appearing throughout the Bible.

An ax head floats.

A young boy kills a nine-foot giant.

An army walks across a sea on dry land.

A man walks across the water in a stormy sea.

The world says, "Seeing is believing." God says, "Believing is seeing."

God's wisdom is counter-intuitive. To our upside-down ears, Satan's lies often sound like they make more sense than real truth: Look out for number one. Only the strong survive. He who makes the gold rules. Evil exists, therefore God doesn't.

So how do we make sure you're getting filled with God's truth and not Satan's trash? I could ask it another way: How do you *know* God?

Read His autobiography. He included a whole section in it called the Wisdom books.

Job teaches us that our purpose on earth is God's glory, not our comfort.

Proverbs is wisdom on steroids.

Ecclesiastes describes the futility of life in the upside-down world—without God.

Song of Songs is a love story, and God is all about love.

There's also the "Proverbs of the New Testament," James. In one verse, James tells us how to recognize the kind of wisdom that comes from God: "But the wisdom from above is first pure, then peace-loving, gentle, compliant, full of mercy and good fruits, without favoritism and hypocrisy" @James 3:17. From just this one verse, we learn the earmarks of the real thing. Wisdom is:

1. Pure, undefiled
2. Peace-loving
3. Considerate, gentle, courteous
4. Submissive, reasonable, yields to reason
5. Full of mercy, compassion
6. Full of good fruit
7. Impartial, unwavering, whole-hearted, straight-forward, unfeigned
8. Sincere, without hypocrisy, free from doubts

If the wisdom you're operating with doesn't live up to these qualities, it's upside down.

Still not sure you're being wise? Just ask God.

> Now if any of you lacks wisdom, he should ask God, who gives to all generously and without criticizing, and it will be given to him. @James 1:5

Solomon found out the offer is for real. Pleased by his godly character, God said, "Ask. What should I give you?" Solomon could have asked for long life, riches, revenge on his enemies. Instead, he asked for wisdom "to discern between good and evil" @1 Kings 3:9. He wanted to be able to know which way is up. God granted him wisdom—plus everything else he didn't ask for to boot. Want to *be* wise? Ask the Source to give it. He's got plenty to go around.

HOW DO YOU *DO* WISDOM?

So you're getting to know God and His all-wise ways by saturating your mind with His words of wisdom. You are growing and being filled with wisdom; you are *being* wise. How do you *do* wisdom? How do you navigate through a world that's upside-down?

Live inside-out.

What do I mean by that? It's really just another way of saying let be = do. Let who you *are* in Christ define what you *do*, what you say, how you live.

Most people are living their life from the outside in. They walk around and let all the external stimuli penetrate their innermost being. This bombarding from the outside world shapes their inner self. The inner self conforms to the outer-world mold.

God's wisdom tells you are forgiven and fully pleasing to man. An unloving Christian brother tells you are a failure and you'll never measure up. Do you live in defeat? Or let the inner wisdom win out?

God's wisdom tells you that marriage is one man plus one woman for life. But the Christian divorce rate is 50 percent, and more than 55 percent now approve of gay marriage. Do you conform? Or let the inner wisdom transform you and then you impact the culture?

God's wisdom tells you to think on what is pure and righteous. But the media barrages you with sex and violence. Do you lower your standards? Or keep your guard up?

God's wisdom tells you that you're valuable because of Whose you are. The culture says your value is measured by what you make and what you own. Do you live in discontentment? Or look to Christ for your self-worth?

God's wisdom tells you to show kindness to that coworker who keeps stepping on you on his way up the corporate ladder. But your friends tell you how to tear him down in the boss's eyes. Do you seek revenge your way? Or love your enemy?

In every case, the temptation and pressure to do things the way of the upside-down world is immense. But remember you are right-side up. Remember the One Who never leaves your side. Get stepped on?

> *Don't say, "I will avenge this evil!" Wait on the LORD, and He will rescue you. @Proverbs 20:22*

There's wisdom for every situation in God's Word. Value it. Seek it like silver. The more you *are* filled with His Spirit and His Word, the more you will transform your world instead of conforming to it.

BUT WHAT ABOUT THE HARD QUESTIONS

You're not always going to have the answers. A friend is going to get cancer and die too young. A child is going to be abused. Someone is going to steal something for which you've worked hard. People are going to starve because God didn't send rain.

The upside-down world is going to turn sideways sometimes, and you can't tell which way is up.

In times like these, what can you do?

Know the Builder.

Go back to beginning. Know that He is sovereign God and that everything that happens is for His glory and our good.

> *We know that all things work together for the good of those who love God: those who are called according to His purpose.... What then are we to say about these things? If God is for us, who is against us?... For I am persuaded that not even death or life, angels or rulers, things present or things to come, hostile powers, height or depth, or any other created thing will have the power to separate us from the love of God that is in Christ Jesus our Lord! @Romans 8:28, 31, 38–39*

Know His purpose.

Know His power.

Know His love.

Know Him.

Sometimes His wisdom is a mystery—a truth once concealed, but someday revealed.

> *"For My thoughts are not your thoughts,*
> *and your ways are not My ways."*
> *This is the LORD's declaration.*
> *"For as heaven is higher than earth,*
> *so My ways are higher than your ways,*
> *and My thoughts than your thoughts."*
> *@Isaiah 55:8–9*

We'll never cram the infinite amount of God's wisdom in our finite minds. A child doesn't understand why a loving parent would take him to a man who would stick a painful needle in his arm. He cries. He bleeds. He feels pain. He feels hurt, maybe betrayed. But one day the mystery will be revealed.

I wouldn't want to worship a God I could fully understand. He would be much too small.

So why does a child die because God didn't send rain? I don't know. I don't know enough to even speculate. Because the more I do know, the more I know how little I know. I don't have all wisdom. I'm not God, and I wouldn't be very good at it, if I tried.

> *Trust in the LORD with all your heart, and do not rely on your own understanding.* *@Proverbs 3:5*

What I do know is Him. I know that God is good, and God is great. And we are neither of these things. *Knowing* God is enough to *be* who He says I am. And to *do* what He tells me to do. I'm not smart enough to know anything else. And that makes me one of the smartest people in the room.

Chapter 9

GOD'S CONNECTIVITY

God is not an extrovert. Nor is He an introvert.

God is an omnivert.

He turns in every direction seeking relationship, fellowship, community—and unity.

Three is never a crowd within the Holy Trinity. Internally, the Godhead is perfectly and eternally complete within the community of God the Father, God the Son, and God the Spirit. Population: 3.

Externally, He is pleased to fellowship with the beings of His created community. In fact, that's the point. God did not create the human race out of need. He wasn't lonely. He wasn't lacking something that needed to be made up. He was perfectly satisfied with the fellowship He enjoyed in the Trinity—Father, Son, and Spirit. But as we have seen, God created us so that we could *know* Him and His glory and connect with Him body, soul, and spirit.

Some people, such as deists, view God as an uncaring, uninvolved "Clockmaker" Who created the clock (universe), wound it up, and let it go.

But does this kind of "Silent Partner" God write an autobiography detailing His history-long interaction with His people—the nation of Israel (Old Testament) and His church (New Testament)?

Does a hands-off Creator become a man Himself, getting His hands dirty—no, bloody—so that He can identify with and redeem man?

Does an absentee Father-type of God care for our smallest need and encourage us to pray and live in constant communion with Him?

No, the God of the Bible is an ever-present God Who highly values community, family, relationships, fellowship, and unity.

God is well-connected.

GOD, THE ORIGINAL INTERNET

I can still remember the first time I connected to the Internet. It was 1992. I had received in the mail one of those CDs with "500 free hours" from AOL or CompuServe or one of those early online services. I bought a 50-foot telephone extension cord which I carefully routed along the wall from our kitchen phone jack to my computer, the first PC I ever owned. I installed the software from the disc, went through the steps, and then heard for the first time that now familiar series of beeps and buzzes that a dial-up modem makes when connecting to the Internet. And then I was connected. I hardly realized what was going on or what to do once I was connected. But I can still remember the thrill of being connected to a network of millions—now billions—of other computers.

Long before bytes and modems and websites and Tweets, God was connecting His mainframe with users far and wide, sending Tweets such as, "It is not good for the man to be alone. I will make a helper as his complement" @Genesis 2:18, and "We who are many are one body in Christ and individually members of one another" @Romans 12:5. He invented social "media."

He started talking and texting from Day One. As early as Genesis 1:3, He speaks, "Let there be light." At this point, the members of the Trinity are talking amongst Themselves. But soon He's connecting with Adam, with Eve, with Cain, and right on down the line. He sends specs for the ark to Noah. He makes promises to Abraham. He helps Joseph save the day. He sends Moses on a mission. He types up the 10 Commandments. He helps the prophets write some blogs.

Then He goes above and beyond merely sending words. He *becomes* The Word. Jesus. The Divine Communication. The Word in flesh. God

Himself becomes the definitive Word on Who He is, Who we are, and what we are to do. It's God's ultimate medium for communicating Himself to us.

Yes, God is a communicator. *Know* this about Him: He wants you to *know* Him. He wants you to be connected to Him, and He wants a free flow of information between you and Him. Far from a disinterested clockmaker, God went out of His way to make sure that He was revealed, not concealed. God wrote the Book on community and communication.

WHAT IF?...

One of the most terrifying thoughts I can imagine is, What if God had not been so connective? What if He *had* created us, then walked away. What if He had never written the Bible? What if He had no desire to have a relationship with us? What if the Holy Trinity couldn't agree on what to do about man's sin? What if God was out of fellowship with Himself and with us? What if there was no community nor unity?

God can sometimes seem hard enough to figure out *with* the Bible. Imagine life without it.

Meet Job.

The Book of Job was probably the first book of the Bible ever written. Yet, even without the rest of the Scriptures, Job knows and has a relationship God. But it's not easy. And the message of the book is essentially God letting man know, "You are Man, and I am God. You're going to have a devil of time figuring Me out sometimes. But I'm going to help all I can."

Me? I already like Him.

For Job and his three so-called friends, who were getting to know God without the benefit of the Bible or any of the backstory we get in Job 1–2, they indeed had a devil of a time figuring Him out.

God doesn't clue Job in about the big summit meeting in Heaven that He had with the devil. He doesn't tell him that his faith is being tested, even put on display. That might have made it easier on ol' Job. But, ah-hah, we just learned something about God: Our ease is not His first concern. His glory is. Our ultimate good and well-being is important to Him, but only as *He* defines it. In the end, God explains all this to Job. He wants Him to understand. He wants Job to *know* Him more.

From the beginning, God yearns for man to *know* Him. Not a sanitized, PR-polished, politically correct, put-on-your-best face-for-Facebook post. God *is* Who He *is*. Sometimes He seems awfully hard to predict. At times, His grace is lavish. Other times, His justice seems harsh. At times, He's long-suffering and merciful. Other times, He overturning tables and using wicked people to discipline His own children. At times, He seems to be letting us exercise our free will. Other times, He's ruling, overruling, and ordering every step of our way. His ways often seem to stretch from one extreme to another.

But like strings on a guitar, each strand is a string of truth held in divine tension between the poles of His nature. And the most soothing music is a product of tension. Just look at the strings on a guitar, violin, harp, or piano. Each string has the precise amount of tension needed to create the perfect pitch. A little more or a little less, and the note would be off-key. But stretched straight and true, the strings produce soaring sounds that belie the stress they bear. Even the human voice itself creates sound because of vocal cords held in tension.

God orchestrates His World with the same kind of Divine Tension, playing a Love Song for His Creation that resonates in perfect pitch for all eternity.

Clearly, there are limits to how much we can wrap our finite mind around His infinite mind. But, the more we *know* Him, the more we see that He never changes, and His nature is consistent with His every attribute.

NOT LISTENING

Yet, even as the divine orchestra fills the universe with His music, some people still don't know Him. Some people still don't believe. To those who crown Human Reason as their ultimate authority, seeing is believing. Why couldn't He have written His name across the back of every man's hand? Why couldn't He have engraved it in the sky? Why didn't He? Well, come to think of it, He actually did. In fact, He went further. He created matter, an entire universe actually, out of nothing; something man can't do nor explain. He created life out of inanimate matter; something man can't do and feebly tries to explain. Then He stamped His own image on man himself. His DNA is all over the place. To miss it, you really have to close your eyes, cover your ears, and start speaking gibberish like a little kid trying to drown out something he doesn't want to hear. And that's just Creation. Add God's Word and the Word become flesh, God's Son, and well, it couldn't get any plainer that God wanted man to *know* Him. He's dying for you to get the message. In fact, He *did* die so you could *know* Him.

> ## He's dying for you to get the message. In fact, He *did* die so you could *know* Him.

But what about people in remote areas or from obscure ages? What about those who never got the message? Those who have never seen a Bible, heard a preacher, or even heard the name of Jesus? God makes Himself known to them and makes a promise to them, like He does to everyone.

His promise: If you respond to the light you have, He will send more.

"Draw near to God, and He will draw near to you." @James 4:8

God makes this plain in the book of Acts as the Gospel was spreading to pioneer areas, just like it does today.

> *In past generations He allowed all the nations to go their own way,* **although He did not leave Himself without a witness,** *since He did what is good by giving you rain from heaven and fruitful seasons and satisfying your hearts with food and happiness.* @Acts 14:16

God graciously gave them good things: rain, fruit, satisfaction, food, happiness. The human race understood that these benefits came from a source outside themselves. They yearned within themselves to know God. Yet sadly, many cultures invented false gods in a misguided attempt to connect with the true God.

Couldn't God have been more specific it was Him, the Great I AM that was behind all these benefits of creation?

Again, respond to the light you've received, and He will send more. Listen as Paul points them to this Unknown God:

> *For as I was passing through and observing the objects of your worship, I even found an altar on which was inscribed:*
>
> *TO AN UNKNOWN GOD.*
>
> *Therefore, what you worship in ignorance, this I proclaim to you. The God who made the world and everything in it—He is Lord of heaven and earth and does not live in shrines made by hands. Neither is He served by human hands, as though He needed anything, since He Himself gives everyone life and breath and all things. From one man He has made every nationality to live over the whole earth and has determined their appointed times and the boundaries of where they live. He did this **so they might seek God, and perhaps they might reach out and find Him, though He is not far from each one of us**. @Acts 17:23–27*

Reach out. He's not far. Respond to the light you've received, and He will send more. Paul expands on his message in his letter to Romans:

> *For God's wrath is revealed from heaven against all godlessness and unrighteousness of people who by their unrighteousness suppress the truth, since what can be known about God is evident among them, because God has shown it to them. For **His invisible attributes, that is, His eternal power and divine nature, have been clearly seen since the creation of the world, being understood through what He has made. As a result, people are without excuse.** @Romans 1:18–21*

God knew that as the human race spread, His message would sometimes get lost in the clutter. Be distorted, discounted, and denied. And people would try to make excuses. So He proclaimed Himself in a universal language: creation.

> *The heavens declare the glory of God, and the sky proclaims the work of His hands. @Psalm 19:1*

But He didn't stop there. Designing man in His own image, He also lit the spark of His Spirit in man: man's conscience. Before a person becomes a believer, this spark lights the way dimly. By the grace of God, it provides enough light for man to see God and follow His moral compass. The conscience is like a pilot light that barely stays lit until a person is born again. Then God turns on the gas, and the life bursts into full flame. The flame of the believer's spirit is fueled and fanned by God the Spirit. Together, they turn life into a brilliant light that brightly illuminates God's character and lights the way for you and others to follow.

> *You are the light of the world. A city situated on a hill cannot be hidden. No one lights a lamp and puts it under a basket, but rather on a lampstand, and it gives light for all who are in the house. In the same way, let your light shine before men, so that they may see your good works and give glory to your Father in heaven. @Matthew 5:14–16*

Creation. Conscience. Christ. Indeed, He went to great lengths so that you, I, the entire world would acknowledge Him and *know* Him. He communicates. He connects.

What if He hadn't? It would be a dark world indeed. But perish the thought. His first recorded words are "Let there be light." And He's been lighting the way ever since.

CREATED FOR COMMUNITY

After World War II, my dad headed home from the Pacific with a pocketful of money and a penchant for redheads. He spent a chunk of it pursuing my red-headed mother, and they were married in less than a year. They moved into a sparkling white, four-room house on a brand new street, Meadow Park, lined with cookie-cutter houses, all standing in a row like soldiers at attention, built to accommodate the waves of returning servicemen, eager to start their new lives. They were surrounded by young couples just like them, all doing their part to get the baby boom booming. Every morning, after the men went to work, the women would meet at one of the houses, kids in tow, for coffee talk. Magpie moms in their tidy nests, they traded stories, laughed, cried, talked about their men, their children, their futures. The group of eight ladies began calling themselves the Meadowlarks.

One by one, the families moved away. Families grew and busted out of the tiny foursquares. Husbands got promotions and moved on to larger houses. But the Meadowlarks stayed in touch. For more than 64 years. Over the years, their busy lives made the meetings less frequent, but they always met at least once a year to exchange presents at Christmas, catch up on each others' lives, and reminisce about the fresh-cotton-dress days back at Meadow Park. As time marched on, more of their meetings were sad gatherings at funerals. And today, at age 89, my mother is the oldest of two living members of the Meadowlarks.

One of the things that made this Greatest Generation great was their sense of community. Part of it was necessity. They'd been thrown together by history into a fight against common enemies—the axis of evil. Nothing creates a sense of community like a common cause. In my lifetime, the only thing I've experienced that comes close was 9/11.

I can still remember the days following the terrorist attacks. The churches were packed. And a people previously splintered by diverging politics and divisive class wars was suddenly pulling together, united by a common enemy, common hurt, common goals—justice and freedom.

But it wasn't long before people were arguing about our response, the patriotic spirit waned, and people were divided again. It's such a tragedy that only tragedy seems to bring community to our nation.

God made us for community. It begins with God Himself. God sets the

> God made us for community. It begins with God Himself. God sets the example. He Himself is a community. God the Father, God the Son, and God the Spirit live in constant fellowship.

example. He Himself *is* a community. God the Father, God the Son, and God the Spirit live in constant fellowship. Always communicating. Always in one accord. They're united by a common enemy—Satan—but that's not their main connection. They focused on the creation they made to bring themselves glory. The Holy Trinity was all active in creation. They were all active in redemption. And they are all active in our sanctification, our becoming more like God.

Two things build community: One, a common enemy. Two, a common achievement.

I'm wild about the Wildcats—the Kentucky Wildcats basketball team. I'm part of the Big Blue Nation. Nothing brings us together like a common enemy, such as the Duke Blue Devils. My two favorite teams are Kentucky and whoever's playing Duke. But common achievement bonds us like nothing else. There's no other way to explain why 23,000 people packed into Rupp Arena, most of whom you've never met, will talk like best friends, high five, hug, yell their lungs out together at three nervous officials, and otherwise act like a crazed band of Big Blue brothers. Until you've felt it yourself, it's hard to put into words the sense of camaraderie you experience when your team wins the big game. You've lived through it together, and now you have a story to share forever.

God wants His people to share this kind of community. High five someone over that young person who goes to the mission field. Yell your lungs out at that husband who walks out on his wife. Revel in the sense of community when the church pulls off a tiring week of Vacation Bible School. Cry when that mother loses her baby. Celebrate when that alcoholic becomes a believer. Spend time on your knees while that friend is sharing his faith with his lost father.

Community is how the first century church exploded from a rag-tag bunch of fishermen and tax collectors to a thriving church that was adding thousands rapidly.

But rewind a few months. See the disciples as they argue about which among them would be the greatest in the Kingdom of Heaven. Watch as a short time later, James and John, spurred on by their pushy stage mom, lobby to sit in honored positions, one at Jesus' left and one at His right. The other 10 get indignant. It's every man for himself. A few pages later, Peter brags that even if everyone else runs away, *he* never will. Verses later, *all* the disciples desert the Lord and run away. Finally, Peter, following Christ "at a distance," is questioned about being one of Jesus' followers, curses, and denies Christ. Cue the rooster crowing.

Not much community going on here. Community isn't fighting over the best seats. It's not bragging about how much better you are than the others. It's not breaking up the group when one member is in trouble. It's not running away. It's not following "at a distance."

I think about Peter after his denial, broken and alone. "He went outside and wept bitterly." Where was his band of brothers? No one was there to help him pick up the pieces. No one was there to lend an ear or offer an encouraging word. No one was even there to yell his head off at Peter and his betrayal. No one was there.

Christ faced loneliness as well. His disciples sleep as He sweats blood, pouring out His heart to His Father. He's thrown under the bus and deserted by His closest friends as He stands trial alone. And finally in the supreme humiliation, He hangs from a cross, crying "My God, My God, why have You forsaken Me?"

Has community broken down even within the Trinity?

In that single poignant moment, as Christ became sin for us, God the Father's wrath over sin caused the community within the Trinity to be temporarily suspended. Yet simultaneously, the community between God and His children was restored. His wrath over sin was propitiated. His welcome to sinners was pronounced. "It is finished!" cried Christ, as He hung between two communities—Heaven and earth—that were about to become one.

UNITY IN COMMUNITY

One isn't the loneliest number. One is exactly what you want to be when it comes to community.

One body. One Spirit. One hope. One Lord. One faith. One baptism. One God and Father of all (@Ephesians 4:4–6).

One day changed everything. The resurrection was the ultimate community-building event. Common enemy defeated. The crowning achievement of all history.

In the 50 days from Jesus' arrest to Pentecost, the Christian community made a comeback. One day, an anemic group of disciples is running scared in every direction like rats when the light's turned on. A few weeks later, they're on fire for God—literally!—and filled with so much zeal people mistake them for drunk. What happened?

Unity.

"When the day of Pentecost had arrived, they were all together in one place."

All together. One place. The stage was set for this group to be "*comm-unified.*" God came down and communed with them, filling them with His Spirit. Their hearts were melded together, and they discovered there's unity in community. And there's power in unity. Peter, yes the one who denied Christ to a slave girl, stands up and preaches one of the most powerful sermons every uttered. He gives credit to the entire community of the Trinity:

> *"Therefore, since He (Jesus) has been exalted to the right hand of God and has received from the Father the promised Holy Spirit, He has poured out what you both see and hear." @Acts 2:33*

God the Father. God the Son. God the Spirit. God's people. All in community. All in unity. All for One, and One for all.

BEING IN ONE ACCORD

It took 17 books, Genesis through Esther, for God to tell the story of the nation of Israel. Throughout their history, the sense of community and unity came and went—mostly went.

How many books of history in the New Testament?

One.

Not counting the Gospels, which are accounts of the ministry of Jesus, God tells the story of the early church in one concise book: the book of Acts. What an amazing story it is! It's a story that can be summed up in two words:

One accord.

Not 12 in-fighting tribes. No divided Kingdom of Judah and Israel. No endless, aimless wandering, grumbling, mumbling, and murmuring. In the Old Testament, God's light went forth like a floodlight. Wide, but not very intense. In the New Testament, the Gospel shot out like a laser beam. Focused and powerful. That's the power of unity.

The book of Acts introduces us to a new word: *homothymadon*. It's translated "with one accord" or "with one mind." It's used 11 times in the Bible. Ten are in the book of Acts. Seven refer to the sense of unity and community in the early Christian church. A sampling of the "one accords"...

> *These all continued with* **one accord** *in prayer and supplication, with the women and Mary the mother of Jesus, and with His brothers. @Acts 1:14*

> *So continuing daily with* **one accord** *in the temple, and breaking bread from house to house, they ate their food with gladness and simplicity of heart. @Acts 2:46*

> *So when they heard that, they raised their voice to God with* **one accord** *and said: "Lord, You are God, who made heaven and earth and the sea, and all that is in them. @Acts 4:24*

> *And through the hands of the apostles many signs and wonders were done among the people. And they were all with* **one accord** *in Solomon's Porch. @Acts 5:12*

Their unity was the secret of their power. They were connected to God and to each other. They held all things in common. There was no *yours* and *mine*. Only *ours*.

> *Now all the believers were together and held all things in common. They sold their possessions and property and distributed the proceeds to all, as anyone had a need. @Acts 2:44–25*

This was more than a bake sale. This church was taking community to a whole new level. Selling property and distributing to those in need— and being glad about it! I'm not even going to try to water this down to suit our 21st century American political sensitivities. It's starting to sound kind of radical. But so is baptizing 3,000 new converts at one time. The price for this kind of unity and community is high, but the dividends are out of this world.

DOING LIFE TOGETHER

So we've seen it start at the Top. The Holy Trinity enjoys their community so much they invite us to the party. God loves company and really wants to connect with us, so He reveals everything we need to know about Himself. He's an open book. He gives us His Word. His written Word. And His living Word—Jesus. It's a multimedia campaign that goes viral.

But communication is not enough. He creates institutions that foster community: the family, a chosen nation, government, and finally, the church. Throughout His story and history, the theme of community keeps coming up. We are created to be better together. One big family centered around one big God. Hear Jesus' prayer:

> *I am no longer in the world, but they are in the world, and I am coming to You. Holy Father, protect them by Your name that You have given Me, so that they may be one as We are one. @John 17:11*

May we be one as They are one.

That's Jesus' prayer for us. How do we *be* one? How do we *do* community?

One comes up again.

The "One anothers" of the Bible.

God gives us at least 59 of them in the New Testament. Another sampling:

> Be at peace with one another.
> Love one another.
> Honor one another above yourself.

Accept one another.

Instruct one another.

Serve one another.

Carry one another's burdens.

Be kind and compassionate to one another.

Forgive one another.

Submit to one another.

Do not lie to one another.

Encourage one another.

Spur one another on to love and good works.

Confess your sins to one another.

Wow, that's sounds like a lot of responsibility. Merely selling everything and divvying it up is actually starting to sound easier.

The "one anothers" are a radical departure from, "Look out for number one." If everyone in my church looks out for one another, I have about 729 people looking out for me. If everyone looks out for "number one," I have one person looking out for me. Me.

I like God's networking plan better.

If only we believers could harness the power of unity and community, we really would shine in the world. Today's world hungers for community and desperately seeks a surrogate in social media. But for all its benefits, being connected online is not the same as being connected face to face. The church has an opportunity right now to meet the need for community in a way that no other institution is doing. Seize it, church. Be connected. Be one as He is one with the Father. Do life together. Love one another.

> If everyone in my church looks out for one another, I have about 729 people looking out for me. If everyone looks out for "number one," I have one person looking out for me. Me.

A while back, a man who was a church pillar in our congregation for decades passed away. A victim of Alzheimer's in his waning months, I watched him fade into a shell of the man he used to be. Yet up till the very end, when he saw you, he'd grin widely, open his arms even more widely, and say, "Did you bring one?" He meant, "Did you bring me a hug?" He hugged you every time he saw you.

When I read his obituary, I was astonished. I'd know the man all my life, but I had no idea of all his accomplishments. A bricklayer and owner of a masonry company who had built several prominent buildings in town. A photographer and movie producer who had won awards for his work. A Boy Scout leader. A 17-year volunteer for the Center on Aging. To get more exercise during his retirement years, he became a newspaper carrier, and was named "Carrier of the Year" twice in his late 60s. And on and on. I had no idea. I longed for one more day with him when I could invite him to lunch and hear all about his story. But it's too late now.

I'm a bit of an introvert. No excuse. I want to be more like God, an omnivert. Connecting Who He is with who I am, and connecting who I am with everyone who is around me. Being one with God and with the body of Christ. Doing life together with one another. One for all, and all for one.

Chapter 10

GOD'S ETERNALITY

Sometimes God has to make you smaller to make you bigger.

I'll always remember the day God did that to me.

It was an ordinary Sunday. I was in church, listening to a sermon, just like every Sunday since nine months before I was born. The preacher, the late Dr. Dick Vigneulle, was delivering a message entitled "The Greatness of God." To make his point, he was describing the vastness of the universe. The numbers made my brain hurt.

The size of our universe and the numbers of stars and galaxies are impossible to truly comprehend. Let me try to give some perspective. If the earth was the size of a peppercorn, then our sun would be the size of an 8-inch ball and would be 26 yards away. It would take an airplane 21 years to reach it.

Let's go out further. The closest star to our peppercorn earth would be 4,000 miles away. So if the Earth is a tiny peppercorn in my office in Kentucky, the closest star is in London, England. To reach that star in an airplane, it would take 51 billion years.

At this point, using any kind of scale we can relate to begins to break down. Distances have to be measured in light years. A light year is the distance it takes light to travel in one year, traveling at a speed of 186,282 miles per second. That closest star? The one it would take 51 billion years to reach in an airplane? It's "only" four light years away. And that closest star is just one of 300 billion stars in our Milky Way galaxy, which is 100,000 light years wide.

Is your mind numb yet? We're just getting started.

Our galaxy is only one of 500 billion galaxies in the observable universe. The observable universe is 93 billion light years across. And the observable universe may be only a fraction of the entire universe containing stars whose light has not even reached Earth yet. What an amazing God Who doesn't mind creating a star or an entire galaxy that no one on Earth may ever see.

That peppercorn is starting to look pretty small now. And I'm just a speck on a speck on a speck on that peppercorn.

My pastor went on and on about the immenseness of the universe and the awesomeness of God, and by the end of the message, I was thinking, "I'm so small, and the way I'm spending my life is so small." Then, God overwhelmed me with this clarion calling: "I want you to do doing something with your life that has eternal consequences."

Whoa! I'm serving the Lord here. Praying and reading my Bible. Giving my tithes and offerings. Going to church—three times a week!

But as I took a closer, more honest look at my life, I really wasn't focused on eternity. My focus was firmly fixed on making a comfortable life for myself and my family in the here and now.

My career was going great, and we had just built our dream house. Still in our 20s, we had two kids and two cars, a 30-year mortgage, and that was about as far down the road as I was looking. Life was good, and looking better all the time.

Time. That was the problem. My focus was living in time, not eternity. I was checking the boxes for a healthy spiritual life, but those were just more things I made time for. God was about to relocate my focus about 93 billion light years away.

ETERNITY TIMES INFINITY

Eternity in time is no less mind blowing than infinity in space. We can't conceive of something that has no beginning and no ending.

Since we've always existed immersed in time, we can't fathom existence outside of time any more than a fish can conceive of life outside water. For centuries, man has grasped at understanding the ever present, yet always elusive dimension of time.

Augustine of Hippo, in the 4th century, writes in his *Confessions*:

> "How can the past and future be, when the past no longer is, and the future is not yet? As for the present, if it were always present and never moved on to become the past, it would not be time, but eternity."

If one of the greatest minds of Christendom can't figure out time, then I'm not going to either. But this I *know* about God. Time serves God. God doesn't serve time.

It's why God never seems to be in a hurry. He's not worried about doing things on our time schedule. He's never early. And He's never late. His concern isn't good timing, it's His timeless glory.

> **He's never early. And He's never late. His concern isn't good timing, it's His timeless glory.**

Time is a tool for God. Jesus used time like a prop—for dramatic effect. Lazarus is sick. His sisters send a message to Jesus, Who's only two miles away. Jesus takes His time getting there, and by the time He arrives, Lazarus is four days in the grave.

Jesus is right on time.

His absence is like a pregnant pause made before you state an important point. "Lazarus has died," Jesus explained. "I'm glad for you that I wasn't there so that you may believe" @John 11:14–15.

Some of the bystanders criticized Jesus' tardiness. "Couldn't He Who opened the blind man's eyes also have kept this man from dying?" Even Mary and Martha, Lazarus' sisters, questioned Him. "Lord, if You had been here, my brother would not have died!"

He missed their deadline. But Jesus is Master over the dead.

What if Jesus had hurried there as soon as He heard Lazarus was sick? What if Lazarus had gotten well and not died? What if Jesus had resuscitated him right after he died?

We wouldn't have a story like this! Four days in the grave!

"Didn't I tell you that if you believed you would see the glory of God?" Jesus reminded Martha.

"Lazarus, come out!" He shouted.

"The dead man came out."

Why did Jesus act like He had all the time in the world while Lazarus dies? Because He *does* own all the time. Jesus Himself provides the commentary on His perfect timing as He prays to His Father.

"So they may believe You sent Me."

That's the whole point. For God, Who sees all the past, present, and future simultaneously, time isn't a line, it's a point. And the point is... *knowing* God.

Time melts away when we step back and gaze at the eternal God. Listen in on Moses' prayer @Psalm 90:1–4:

> *Lord, You have been our refuge in every generation.*
> *Before the mountains were born,*
> *before You gave birth to the earth and the world,*
> *from eternity to eternity, You are God.*
> *You return mankind to the dust,*
> *saying, "Return, descendants of Adam."*
> *For in Your sight a thousand years*
> *are like yesterday that passes by,*
> *like a few hours of the night.*

Time? Just a tool. That's why the Bible says, "With the Lord one day is like a thousand years, and a thousand years like one day" @2 Peter 3:8. God transcends time.

God is eternal. His purposes are eternal. The kind of life He gives is eternal. And if we are going to truly *know* Him, we need to think in terms of eternity, not time.

To *know* Him is to get on His timetable, which is not concerned with time at all. It's an eternity-table.

We must see the world from God's perspective, an eternal perspective, a view that sees the value of time and the value of things in this world only in terms of how it brings glory to God.

> *"So we do not focus on what is seen, but on what is unseen. For what is seen is temporary, but what is unseen is eternal." @2 Corinthians 4:18*

Yes, God is eternal. Because we are made in His image, we, too, are eternal in the sense that we exist from now on. We are not eternal as God is eternal—past, present and future, the same yesterday, today, and forever. But as created beings, we will exist now and forever. For the non-believer, that means eternal death. For the believer, we have eternal life.

For the Christian, we must live in the light of eternity. We must be eternal, not focused on time, but on eternity. We must *be* who we are in Christ—eternal. *Be* eternal.

NEARSIGHTEDNESS

A man's father came to him one day and said, "Son, I'm going away for a year, and while I'm gone, I want you to build a wonderful new home for me. I want it to last a lifetime and beyond, so I want it to be first class and built to last. Hire the best contractors. Use the best materials. The budget is unlimited. Just make it a home you would be proud to live in."

The son saw an opportunity to pad his own bank account. So he used second rate contractors and skimped on the quality of the materials, making sure to cover up the shoddy work with a veneer of fine finishes. When he was finished, he had built a house that looked pretty good on the outside. But was built so poorly, it wouldn't last long. His bank account, however, was piled high.

When his father returned, he said, "Son, the house looks great. Is it a place you would be proud to live?"

"Absolutely," the son lied.

"Then here are the keys. The house is yours. I wanted you to have the very best, son. So I pretended it was for me. But I'm giving it to you to enjoy for the rest of your life."

Shortsightedness and selfishness tend to go hand in hand. Think Esau who sold his birthright for a bowl of soup. Think of Achan who hid the spoils of victory under his tent and guaranteed defeat. Think of the rich young ruler who wouldn't trade his kingdom for the eternal Kingdom of God. Think of Judas who sold out his teacher for 30 pieces of silver. Think of Ananias and Sapphira who held back part of their offering and dropped dead.

When we hold on to temporal possessions, it just demonstrates that we don't really *know* God. If we really *knew* Him, we'd know that He doesn't withhold good gifts from His children. (*He* defines "good.") He's not the type Who hands out snakes when we ask for fish or a stone when we ask for bread. He's not the type Who shows up for a funeral four days late and makes excuses about the traffic.

He *is* the type Who will take away a family and all your riches to prove to Satan and the world that you love Him. He is the type Who will leave the glories of Heaven to be born in a stinky stable, get ridiculed, beaten, and crucified to show that He loves you. He is the type Who will make 500 billion galaxies, a half a million species of flowers, a funny looking fish with a headlight, sunsets so amazing you want to cry, a man who can do a 360-degree windmill dunk shot, a woman so beautiful you just have to marry her, and a Down Syndrome child who will never live on her own—all for no other purpose than His eternal glory.

Yes, God thinks on an eternal scale. Considering our life is less than a peppercorn in this vast universe, it's time we get to *know* Him and His eternal perspective.

INVESTMENT PORTFOLIO

In the 1970s, a brokerage firm ran a series of commercials that produced a famous tagline, "When E.F. Hutton talks, people listen." A typical spot would show two men in loud, crowded areas like an airport or restaurant. They'd be talking about investments. One would relay the advice he'd received from his broker. The other would say, "Well, my broker is E. F.

Hutton, and E. F. Hutton says,…" Instantly, a hush would come over the entire area as everyone leaned in to hear the priceless advice from E. F. Hutton. The voiceover would end each spot with "When E.F. Hutton talks, people listen."

The firm later ran short of cash and had to be sold, so apparently the commercials were better than the investment advice.

But there's another Investment Advisor whose investment tips are always spot on. He's an expert on "futures." He always has your best interest at heart, not His own commissions. And the dividends His clients earn are truly "out of this world."

Lean in and listen to an investment seminar conducted by the ultimate Investment Advisor, Jesus:

> *"Don't collect for yourselves treasures on earth, where moth and rust destroy and where thieves break in and steal. But collect for yourselves treasures in heaven, where neither moth nor rust destroys, and where thieves don't break in and steal. For where your treasure is, there your heart will be also."* @Matthew 6:19–21

> **There's an Investment Advisor whose investment tips are always spot on. He's an expert on "futures." He always has your best interest at heart, not His own commissions. And the dividends His clients earn are truly "out of this world."**

It's a remarkable piece of investment advice. Don't invest in Earthly Treasures, Inc. Instead, invest where the risk is lowest and the return is the highest: Heavenly Treasures Unlimited. Think long-term, low risk—not short-term, high risk—in building your "investment portfolio."

Later, Jesus gives us a prospectus for the return on investment:

"Everyone who has left houses, brothers or sisters, father or mother, children, or fields because of My name will receive 100 times more and will inherit eternal life." @Matthew 19:29

How much is "100 times more"? That equates to 10,000% interest. Know anywhere else you can get 10,000% interest on a guaranteed investment managed by Someone Who can see into the future? If I knew a broker I trusted who could see only *one* day into the future, I'd hand over every penny I had.

We don't have to know the future. We only need to *know* the One Who holds the future. Once we acknowledge His eternality and His power, we're free to *be* the kind of eternal being that we are created to *be*.

In His investment seminar, Jesus offers a remarkable insight that helps us connect the dots between *being* eternal and *doing* eternal things.

"For where your treasure is, there your heart will *be* also."

In my earlier years, I couldn't care less what the stock market did. I never checked the stock report. I paid no attention to the Dow Jones, S&P 500, or NASDAQ. Then I started putting money into a 401K that was tied heavily to the stock market. Suddenly, I am vitally interested in whether the Dow went up or down today. When it goes up, my heart goes up. But rust, moths, thieves…they take their share. And when it goes down, my heart goes down. That's where my treasure is—at least the part I've invested in Earthly Treasures, Inc.

Want to possess an eternal perspective like God has? Invest in Heavenly Treasures. Your heart will follow. It works both ways. When your heart is invested in God's Kingdom, your treasure will be sure to follow.

Know God's eternal perspective. Be eternal in your perspective. Invest your treasures, your time, your talents in Heavenly Treasures Unlimited.

Don't work for the food that perishes but for the food that lasts for eternal life. @John 6:27

In the words of missionary martyr Jim Elliot, "He is no fool who gives what he cannot keep to gain what he cannot lose."

FOCAL POINT

Alexander the Great set his sights on conquering the entire world. By age 30, he was well on his way. His empire stretched from Europe to Asia and down into Africa. His expanding kingdom was in constant need of new leaders. The story is told that one day, he sent an assistant out into the midst of the rank and file to discover new candidates for officer training. The headhunter happened upon three laborers who we're building a stone fortress wall around one of the cities. All three were stone layers. He asked one of the men what he was doing.

"Laying stones," the man replied.

The recruiter went on to the next man, who was doing the exact same work. "What are you doing?"

"I'm constructing a wall that will help protect the city."

Ahh, the officer thought to himself. This man has a little more vision than the first. He went to the final man who, again, was doing identical work, simply laying stones. "What are you doing?"

"I am a servant of Alexander the Great, and I am helping him build his empire."

"Come with me," the officer exclaimed. He had found a man who had the big picture vision of the true task at hand.

It's easy to get overwhelmed with the details of the Christian walk. Daily quiet time. Bible reading plans. Memory verses. Worship services. Ministry programs. Witnessing opportunities. Christian books to read (here's another one!). People to visit. Notes to write. Missions trips. Offering checks. Sunday school lessons. Whew! Almost lost my joy there!

It's easy to stay so focused on the next stone we're putting in the wall that we forget about the big picture—God's eternal Kingdom that we are helping to build.

Doing eternal things doesn't make you an eternally minded Christian any more than doing financial things makes you a tycoon.

Doing is not the objective here. It never is.

Before you lift a finger to do anything, focus on the One for Whom you are doing it: Jesus the Great.

And whatever you do, in word or in deed, do everything in the name of the Lord Jesus. @Colossians 3:17

Know that He created you for His eternal purpose and His everlasting pleasure. Know that He created you in His image: kind, powerful, wise, connected. Abide in that ability. Accept your position in Him. Be who you are in Christ.

Then, when you go to put a stone in the wall, the stones will feel like feathers. The early morning quiet times will fly by like they have wings. You'll begin to view the people you minister to as precious, timeless vessels, made in His image, who may live with you forever. Viewed in the light of eternity, the tasks will have purpose and significance—now and forever. Never mind the timeline. Have a focal point, and make it eternity.

Are the stones you're laying getting heavy? Are you tiring of the "mundane," over and over and over again, picking up a stone from the pile, putting it in the wall, and then doing it all over again. Day in and day out. Month upon month. Year after year.

Stop what you're *doing.*

And start *being.*

Be the servant of the One Who conquered all. Be the partner of the greatest enterprise in the universe: God & Sons. Be the prince or princess of the King Who invites you to His table. Be the stone layer who sees beyond the wall and knows the Creator Who made the stones.

20/20 VISION

I've got one eye that's nearsighted, and one's that's farsighted. If I close my right eye, my left eye can see close-up text crystal clear. If I close my left eye, my right eye can see a detail 100 yards away tack sharp. I've never worn glasses because I get along pretty well at any distance as one eye makes up for the deficiency of the other.

Many of us think we can go through the Christian walk much with the same type of vision. Most of the time, our focus is what's right in front of our face. So we close our eternal eye and focus pretty well on the task at hand. On Sundays, we try to take a little glimpse of eternal things, and we might close our temporal eye and focus on the long range.

We might think this works pretty well, except for one problem. In the Christian life, "We walk by faith, not by sight" @2 Corinthians 5:7.

Eternity may seem as distant as a galaxy billions of light years away, whose light still hasn't reached earth. But it's there. In fact, it begins the moment eternal life begins. It's not something we experience *after* we die. Eternal life is something that's present as soon as we begin to live.

We don't have to grope and trip through life with one eye open at a time. We just open our faith eyes wide and see the eternity that is God's. Faith is 20/20 vision for our spirit. With our faith eyes, the here and now is always seen through the lens of eternity.

As I sat in that worship service years ago, listening to my pastor give a guided tour through the universe. I tried to close one eye, my near-sighted eye, but still I could not see clearly. So I closed both eyes, and then everything burst into clarity.

"I want you to do something with your life that will have eternal consequences," God told me. But before you *do* a thing, I want you to *be* who you are in Me, and I want you to *know* Who I am in you."

Faith didn't open my eyes, it *closed* them. Now it's so clear with my eyes closed, I can see forever. Live in the light of eternity. It will make light years of difference in your perspective.

Chapter 11

GOD'S SERVICE

Disclaimer: Service is not my bailiwick.

My spiritual gift is selfishness with a minor in discouragement.

My self-centeredness is not from lack of positive examples. The closest people in my life are genuine servants.

My wife is the kind of person who spends the afternoon in the kitchen baking a cake from scratch for a restaurant owner she's trying to reach for Christ.

My best friend is the kind of person who gets mad, sincerely peeved, when I take my vehicle to the shop for a new alternator instead of calling him.

My mother is the most selfless person I know. She always takes the worst of everything for herself so that others can have the best.

My brother takes care of handyman duties and computer technical support for about a dozen households. He's helped me move so many times, U-Haul put his picture on one of their trucks.

But it's this very deficiency in my life that causes me to stand in such awe of God's attribute of servanthood.

Here's my definition of *service*: taking something that costs you and giving it to others.

That something might be a weekend you could have spent reading or relaxing. But you helped a neighbor clean out his garage.

It might be a $1,000 that could have bought a new TV. But you gave it for a new mission church in Peru.

It might be the stature you'd gain hanging out with the cool kids. But you went and sat by the awkward kids.

It might be leaving your Father's mansion to be born in a feed trough, trading a throne and crown for a crown of thorns.

THE MIND OF CHRIST

You can encapsulate the whole concept of Know Be Do into the idea of having the mind of Christ.

> *Let this mind be in you which was also in Christ Jesus, who, being in the form of God, did not consider it robbery to be equal with God, but made Himself of no reputation, taking the form of a bondservant, and coming in the likeness of men.* @Philippians 2:5–7

Having the mind of Christ means *knowing* Him. You must have intimate, *ginosko* knowledge of His mind in order to saturate your own mind with its truth.

Having the mind of Christ means *being* who you are in Him. "Let this mind *be*..." Let it *be*. In you. Abide in Him, and He in you. Accept your position in Him.

Having the mind of Christ means *doing* things for others. It means not using your status for your own advantage. It means taking no concern for your own reputation. It means dedicating your life to serving. It means humbling yourself, laying aside privileges, to serve in the lowest of circumstances.

Yes, Jesus certainly set the bar high for servanthood. Or, since He was becoming a humble servant, perhaps I should say He set the bar low.

How do you let Christ's mind be in you?

First, you've got to *know* what's in there. Christ's mind is full of noble thoughts and motives. He perfectly fulfils Paul's lofty admonition: "Whatever is true, whatever is honorable, whatever is just, whatever is pure, whatever is lovely, whatever is commendable—if there is any moral excellence and if there is any praise—dwell on these things" @Philippians 4:8.

Me? I'm much more comfortable with someone examining what I *do*, not who I *am*. I'd rather have people watching my actions, not reading my mind.

Exactly one year after 9/11, I had my own crisis. I woke up in the middle of the night feeling like someone had just dropped a cannonball on my chest. My wife called 911. The paramedics came, put a nitroglycerin tablet in my mouth, and rushed me to the emergency room. The EKG showed that I probably had a heart attack, so they immediately took me in for a heart cath. It was one of the strangest experiences I've ever had.

I was fully alert and feeling fine by this time. I laid there on the gurney, looking up at a monitor, as the tiny camera snaked through my veins, navigating its way to its destination. Then it arrived, and there I was, watching the inside of my heart. It wasn't much to look at. It pulsated and rested, expanding and contracting. The whole team of doctors and nurses watched with me, looking into my heart.

Imagine if you had to undergo a spiritual heart cath. The Bible often uses the word *heart* in the same sense we use the word *mind*. Think of your inner thoughts and motives coming up on the IMAG screen on Sunday morning as the whole church looked on. The service opens in prayer, and after about five seconds, the video displays your mind drifting off to which restaurant you're headed after church. The singing begins, and you're focused on how hot that woman in the choir looks today. The offering plate passes and you drop your check in—begrudgingly given by a motivation of guilt and obligation. The preacher gets up and begins to speak, but your mind is applying the message to your wife. I hope she's listening to this, you think to yourself. The announcements are made about the missions project this weekend, but you're thinking about how it conflicts with the big game. You're already formulating your excuse. After church, you see that guy you said you'd pray for, so you offer up a quick, "Lord, please help Bill. Amen." And then exclaim with a big grin, "Hey, Bill, been praying for you!"

Were it not for the spiritual heart cath monitor, people might think you're a model church member. But the mind of Christ is not in you.

The focus is on you. Not God. Not serving others.

Contrast your mindset with Christ's. He didn't mind leaving the comforts of Heaven to take a missions trip to earth. It wasn't beneath Him. Take a look at Philippians 2:3–8 from *The Message*:

> *Don't push your way to the front; don't sweet-talk your way to the top. Put yourself aside, and help others get ahead. Don't be obsessed with getting your own advantage. Forget yourselves long enough to lend a helping hand. Think of yourselves the way Christ Jesus thought of himself. He had equal status with God but didn't think so much of himself that he had to cling to the advantages of that status no matter what. Not at all. When the time came, he set aside the privileges of deity and took on the status of a slave, became human! Having become human, he stayed human. It was an incredibly humbling process. He didn't claim special privileges. Instead, he lived a selfless, obedient life and then died a selfless, obedient death—and the worst kind of death at that—a crucifixion.*

That's service. Jesus took something that cost Him—*His life*—and gave it to others. He was literally the very embodiment of servanthood.

CHRISTIAN CONSUMERISM

Giving is the heartbeat of service. "For God so loved the world He *gave*." God the Father gave His Son. God the Son gave His life. God the Spirit gives comfort and direction. Yes, God is a giver.

People, on the other hand, are basically consumers. My wife uses 15 different products to get ready before she'll leave the house. Men aren't as bad about beauty products, but I have a closet full of tools, many of which I've used only one time in years. Our appetites for more stuff are never satiated. We strive to supersize our stuff and minimize our service. First our stuff serves us. Then we begin to serve our stuff. We serve our stuff and use people when we should be using stuff and serving people.

We're a disposable society that throws things away rather than fix them or reuse them. My mother, who grew up in the depression, still washes out bread bags to reuse instead of buying baggies. Not because she can't afford to, but because not wasting, not throwing away is ingrained in her. She was married to my father for 51 years before he passed away. Their secret: They gave more than they took.

Consumerism has infiltrated the American church. People shop for churches the same way they'd shop for a new computer. They check out the features. They want to know what the church has to offer. They make a selection based on what's in it for them. It's an upside-down-world approach that puts the focus on the bride of Christ, instead of on the Bridegroom, where it belongs. The American church has turned into bridezilla.

> **It's an upside-down-world approach that puts the focus on the bride of Christ, instead of on the Bridegroom, where it belongs. The American church has turned into bridezilla.**

How unlike Christ, the Suffering Servant. Can you imagine if Christ had the consumer mentality of today's church member?...

"OK, Father, you're sending me on a mission to redeem man. What? Born in a stable in Bethlehem? That simply won't do. I was thinking Rome. I'll need reservations for the best inn in Rome. Oh, and I think a nice royal family would do nicely. I want the best known name, the finest home, and the best education. I'll need all that if I am to be King one day.

"Now, about these protégés of mine...I know you have in mind a motley crew of fishermen and the like, but I've been perusing resumes, and I believe I've found some better qualified applicants amidst the Sanhedrin. I'll need a state-of-the-art training facility to get these men up to speed, so I'll need a healthy trust fund and a board of well-heeled sponsors. I've got the entire complex planned out, and I've developed this Master plan that shows where the Seminary will be, the medical center, administrative offices, and recreational facilities. I'll need a staff of approximately 500 to help me run it. There's no need for me to do all the work. I can farm a lot of this out.

"Finally, I read that little preview in Isaiah that you wrote of Your plan for me redeeming mankind. A little melodramatic, I believe. And it sounds painful. Now, is it really fair that I be the scapegoat for all these murderers and adulterers and liars and their ilk? Let's negotiate this a little. Each person spends a few years in hell paying for their sins. I'll oversee the whole deal and make sure You're satisfied. So, do we have a deal, Abba?"

It hurts to even imagine Christ the Consumer. Everything I know about Him is the exact opposite. He's never loud and proud, barking orders to servers and walking around with an air of entitlement. To the contrary, He's always the One stooping down low. Washing feet. Kneeling down to heal a cripple. Bowed in prayer. Stepping down from Heaven to earth.

I thank God the Father, God the Son, and God the Spirit for being givers, for being Servants. For taking what costs Them so dearly, and giving it to us. For being exactly what we strive to *be*.

THREE TYPES OF PEOPLE

Look around and you'll find three types of people when it comes to serving.

1.   You serve me.
2.   You serve me, and I'll serve you.
3.   I'll serve you.

You serve me.

I can tell a lot about a person by going to a restaurant with them. I watch how they treat the server. Some people never really acknowledge the server. They act as if the server was a robot, part of the décor. They're demanding and demeaning. They never look the server in the eye, let alone smile. They act like kings and tip like paupers. They're self-important, self-absorbed, and self-promoting. Their attitude, often well outside the restaurant, is "You serve me."

On the other hand, some of the most important, and often wealthy people I know, go out of their way to *serve* a server. They remember their name, ask genuinely interested questions about their lives, and leave good tips. I worked for one CEO who was especially servant-hearted in this area. If he went into a meeting room and encountered a man cleaning or doing other service work, he would make it a point to introduce himself, shake their hand, and treat them like an equal.

> *Don't be selfish; don't try to impress others. Be humble, thinking of others as better than yourselves. @Philippians 2:3*

The "You serve me" person is thinking of self, not others. He's driven by pride and, at the same time, insecurity that make him believe that putting others down somehow lifts him up. But only in the upside-down world. In reality, in the true right-side-up world, exalting yourself actually *lowers* your status.

> *Whoever exalts himself will be humbled, and whoever humbles himself will be exalted. @Matthew 23:12*

Haman discovered this truth the hard way. The Book of Esther tells the story with all its ironic brilliance. Haman is indignant because Mordecai won't bow down to him. So he misleads the king into ordering his execution. Haman prepares a gallows to hang his enemy.

I wouldn't want to be a server in a restaurant where Haman dines.

Meanwhile, however, the king learns that Mordecai had foiled a plot to have him assassinated. The King asks Haman what should be done for a man the King wants to honor. Thinking the King is referring to himself, Haman suggests the royal treatment. In the end Mordecai is exalted, and Haman gets hung on the same gallows he prepared for Mordecai.

Are you a Haman or a Mordecai?

Do you long to be bowed down to and honored? Do you want to see your enemies hung?

Or are you more interested in serving the King?

> *The greatest among you will be your servant. @Matthew 23:11*

Be served.

Or *be* a servant.

Which one makes you more like the King?

You serve me, and I'll serve you.

Another type of person is eager to serve—as long as there's something in it for him. You scratch my back, and I'll scratch yours. The truth is, however, that if you serve merely to get something in return, you're not serving *others* at all. You're serving your*self*.

Sadly, churches, especially larger churches, attract these types like frat boys on sorority move-in day. How can I help you? Let me carry that for you. Can I show you around? They're all too zealous to help—with an eye towards helping themselves to what they want later.

There's the Christian businessman who views the new church directory as his personal prospect list. He signs up for every committee, but he's not really serving. He's networking. There's the Approval Addicts. They'll go above and beyond the call of duty—as long as there's plenty of recognition as the pay-off. There's the VDPs, as one pastor calls them: Very Draining Persons. They're dynamos of service at the start. But it's just an initial investment. Soon enough, they become draining, demanding, and dependent. The list of dysfunctional servants goes on and on.

To *be* a true servant is to *know* the Suffering Servant. His service involved an exchange alright. But it wasn't mutually beneficial. Christ's idea of service is this: I'll take your sins. And you take My righteousness in exchange. I'll give you something that cost me dearly. You owe Me nothing. We could never repay anyway.

No "You scratch My back, and I'll scratch yours" here. Jesus got His back scratched—but with a Roman executioner's cruel whip.

To *be* a true servant, we must *know* the mind of this Suffering Servant. We must let His mind be in us. His mind is

> No "You scratch My back, and I'll scratch yours" here. Jesus got His back scratched—but with a Roman executioner's cruel whip.

selfless. Ours is selfish. His mind is giving. Ours is taking. Having the mind of Christ is not hard. It's impossible…as long as we're content to *be* who we are naturally. We must *be* who we are *in Him* supernaturally.

> *I no longer live, but Christ lives in me. The life I now live in the body, I live by faith in the Son of God, who loved me and gave Himself for me.* @Galatians 2:20

Next time you're "tempted" to do something nice for someone, let the Holy Spirit pull up the heart cath and take a look at your motives on the monitor. Will this move benefit you in any way? Red flag. Are you looking for recognition at the end of the day? Red flag. Are you making a "deposit" that you expect to pay dividends at some time in the future? Red flag.

Would you do it even if no one ever knew you did it, including the person you're serving?

Give yourself a heart check. Make sure your heart lines up with the Giver's heart. Full of kindness, compassion, and charity. If it does, then you *are* a servant. You won't have to muster up a humble, helpful attitude. You'll do what comes naturally—supernaturally.

I'll serve you.

Say you did something so great that it got recorded by God in the Holy Scriptures. It would be nice if your name got mentioned, would it not?

Meet Abraham's servant.

Nameless. But selfless.

He gets no byline, no credit at the end of the movie, not even a hint of his true identity.

He's known simply as Abraham's servant.

This nameless servant, however, leads the league in assists. His picture is front and center in the Bible's Hall of Fame for Servants (which would never exist because true servants aren't looking for fame).

Our anonymous aide enters the stage by getting a tough assignment from his boss, Abraham (@Genesis 24). He's got to go find a wife for Father Abraham's son Isaac. A lot is riding on this. The wrong woman can really bring a man down. And the future of the nation of Israel depends on

Abe's servant pulling a matchmaking masterpiece. Abe even makes him take an oath by placing his hand under Abraham's 140-year-old thigh. Ugh! That alone shows the man's servant heart!

Abraham provides the profile of the kind of girl he wants for Isaac. It's not exactly the girl next door. The servant boards a camel and takes off across the desert on a 500-mile trek. His mission is to find a non-Canaanite woman from among Abraham's relatives.

Oh, and one other little detail. Isaac is not going. Abraham's servant is on his own.

Abraham obviously put a lot of trust in this servant. The Bible says the servant managed all that Abraham owned, which was a considerable estate. Now he was also entrusting the future of his blessed son, "the son of the promise," a forefather of Christ.

Abe would not have picked just any man for this critical task. No doubt he selected a servant who knew his master well, who shared the same values, who would make the same decisions.

A servant who would *be* his master in proxy.

Abraham didn't give much detail as to precisely how he would *do* the job. His concern was much more with *be* than with *do*. He simply gave a general objective, and trusted his servant to *be* his ambassador in the field.

Abraham's servant served well. *Knowing* His master well, he began with a prayer:

> "Lord, God of my master Abraham," he prayed, "give me success today, and show kindness to my master Abraham." @Genesis 24:12

God gave the servant a plan. He waited at the town spring till the women came to draw water. He would ask one for a drink, and the girl who gave drink and offered to water his camels as well would be the one. Instantly, Rebekah appeared, and she fit the bill, a perfect answer to prayer, herself showing what it means to be a servant.

Mission accomplished.

Abraham's servant praised the Lord for the success. He brought Rebekah home to his master. Isaac loved her, they were married, and the messianic line continued.

We still don't know the name of that magnificent matchmaker, but it's only fitting that he remain nameless. Because a servant is really only concerned with one name: his Master's.

SERVING GOD AND SERVING OTHERS

Abraham's servant is an amazing model for **serving our Master**. He knew his master well. He understood his commission. He was trustworthy. On task. Reliant on the Father. Tuned in to His plan. Resourceful. Ultimately successful. Knowing. Being. Doing. Abraham's servant is a remarkable example of Know Be Do.

Rebekah is an outstanding pattern for **serving others**. She was where she should be. She was sensitive to needs around her. She was responsive, quick to serve. "She quickly lowered her jug…quickly emptied her jug…hurried to the well again" @Genesis 24:18–20. She was generous. Humble. Hard-working. Selfless.

Both are wonderful examples of the "I'll serve you" person. Contrast them with "You serve me" types.

The You-serve-me person has the attitude "What's yours is mine."

The You-serve-me-I'll-serve-you person has the attitude "What's yours is yours. What's mine is mine."

The I'll-serve -you person has the attitude "What's mine is yours."

Meet John. He's a What's-mine-is-yours type of man. He's given away his entire life. He started out by giving three years of his life to serving his country as a Merchant Marine during World War II. He came home and met his wife Alta at college. They began giving their life away together.

They started working as missionaries at a small mission in Kentucky. "The first day there was the big crowd of one 12-year-old girl," John remembers. "(God) answered my prayer, and the next week there was a 100 percent increase in attendance. The girl brought her 8-year-old brother. I was hooked on church planting ministry." In a year and a half, 47 persons were baptized, and the Second Street Baptist Church was established.

The giving was only just beginning. They soon felt called to a new field and in 1955 moved their family to Brazil.

They gave the bulk of their life to the nation of Brazil—59 years on the field there. Giving up all the amenities of a comfortable life in the United States, they endured disease. Outrageous living conditions. Sometimes cynical and fickle supporters. Meager resources. Constant relocating.

Brazil has 26 states and territory larger than the 48 continental United States. John and Alta have started works in half of these states. They've planted 70 churches that are still in existence. Founded in 1956, the first church they started currently has a weekly attendance of about 3,000. One of their sons, David, is the pastor. Another son, Paul, pastors another church in Brazil, and he and his wife have established more than 40 new churches.

"I have 64 years of ministry," John says. "Alta has more than 250. She has been a godly wife and godly mother who produced and trained five children to be missionaries."

I asked my friend John one day what books he'd read lately. I wanted whatever was in him to rub off on me.

"I read only the Bible anymore, Larry." he replied. His desire is only to *know* the Savior better. To commune with Him. To hear His heartbeat. To become more like Him.

John has *done* a lot of mission work.

But what he *is* is a servant.

Taking what costs him and giving it to others.

"The work is the Lord's," he says.

Knowing. Being. Serving.

Chances are, you've never heard of John Hatcher, missionary to Brazil. To millions in the United States, he's as anonymous as Abraham's servant.

Both servants served faithfully, delivering a bride to his master's son. Abraham's servant delivered a bride to his master's son, Isaac. John Hatcher, the Father's servant, is bringing the bride of Christ to his Master's Son, Jesus.

Scripture doesn't record what Abraham said when his servant returned successfully from his long journey. But I'm sure it was similar to what John Hatcher will hear after his long journey to another country.

"Well done, good and faithful servant."

Not well known. But well done.

Chapter 12

GOD'S PURITY

"I wouldn't trust the best 15 minutes of my life to get me into Heaven."

This. From the godliest man I've ever known. I believe he really meant it. And it was probably the truth.

If sins of commission don't get you, sins of omission will.

If sins of omission don't get you, wrong motives will.

If wrong motives don't get you, original sin will.

> *"If you, LORD, kept a record of sins, Lord, who could stand?"*
> *@Psalm 130:3*

No one.

But then... *This...*

> *"Be holy, because I am holy." @Leviticus 1:44, 1 Peter 1:16*

Something's got to give here. God is holy. That's a given. But man is not. That's a given.

So how can we *be* holy?

Answer that and you will begin to understand the concept of Know Be Do.

I FEEL LIKE MUD

Suppose you were thirsty, and I offered you a cool glass of 100% pure water. You'd drink it, right? Yes.

But suppose I put two handfuls of dirt in the water, turned it to mud. Would you drink that? No way.

Suppose I put just one teaspoon of dirt in the water. Would you drink that? Maybe, if you were dying of thirst.

Suppose I put just a trace of dirt in the water. Would you drink that? Probably. Bottled water has thousands of chemicals in it.

Now suppose I put just one nanogram (one billionth of a gram) of dirt in the water. Would you drink that?

God wouldn't. Not if dirt was sin.

God is so holy, that 99.999999999% pure is not good enough.

Every person has some threshold for how much sin he or she is willing to tolerate. Some will drink the water with a teaspoon of dirt. Some drink only bottled water. Some sip mud. But the more time we spend around God, the more we realize that He doesn't tolerate any sin.

Not one nanogram. Not one yoctogram (1 in 10 with 24 zeroes behind it). He won't put up with one sin in Heaven. Not one. Not one little white lie. Not one proud look. Not one evil thought.

Make no mistake, God has a zero tolerance policy toward sin.

One sin got Adam and Eve kicked out of the garden. One sin (Achan's) caused God's wrath to fall on all of Israel. One sin kept Moses out of the Promised Land.

Ask Uzzah if God winks at sin (@2 Samuel 6). Ask Ananias and Sapphira if God looks the other way (@Acts 5). Ask Nadab and Abihu if you can make your own rules (@Leviticus 10).

God's holiness is absolute. God's righteousness is relentless. God's justice is impeccable.

The more I'm around Him, the more I feel like mud.

A few years ago, my wife and I bought a 170-year-old home. When we moved in, it was very livable, but there were plenty of problems that were obvious to see. The carriage house needed a new roof. Some of the walls needed repair and repainting. The gutters needed replacing. We fixed all those. But then new flaws came to light. Some of the plumbing needed to be replaced. The foundation needed to be shored up in a few places. The air conditioning system had issues.

We watched *This Old House* on TV and subscribed to the magazine. We saw the beautifully historic homes that had been restored to perfection. Their shiny copper gutters. The pristine walls. The leveled floors. The up-to-code plumbing. The more we compared our house with the ideal, the more we discovered needing fixing. The more we lived with the house, the more we discovered its imperfections. We really got to know the house. We thought we knew it when we bought it. But now we really *know* it and its shortcomings.

God sees all our dirt and damage. The closer we get to the expert Creator, the more we really get to *know* Him. The more He shines the light of His Word on our lives, the more we begin see these imperfections for ourselves. Over there are some morals that are sagging. Over here is some damage that we just let go. That dark corner once looked OK. Now I can see how much dirt is piling up. I fixed that leaky plumbing once, but did a halfway job; now it's dripping again. Those windows looked fairly clean late in the evening, but in the noonday sun they show every streak. God is a tidy housekeeper. He wants a perfectly clean house to live in. And we keep tracking in mud.

> *"Do not come closer," He said. "Remove the sandals from your feet,*
> *for the place where you are standing is holy ground." @Exodus 3:5*

Not one speck of dirt allowed in God's presence.

I *know* God is holy. But do I truly *know—ginosko* know—just how holy He is? Sure, I share God's disdain for sin. But do I really understand just how much God is offended by sin? Here's a test that separates the men from the boys. Does sin make you angry? I'm talking about *all* sin. Not just the Holocaust. Not just child abuse. Not just when someone hurts *you*. I'm talking about all sin. Your sins. Your pet sin. Does it make you *mad*? I'm talking ripsnortin', hot-under-the-collar, fire-breathing livid. Three Hebrews words are used to depict God's anger. One originally meant "to snort." The other two relate to heat. So I literally mean it when I say sin should make us ripsnortin', hot-under-the-collar, fire-breathing incensed.

My wrath will break out like fire and burn with no one to extinguish it because of your evil deeds. @Jeremiah 4:4

We laugh at sin. We make sit coms and rom coms about it. And once you've laughed at sin, you can't take it seriously. Let alone be angered by it.

We excuse sin. We blame it on others. We justify it. We amplify it. We strut it. We wink at it. We pacify it. We tolerate it. We harbor it. But we don't get enraged by it.

And that is a sin in itself.

It doesn't get much better in the church. *Decision* magazine interviewed pastors from countries where believers are persecuted for their faith. Humbly yet with keen perspective, one pastor observed, "One of the things we see in America is that the church is considering sin as something that is part of the everyday Christian life—everyone just puts up with sin. But we know that where there is sin, God cannot bring His blessing."

Oh, that what breaks God's heart would break ours! If only we got just a glimpse at the holiness of God, our hearts would be broken. Our spirits would be white hot with anger over what offends our God and brings self-destruction to ourselves.

All sin is self-destructive behavior. In fact, that's a major reason why righteous God is offended by sin, because sin is destroying His creation. One year, we planted tomatoes in our backyard. We nurtured them. We watered. We weeded. We carefully and gently staked them so they'd grow tall and strong. Finally, yellow buds appeared at the end of the branches, and we knew fresh tomatoes wouldn't be far behind. But one day, we went out to our garden and all the blossoms had disappeared. Something—birds, we suspect—had eaten them. We got no tomatoes from those plants that year. Believe me, after all the effort we invested in those plants, we were ripsnortin' hot under the collar!

> **All sin is self-destructive behavior. In fact, that's a major reason why righteous God is offended by sin, because sin is destroying His creation.**

Holy God is furious about sin. It gnaws away destructively at His creation. We were designed to be uncorrupted. Holy. Whole. Healthy. All three words come from the same original word *hal*. Our **spirit** is made to be *holy*. Our **soul** (mind, will, and emotions) is designed to be *whole*. Our **body** is intended to be *healthy*. Sin destroys all that. It steals our flowers. It thwarts our fruit. It spoils our purpose.

Know God's anger over sin. Feel the heat. Then reflect the heat. *Be* angry over sin.

"Be *angry, and sin not.*" @Psalm 4:4; Ephesians 4:26

Sharing God's white hot anger over sin is one way we can purify our lives. But can we ever truly *be* pure?

BE HOLY BECAUSE I AM HOLY

Back to our perplexing question from the beginning of this chapter. Given the fact that we track muddy sin everywhere we go, how can we *be* holy?

The answer lies at the heart of Know Be Do.

God is holy. His holiness makes Him righteous. His righteousness makes Him just. His justice demands penalty for sin. He sits as Chief Justice on the Supreme Court of the Universe. And someone must pay the penalty for sin. In fact, the penalty required by holy God is the death penalty.

"*For the wages of sin is death*" @Romans 6:23

I used to go around quoting the Christian cliché, "God hates the sin, but loves the sinner." I've gotten wiser. Actually, I started paying closer attention to the Bible.

For You are not a God who delights in wickedness;
evil cannot dwell with You.
The boastful cannot stand in Your presence;
You hate all evildoers.
@Psalm 5:4–5

The LORD *examines the righteous and the wicked. He hates the lover of violence.* @Psalm 11:5

"I loved Jacob, but I hated Esau."
@Malachi 1:2–3; Romans 9:13

Strong words. But I want you to have a full appreciation for a God Who is so pure, so holy, that sin makes Him boiling mad, that His wrath is on the sinner, that He even hates sinners. Because the more we *know* God and how He hates sin, the more we will stand in awe of God and His equally hot passion for grace, mercy, forgiveness. You will never fully appreciate God's kindness until you can begin to plumb the depths of His holiness, His purity, His righteousness, His justice, His wrath.

If you don't fully *know* God and His holy wrath, you haven't truly scaled the heights of His pure mercy. Did you know that Mount Everest is actually not the highest mountain on earth? It is 29,028 feet above *sea level*. But measuring from sea level doesn't really give the whole picture. Hawaii's Mauna Kea rises an astounding 33,476 feet from the depths of the Pacific Ocean floor. That makes Mauna Kea the tallest mountain on earth.

If you want to experience the rarified air of God's grace, don't start at sea level. Start at the bottom of the ocean. The lightless lowpoint of man's depravity and sin. The dark depths of God's wrath, ground zero for the unfathomable revulsion that God has for sin.

Then look up at the holy mountain of pure righteousness. Scale the summit of God's glorious grace with Christ. Draw a deep breath of the pure, unpolluted air at the pinnacle of holiness. Then, only then, can you *be* holy. Not your holiness. But Christ's.

This is where *knowing* God comes full circle. We began this section of the book in Chapter 6 getting to know God's kindness. Now we've come full circle, to a point that shows just how kind God really is. God's purity demands payment for the penalty of sin. God's kindness provides the payment.

POSITIONAL PURITY VS. PERFORMANCE PURITY

Between sins of commission, sins of omission, wrong motives, and original sin, you and I don't look very holy to God. You've been sentenced to death, and the death penalty is due. Now that you're on death row, you've got two options:

1. Pay your own death penalty through an eternal death in hell.
2. Let Christ pay your death penalty on the Cross.

> Now that you're on death row, you've got two options:
> 1. Pay your own death penalty through an eternal death in hell.
> 2. Let Christ pay your death penalty on the Cross.

No brainer. Funny how the people with the most "brains" often seem to unwittingly choose option 1.

I used to secretly wonder if it was really fair for one man—Christ—to pay for everyone's sin. But Romans 5:12–21 explains how sin and death came into the world through the disobedience of one man—Adam. So likewise righteousness and life comes through the obedience of one man—Christ. How? Because this one man is the God-Man. He is infinite, so His death is able to pay the penalty for an infinite number of people.

His blood is infinitely pure and holy. God the Father accepts His death penalty as a substitute for me, you, everyone who trusts it.

When you reach up with your hand of faith and take the pardon from His hand of grace, you get the "double cure."

"Save from wrath *and* make me pure," in the words of the precious hymn, *Rock of Ages*.

Christ's death, burial, and resurrection accomplished two holy acts:

1. It saves you from the death penalty, God's wrath on sin.
2. It makes you pure, spotless, righteous, holy.

Mere innocence is one thing. Pure righteousness is another. A criminal may serve his time and pay his debt to society. But that doesn't qualify him to be Citizen of the Year. Christ not only satisfied God's wrath, He gave you His righteousness. In God the Father's eyes, you're as holy as His Son Himself. Not just forgiven. Justified. Just-if-I'd. "Just as if I'd"…never sinned.

The double cure: save from wrath *and* make me pure.

You have no cure in and of yourself. Your best 15 minutes won't cut it.

"All our righteousnesses are like filthy rags." @Isaiah 64:6

You have but one hope of being holy. Have Christ's. Exchange your sin for His holiness. Your death penalty is paid by His suffering on the Cross. And His resurrection guarantees you eternal life.

> *But people are counted as righteous, not because of their work, but because of their faith in God who forgives sinners. @Romans 4:5*

If you have not yet made that Great Exchange—your sin for His sinlessness—I urge you to trust Him today. Trust. Believe. Rely on. Rest in.

> *If you confess with your mouth, "Jesus is Lord," and believe in your heart that God raised Him from the dead, you will be saved. One believes with the heart, resulting in* **righteousness**, *and one confesses with the mouth, resulting in salvation. @Romans 10:9–10*

Know that Jesus is Lord. *Be* righteous, believing with your heart. *Do*—confess with your mouth.

He will save you—spirit, soul, and body—pure and full of life for all eternity.

Finally, we have our answer.

How can you "be holy"?

With Christ's righteousness as your own, you can be holy *positionally* where you will never be holy through your *performance*.

I no longer live, but Christ lives in me. The life I now live in the body, I live by faith in the Son of God, who loved me and gave Himself for me. @Galatians 2:20

Not I, but Christ.

Not I, but Christ's holiness.

Not I, but Christ's service.

Not I, but Christ's eternality.

Not I, but Christ's connectivity.

Not I, but Christ's wisdom.

Not I, but Christ's power.

Not I, but Christ's kindness.

I'd rather have 15 seconds of Christ's position than 15 years of my performance.

NO SWEAT

As a believer, once you embrace the reality that *you are holy,* everything changes.

Don't be afraid to say it: "I am holy."

Don't let some kind of morbid humility stop you from believing it. This isn't about you. This isn't about your baggage. This isn't about your performance. This is all about your *position* in Christ. Accept your position in Him. *Be* holy. Don't even worry about *doing* holy right now. Simply let the truth of God's righteous declaration about you wash all through your being. *Be* holy.

Once that sinks in, the results start rippling out, like waves from a stone tossed in a pond. Or to use another metaphor...

I can break a sweat changing a light bulb. I guess it's a guy thing. Or maybe I'm just that out of shape. It takes very little exertion for me to start perspiring. So once I've taken a fresh shower, I don't want to lift a finger; I want to stay clean. I only want to do activities that I can do calm and collected. Once I'm cleaned up, I want to stay that way.

I've found I have the same tendencies spiritually. Once I've had my quiet time with God in the morning, I'm clean. I'm prayed up. I've asked for forgiveness and cleansing from recent sin. I'm in good fellowship with

God. And I want to stay that way as long as I can. That's why I have my quiet time in the morning, just like my shower, to start the day fresh and pure.

Physically, it's hard to keep that fresh feeling sometimes. After a shower, my wife may have something she wants done. Sometimes I have to go out, and it's hot. Sometimes bad stuff happens, the blood pressure goes up, and the sweat glands kick in. Once I'm no longer feeling fresh, I don't mind get a little more dirty. After all, I already need another shower. I'll mow. I'll clean. I'll overhaul an engine; I don't care. After I'm already dirty, what's a little more dirt?

Spiritually, I've found the same thing. Once I've gotten my hands dirty with sin, I'm feeling dirty. I am dirty. So it's not so hard to give in to more. Temptations that were "beneath me" when I felt clean and holy, suddenly don't seem so repulsive, so remote. My fellowship with God has already been tarnished. What's a little more?

This phenomenon is the reason it's so important to "be holy." To have the awareness of His presence and an acceptance of your position in Christ. As long as you maintain your sense of being holy, it's more conducive to staying holy. *Being* holy, present tense, leads to "will be" holy, future tense. It's spiritual inertia—the spiritual equivalent of "a body at rest tends to stay at rest."

Likewise, a body in motion tends to stay at motion. And once you've got momentum going in the direction of sin, it's only natural to keep going in that direction.

That's when it's time to take a spiritual shower. "First John one nine it," as a friend of mine says.

> *If we confess our sins, He is faithful and righteous to forgive us our sins and to cleanse us from all unrighteousness. @1 John 1:9*

Ahhh, better than a shower with Irish Spring!

My favorite passage for taking a spiritual shower is Psalm 51. The superscription says, "A Davidic psalm, when Nathan the prophet came to him after he had gone to Bathsheba." It's a prayer from King David, the same David whom God called "a man after His own heart." A member of the illustrious Hebrews 11 Hall of Faith. David, the adulterer and murder. The spiritual giant, felled by one tiny stone: a bathing Bathsheba. The prophet Nathan held up a mirror to David, and the King saw just how dirty he was (@2 Samuel 11–12). David's heart cry resulted in one of the Psalm's greatest prayers of repentance and restoration.

I love its language of "getting cleaned up." It was David's turn for a bath.

"Blot out my rebellion."

"Wash away my guilt."

"Cleanse me from my sin."

"Purify me with hyssop, and I will be clean."

"Wash me, and I will be whiter than snow."

"Blot out all my guilt."

"Create a clean heart in me."

After I pray that, I feel clean again. I never stopped *being* holy positionally in God's eyes. But I needed to refresh my own experience of holiness in my own eyes. And I needed to restore my communion with God relationally. In other words, I need to go back to the beginning: to *know* God and to *know* that He knows me.

Once you're a believer—His child—nothing can ever break your *relationship* with God. Not even *you*. But sin can break your *fellowship* with Him. *Fellow*ship, not relationship. Once you're stinky with sin, you don't feel worthy hanging out with such a holy friend. He never stops *being* your Father. You never stop *being* His child. But dirt gets in the way of your connection to His power. And that just will not *do*.

CLEAN ROOM CHRISTIANITY

If you want to email your boss, stream that viral video of the cute baby, buy shoes online, post a photo to your favorite social media site, check your stocks, or text your daughter, you're going to need a computer or smartphone. To build a computer, you need to produce a processor. And to produce a processor, you need to create a chip. And to create a chip, you need to build a clean room.

A clean room is a special room used for precision manufacturing. The air is highly filtered. The workers wear head-to-toe clean room suits, or "bunny suits," as they are called. Every object must be sanitized before it can be brought in. Clean rooms are classified by the number and size of particles in the air. Regular room air has trillions upon trillions of particles in one cubic meter. The highest grade clean rooms have less than 100. That's clean.

When you're sitting perfectly still, you're putting off 100,000 particles every minute. Walking around, you put off 5 million a minute. That's why you wear a bunny suit in a clean room. One tiny particle of dust from your hair could ruin a microchip worth thousands. If cleanliness is next to godliness, these clean rooms are Heaven's abode.

God works in a clean room. Not one particle of sin is allowed in Heaven. To do His work in the Kingdom, He uses clean instruments.

> *So if anyone purifies himself from anything dishonorable, he will be a special instrument, set apart, useful to the Master, prepared for every good work. @2 Timothy 2:21*

God is too holy to use dirty tools. As you walk through this world, it's easy to get contaminated. Before long, you're putting off about 5 million sins a minute. It's time to stop, sanitize, and don your bunny suit. Put on your Christ suit.

> *For as many of you as have been baptized into Christ have put on Christ like a garment. @Galatians 3:27*

In a clean room, the "bunny suit" is designed to keep *you* from contaminating the *work*. A Christ suit not only keeps you from contaminating God's work, it keeps the world from contaminating you. It's like a clean suit and a hazmat suit all in one.

But clothing yourself with Christ doesn't mean *isolating* yourself from the world. It means *insulating* yourself from the world. You can do little work for the Kingdom if you're isolated from people who need salt and light. Being insulated but not isolated means you influence the world rather than the world influencing you.

Spiritual work is precise work. One small contaminant can ruin the entire work.

Don't you realize that this sin is like a little yeast that spreads through the whole batch of dough? @1 Corinthians 5:6

> Run every idea, every worldview, every image, every thought, every sound, every temptation, every argument, every opinion through your Holy Spirit filter. Let Him capture every impurity before it gets inside of you. The better you *know* God, the finer your filter will work.

Want to *do* good works? Remember that you are holy. Set apart. So purify yourself from outside contaminants. Like a filter in a clean room, let the Holy Spirit scrub the spiritual air that you breathe.

We destroy arguments and every lofty opinion raised against the knowledge of God, and take every thought captive to obey Christ. @2 Corinthians 10:5

Run every idea, every worldview, every image, every thought, every sound, every temptation, every argument, every opinion through your Holy Spirit filter. Let Him capture every impurity before it gets inside of you. The better you *know* God, the finer your filter will work.

A while back, I was reading a Christian book. Someone I trusted recommended it to me, so I embraced it fully, knowing little about the author. As I read it, I ran across ideas that I hadn't encountered before, and for the most part I swallowed them whole. As I shared things I was learning, my wife started making remarks like, "You're getting weird on me" and "I'm not sure about you since you've been reading that book." I just wrote it off to me learning and growing. She would eventually come along, I thought.

Later, I learned that the author is regarded by many as a false teacher. My wife's "filter" was finer than mine. She *knew* God in ways that I had not yet experienced. Knowing God more intimately helps you filter out error and let in truth.

One of the errors in the book and that many Christians make is that sin is something to be managed. The more holiness you can muster, the closer you get to God. Sounds OK, right?

Wrong. Holiness isn't the pathway to God. God is the pathway to holiness. All the spiritual discipline in the world won't gain you a relationship with God. The correct order is Know-Be-Do. Knowing God illuminates who we *are* which in turn inspires what we *do*. God's grace leads to our faith which leads to good works.

> *For you are saved by grace through faith, and this is not from yourselves; it is God's gift—not from works, so that no one can boast.* @Ephesians 2:8–9

If you try it the other way around—Do, Be, Know—you'll get hypocrisy, pride, and false faith. You'll get a white-washed tomb of a life that looks like a clean room on the outside, but has mud tracked all over on the inside.

Begin with the holiness of God. *Know* His purity and His unconditional love, grace, and mercy. Let Him lead you to holiness as He saturates your life with His holiness. Forget about trying to manage sin. Let Him mortify your sin with His death and revive your life with His resurrection. Then you can *be* holy, because He is holy. Then and only then you can *do* holy, as you are "set apart, useful to the Master, prepared for every good work."

Chapter 13

CONCLUSION OF BOOK TWO

"Give the other person a fine reputation to live up to."

That's one of the principles in Dale Carnegie's classic *How to Win Friends and Influence People.* (It's a book, by the way, that contains more hidden biblical principles than you might think.)

Carnegie offers the "fine reputation" strategy as a leadership method for "How to Change People Without Giving Offense or Arousing Resentment."

But there's a nugget of truth there that helps us understand the Know Be Do concept.

I've found that many people have at least some grasp of the concept of *knowing* God, of cultivating an intimate relationship with Him, communing with Him moment by moment.

People also often have a pretty good idea of what God wants them to *do.* He spells it out clearly in His Word.

But why don't they *do* it? Because there's a disconnect between *knowing* God and *doing* His will. This missing link is *being. Being* who they are in Christ.

Most people today don't understand the concept of *being*. Maybe it's the lack of integrity in today's world. Maybe it's because our world's culture is more focused on externals than internals. The idea of *being* seems foreign. They want to *know* God. They want to know what He wants them to *do*. But the notion of *being* what He wants them to *be* just seems foggy, esoteric, nebulous.

Take a look at it from another angle:

Give yourself a fine reputation to live up to.

What reputation is that? That's where *know* comes in. *Know*, really *ginosko* know the God Who is kind, powerful, wise, connected, eternal, servant-minded, pure. Commune with Him.

Then, recognizing that He is in you and you are in Him, embrace those attributes in yourself. You're a Christian—a "little Christ." You bear His family name.

Jesus has given you a reputation.

Live up to it.

> *We should live up to whatever truth we have attained. @Philippians 3:16*

That's where the *do* comes in. But don't get the cart before the horse. You can't *do* successfully if it comes from a hollow, hypocritical heart that is trying to *do* one thing and *be* another. Don't try to get *do* before *be*.

There have been several seasons in my Christian life when I felt like I was really hitting on all eight cylinders spiritually. They were times when my identity, who I was (*being*), made it easier to *do* what I *should* do. One was when I was a seminary student. One was when I held the position of a minister on staff at a church. And the most recent was as I wrote this book, filling the role of "Christian author." The times when I viewed myself as a direct ambassador for God, I gave myself a fine reputation to live up to. I communed with Him more closely. I abided in His ability. I accepted my position in Him. My *being* was a reflection of who I was in Him.

Then *do* came naturally—and supernaturally.

As a young boy growing up in my neighborhood, I started hanging out with some kids who were a little older than me. I thought they were cool, and I wanted to be like them. One thing they did was cuss a lot, and I picked up the disgusting habit myself. I still remember the day I broke that habit.

I love souped up muscle cars. One hot summer day, a hot rod came screaming down our street, slammed on its brakes, and skidded a long distance. Cool stuff to an 11-year-old boy. My jaw dropped, and I let out an expletive that shattered the Third Commandment.

Shocked, the girl next door scolded, "Aaaaahhhmmm! I'm gonna tell your mom!"

She did, and my mom called me into the house. The daughter of a Baptist preacher, she was blistering mad about what I'd said. I don't remember all she said, but one statement stands out in my mind. It's the cause for me never uttering that blasphemous phrase again the rest of my life.

"You're a Thompson, and Thompsons don't use those kinds of words. If you talk like that, people will think that we talk like that."

That was enough for me. Our family had a fine reputation. I didn't want to disgrace our family name. I wanted to *be* what the Thompson name stood for.

After that, I never struggled with cussing again. I didn't even have to try hard to watch my mouth. It was easy to *do*. Because of who I *was*, of who I had become, of the position I had accepted. I was a Thompson. Thompsons don't cuss.

I'm thankful that my mom let me *know* what a Thompson was like. Her words that day taught me something about my mom, my family, myself. I learned to *be* who I was in the family.

It's a fine reputation to live up to.

Listen to what the Father is telling you about His family. It's a family full of kindness, power, wisdom, community, eternality, service, purity. *Be* who you are in the family. Embrace the name and all it stands for. You don't want to disgrace the family name. So call on your Big Brother. He'll be there for you when you need help. *Be* Christian.

Then when your *being* is supernatural, the *doing* comes naturally. No more mustering up the strength within yourself. When you're abiding in your *being*, you cannot fail. Because *you* are not trying. *You* are doing nothing. You *can* do nothing.

"Without Me you can do nothing." @John 15:5

How freeing! You can do nothing on your own anyway. So stop trying. Start trusting. Focus on *knowing* Him. *Being* who you are in Him. And then He will *do* it through you. "Not I, but Christ."

Then, in the power and authority of Jesus' name, you're going to *do* just fine.

BOOKTHREE

Chapter 14

US—INSPIRATION

By now, I hope you're getting the idea that Christianity is not a to-*do* list. And contrary to what some think, it's not a "to-*don't-do*" list either. In fact, it's not a list at all, it's a *life*.

It's a to-*know* life, which fosters a to-*be* life, which flows into a to-*do* life.

Life. It's one of my favorite words. It's a word that defies the darkness. Defeats depression. Decimates death.

It's a word that's full of light and love. Promises and possibilities. Revivals and renewals.

And quite literally, life is full of "ifs." L-*if*-e. There are lots of ifs in the middle of life. And that's a good thing. Not regretful *ifs*, as in "If only I'd…" But possibility *ifs* as in "What if I…"

The "What ifs" of life are what keep us growing. They are what helped me go beyond the cold legalism of "to-do" Christianity. "What if there's more to the Christian life than merely *doing*?" I posited. And then, after discovering that *being* supercedes *doing*, "What if there's more to the Christian life than *being*?" Now I explore the Christian life seeking to *know* God more. What facets of His infinite character have I yet to discover? I'll never plumb the depths.

This section of the book explores the "What ifs" of the Christian life. The possibilities. The problems. The prospects. Using Know Be Do as a framework, we'll look at questions, such as:

- How do you discover God's will?
- How do you overcome stubborn sin?
- How do you answer life's doubts and difficulties?
- How do you grow in your Christian walk?
- How do you apply Know Be Do to your work, finances, and relationships?
- How do you study the Bible using the Know Be Do framework?

It's a different approach because you won't find "Seven easy steps" or any other kind of "to-do" list that begins with *you*. That's because it all begins with *Him*. *Knowing* God. Then *being* who you are through Him. And finally *doing* life unto Him.

> *For from Him and through Him and to Him are all things. To Him be the glory forever. Amen.* @Romans 11:36

That's the idea of the next section of the book. In Book Two, we focused on *knowing* God. In Book Three, we focus on *knowing yourself—* from God's perspective. It's letting God's life inspire yours.

Renowned Shakespearian actor John Barrymore once said, "A man is not old until regrets take the place of dreams." He was no theologian, but he was on to something there. Paul put it another way:

> **Indeed, our goal is not a "to-do" list. And certainly not a "to-don't-do" list. Our goal is not a place or a thing. It's a *Person*. Jesus Christ. To know Him is to know God.**

Forgetting what is behind and reaching forward to what is ahead, I pursue as my goal the prize promised by God's heavenly call in Christ Jesus. @Philippians 3:13–14

Indeed, our goal is not a "to-do" list. And certainly not a "to-don't-do" list. Our goal is not a place or a thing. It's a *Person*. Jesus Christ. To know Him is to know God. To have His life is to live in Him and Him in you. Pursue Him, and you will fulfill all the "*What ifs*" of life. It's the only thing to *do*.

Chapter 15

KNOWING GOD'S WILL

Beware open doors.

These inviting opportunities can be one of the most dangerous things in the world.

We had some friends in our Bible Fellowship group once who were growing rapidly in the Lord. They were relatively new Christians, and like an infant you see don't see every day, their growth was clearly noticeable from Sunday to Sunday, month after month.

One Sunday, they cheerfully announced that the husband had received an unbelievable job offer from a company in the New England area. The offer had resulted from an amazing sequence of circumstances that were too good to be coincidental.

It had to be God opening the doors, they said.

They accepted the offer and moved the entire family within weeks. About a year later they came back to town and dropped in to visit their old Bible Fellowship group on Sunday morning. How was it going? Oh, OK, they guessed. Had they found a good church up there? Well, no, there weren't many good churches up in that part of the country. They had visited a few, but none were quite right. They weren't attending anywhere yet. Was everything going well with the family? Well, to be honest, it was stressful. Things were not working out like they thought. You could see in their countenance that the once bright light in their lives was barely still burning. When that "open door" shut behind them, it nearly blew out their light.

THE WILL OF GOD REMIXED

Did this family miss God's will? Only God knows, of course. But before I address that question, I pose a broader question: Is it better to *know* God or to *do* God's will?

Both are important, you say.

Bingo. But there *is* a divine order: Know. Be. Do.

Always begin with *know*.

The mistake that most people make in discovering God's will is that they focus on the *do* part, and ignore the *know* part.

> The mistake that most people make in discovering God's will is that they focus on the *do* part, and ignore the *know* part.

People are obsessed with the *do* part. They deeply and sincerely want to find what God wants them to *do*. What job does God want me to take? What college does God want me to attend? In what ministry does God want me to serve? What person does God want me to marry?

Do. Do. Do.

It's a noble goal to want to follow God's will. But as we've said before, our goal is not a *place* or a *thing*, it's a Person. We must keep first things first and focus on knowing the Person before we discover what the Person wants us to do.

When I was in college, I discovered a virtually foolproof way to guarantee an "A" on a paper. When the professor assigned a paper, most students spent days fretting about what subject they would write about. I went straight to the professor and picked his or her brain. I would find out what subjects we were mutually interested in. Then I'd get their input on the paper: what resources to explore, how to attack the subject, what the various viewpoints were. By the time I was finished, I had not only gained a lot of insights from an expert, he or she had practically written the paper for me. Anything less than an "A" would have been an insult to their own input. It wasn't really underhanded, I genuinely wanted to *know* and learn as much as I could from my instructors. A good grade didn't hurt either.

Life is like a course with God as the Instructor. All exams are open book—the Bible. God gives us general assignments, like term papers, so to speak. We are writing the story of our lives. We can pick any subject we want, but we are wise to get to *know* the Instructor. He has our best interest at heart. His interests are our interests. And our interests should be His interests. At this point, however, the analogy breaks down, because God the Instructor is also God the Sovereign King. And ultimately, He rules and overrules where He wills, and nothing happens that He doesn't permit. He's the Author of our lives.

> *A man's heart plans his way, but the* LORD *determines his steps.*
> @Proverbs 16:9

We don't have time here to go too deep into mind-blowing theological territory, so let's go back to the beginning and keep in mind that God gives us freedom, in order that we can freely love Him. And that means the ultimate goal is to align *our* will with *His* will. That brings Him the most glory and us the most good.

IS GOD'S WILL A BULL'S EYE?

Is God's will a bull's eye in which there is always one and only one perfect choice for us to make, and all others miss the mark?

Or is God's will more like a "rank these options" question where there's good, better, and best?

Or is God's will more like a buffet where there are lots of good options that are all at our disposal and all equally satisfactory to God?

Fair questions. But again, these questions are focused on *do*, not *know*. And focusing on *do* before *know* can make us hopelessly anxious about every choice we make.

Say you subscribe to the bull's eye view of "God's perfect will." Every moment of life is filled with choices. What if you miss one turn in life? A "big" one, like, you pick the wrong college. Now suddenly, you and the girl you were supposed to marry will never cross paths. The Holy Trinity must call an emergency session and figure out what to do. Should They engineer things so the girl transfers to your college? Should They figure out another way to get you two together? But then, what if you blow it again, meet the right girl, but marry the wrong girl?

You can drive yourself crazy looking for bull's eyes. And every decision, no matter how small, is a do-or-die moment.

On the other extreme, you can career through life with a fatalistic or deterministic outlook, believing your choices don't matter anyway.

We know, however, that humans have freedom to make choices. We can choose to obey God or to disobey God. So what about the "perfect will of God"?

> *Do not be conformed to this age, but be transformed by the renewing of your mind, so that you may discern what is the good, pleasing, and perfect will of God.* @Romans 12:2

The word *perfect* here doesn't necessarily mean "flawless" like we often use it. In this verse and most of the New Testament, *perfect* is the word *teleios*, meaning complete, mature, having reaching the end. The finish line. You don't jump from the starting point to the finish line in one step. The "perfect will of God" is the destination. And the destination is Christ's fullness.

> *This will continue until we all come to such unity in our faith and knowledge of God's Son that we will be mature (teleios) in the Lord, measuring up to the full and complete standard of Christ.* @Ephesians 4:13

Christ is the starting point. Christ is the pathway. Christ is the finish line.

The endgame is the completeness of Christ. We don't get there overnight. It's a journey. Christ is the starting point. Christ is the pathway. Christ is the finish line. God's will is found in a Person, not a place.

So what is God's will for your life? To be as complete as Christ. Feel like you're a million miles away? Join the club. But if you're a believer, you'll get there.

> *And we know that for those who love God all things work together for good, for those who are called according to his purpose. For those whom he foreknew he also predestined to **be conformed to the image of his Son**. @Romans 8:29*

You *will* one day become like Jesus. That is God's sovereign will. That is the finish line. And as a believer, you will cross it. In the meantime, discerning God's will means keeping your eyes glued on Christ.

> *We do this by keeping our eyes on Jesus, the champion who initiates and perfects* (teleios) *our faith. @Hebrews 12:2*

Have you ever driven through farmland and admired the endless rows of crops, each one straight as an arrow. I asked a farmer once how he got those rows so long and straight. Did he measure them? Did he use some kind of gyroscope or some other device? No, he simply fixes his eyes on a point at the far side of the field, and then drives the tractor straight to it. He doesn't look down at every little dip and rise under foot. If he did that, the rows would be as crooked as snakes. He simply keeps his eyes glued to the destination.

Keep your eyes on Christ. Keep moving closer and closer to Him. *Know* Him more and more intimately. That is God's perfect will.

To be perfectly practical I want to share five surefire ways to miss God's will. You'll notice that the common denominator in each one is an obsession with *do* that eclipses *know* and *be*. Finally, I offer three principles for discovering God's will. The common thread there is an emphasis on *know* and *be*.

HOW TO MISS GOD'S WILL

God's will isn't in the Lost & Found.

It's not missing in action. It's not AWOL or hiding or incognito. Sometimes when we say we want to "find" God's will or we don't want to "miss" God's will, it sounds like it takes a search and rescue team to uncover it. But God isn't playing hide and seek or cat and mouse. He wrote 66 books to reveal Himself, gave us hundreds of commands, instructional letters, and wise proverbs. He's made every effort necessary to make sure we "discern what is the good, pleasing, and perfect will of God." All it takes is to "be transformed by the renewing of your mind." Unfortunately, there are pressures for us to "be conformed to this age." Here are five sure ways to be *con*formed, instead of transformed—and miss God's will.

TOO FOCUSED ON THE FUTURE

God teaches us to make plans and prudent provision for the future. But it's possible to trust more in a secure future than the sovereign Father. The Christian life is lived primarily in the present. Sure, sometimes what we should be doing right now is planning for tomorrow. But constantly obsessing about future plans robs us of today's joy and usually kindles anxiety about tomorrow.

I'm a member of a generation who by and large will be retiring without a lifetime pension plan like my father had. I'm hopelessly behind on retirement savings. A lot of us are going to be in the same (sinking) boat. The average American has only one year's salary saved for retirement. A third has less than $1,000 saved. I've tried to save some for retirement. But I've been busy paying for college, weddings, the mortgage. It's easy to get anxious about the future when I check my 401K balance.

You might have your own future concerns. Who should I date? Who should I marry? What should I major in at college? What career should I choose? Should I sell the house and buy a bigger one? Or a smaller one?

Sometimes I think it would be nice to know the future. Then I wouldn't have to worry about what might happen. But the reality is that we would worry more, especially if it was bleak. Better than knowing the future is *knowing* the One Who holds the future.

> *I have been young and now I am old, yet I have not seen the righteous abandoned or his children begging for bread. @Psalm 37:25*

That verse is a lot more comforting to look up than my 401K balance.

There's a time for everything. And there's a time to seek God's will for future decisions. There is a time to plan and provide for future needs. But God is sovereign. He is good, and He is great. Therefore, keep focused on knowing Him—here and now—and He will lead you through the future, one present moment at a time.

Multi-billionaire Warren Buffet has a wonderful plan for how he will distribute his vast estate. He realizes that leaving his children too much is the most unloving thing he could do. It could dampen their ambition today and destroy them after he's gone. So he's already declared that he will give away nearly all his money to worthy causes before he dies. Then, when he's gone, Buffet says, "I want to give my kids just enough so that they would feel that they could do anything, but not so much that they would feel like doing nothing."

Our wise Father knows how to secure the future for us. And He will gladly help us navigate through it, prudently providing for our present needs and personally guaranteeing our future is safe in Him. He won't give us more resources and more knowledge about the future than would be good for us. He wants us to depend on Him moment by moment. He will guide. He will provide. Follow the Wayfinder, and you'll find the way. *Know* the Father, and you know the future.

> *Trust in the LORD with all your heart, and do not rely on your own understanding; think about Him in all your ways, and He will guide you on the right paths. @Proverbs 3:5–6*

NOT ASKING FOR GUIDANCE

Most everyone knows "You have not because you ask not." And "If you lack wisdom, ask God." Yet many of us find ourselves operating for long periods of time under our own direction. We call on God for guidance only on the "biggies." I've actually heard people seriously say they don't want to bother God with the little things. He's too busy, they say, for that.

What a small view of God. This is a God who keeps an up-to-the-second inventory of how many hairs on your head. Not a sparrow dies without His consent (@Matthew 10:29–30). I think He's got time for you to consult with Him about anything and everything.

Our wedding anniversary was coming up one year, and I prayed and asked God where I should take my wife for dinner. He impressed on me a certain restaurant, and I made reservations there for two. I should have said three; God showed up. During our meal, they played "our song" out of the blue—a relatively obscure song that was no longer popular. What's more, at the end of our meal, someone we didn't even know approached us and handed us a gift certificate they said they couldn't use. It covered the price of our meal. I got to know God a little more that day. He likes Italian, and He's never too busy to offer a good restaurant recommendation. Needless to say, I now pray about where to take my wife on our anniversary.

God has answered so many prayers about "mundane" things that I know He's listening. I believe in asking God for guidance on all decisions, no matter how small they may seem at the time. You never know when one small decision may be the start of something life-changing down the road.

EMOTIONAL DECISIONS

Emotions are not bad. God gave them to us. They bring passion to life the way spices do to food. But a little goes a long way. And God never intended for them to master us. We must learn to master them. And to do that, we have to let *The* Master guide us when emotions begin to take control.

Anxiety. Fear. Anger. Loneliness. Sadness. Confusion. Shame. Even positive emotions like happiness. Confidence. Desire. Relief. Excitement. All these powerful forces can feed deceptive information to your will.

> *The heart is more deceitful than anything else, and incurable—who can understand it? @Jeremiah 17:9*

Emotions are merely symptoms of a deeper reality. Like the pain you feel when you touch a hot stove. The pain merely informs you that something is wrong: Your skin is burning! Emotions are surface issues. The problem with letting them lead your will is our tendency to assuage the emotion and ignore the deeper issue. When God works in our life, He works at all levels, including the deep ones.

A young single woman desperately wanted to get married. After one relationship went south, she wisely consulted God and decided that she needed to work on her relationship with Him for a year before engaging in any more relationships with men. She made a vow to God not to date anyone for 12 months. After only a few months, however, a young man who met all her qualifications asked her on a date. What was she to do? Her emotions were running wild. The man was exactly what she was looking for. She sought God's will in the matter.

On one hand, she had God's will, clearly stated in His Word:

> *When you make a vow to God, don't delay fulfilling it, because He does not delight in fools. Fulfill what you vow. @Ecclesiastes 5:4*

On the other hand, this man had entered her life. Was it a door God had opened? He was a godly man. And she desperately wanted companionship.

What did she do? She let her emotions deceive her into rationalizing that God wanted her to date the man now. She didn't want to be "legalistic," she said, about keeping the vow.

She failed the test.

We've all let our emotions master our will. I've seen otherwise godly people do all kinds of mental gymnastics with Scripture to justify doing what their emotions told them to do.

Again, their focus is on *do*. When it happens, take a step back. Focus on *knowing* God. "Emotions are the shallowest part of our nature," said Adrian Rogers. "God doesn't do His deepest work in the shallowest part." Let God shape your will at the deepest, most intimate level. Let your emotions follow your faith, not lead it.

CIRCUMSTANTIAL EVIDENCE

The heart may be deceptive, but circumstances can be downright duplicitous. They may be a door God opened. Or they may be a trap door that Satan set.

The God of Providence certainly uses events, even *causes* events, to steer us. He used plagues to send a message to Pharaoh. He used persecutions to scatter the early church from Jerusalem and spread the Gospel. He even controlled the outcome of instruments of chance, such as the urim and thummim and the casting of lots, to communicate His will.

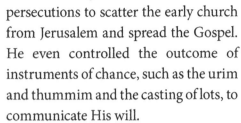

The heart may be deceptive, but circumstances can be downright duplicitous. They may be a door God opened. Or they may be a trap door that Satan set.

But not so fast. Plenty of stories in the Bible reveal the danger of an open door. For example, Joshua was deceived by the people of Gibeon into making a peace treaty with them. Joshua's error: He "did not seek the LORD's counsel" @Joshua 9:14. Appearances can be deceiving. I've known a lot of people who tragically take a circumstantial, hyper-mystical, virtually superstitious approach to following God.

It's tempting to walk through that open door when someone makes an unbelievable job offer. Or that perfect man or woman comes along. It's easy to misinterpret circumstances. It underscores the absolute necessity of *knowing* God before *doing* anything.

God never contradicts Himself. And He always gives a Word that interprets the circumstance. Take Joshua's case. God had already told Him to destroy every nation with certain boundaries. Take the young single woman who made a vow not to date for a year. God had already told her not to break a vow. His Word always trumps every circumstance. Look to His Word first to rightly interpret circumstances. Not vice versa.

Interpreting circumstances is often counter-intuitive. Opportunity and opposition are often signs hanging over the same door. Paul writes, "I will stay in Ephesus until Pentecost, because a wide door for effective ministry has opened for me—yet many oppose me" @1Corithians 16:8–9. This is where *knowing* God and how He works will lead you down the right path. Not the easy path, but the right one.

ACTING TOO FAST—OR TOO SLOW

Discovering God's will can be summed up in two words…

Follow Me.

I got a little taste of how God must feel when He says, "Follow Me," and we try to do things our own way. I recently bought my wife a bicycle. She hasn't ridden much in the past 40 years, but I'm a fairly experienced cyclist. So when we go on a trip, I take the lead. She's back there fretting the whole way, however, about what route we take, where the hills are, whether we ride on the sidewalk or the street, and on and on—instead of just enjoying the ride!

Because I'm experienced, I know the best route for safety, for enjoyment, for travel time. I tell her to just follow me and stay about 20 feet behind me—no more no less. Lag back too much, and she might wind up on her own instead of in my wake, going through an intersection, for example. Or if she peels off on her own route, she might encounter hazards that I foresee and avoid. Just follow me—and enjoy the ride!

How much more an infinite wise and loving Father can lead us safely, for our enjoyment and efficiency. Just follow Him and enjoy the ride.

Sometimes we get inpatient and try to make our own way. Like Abraham and Sarah. Like Peter. Like my young single friend.

Wait on the Lord.

> *But they who wait upon the LORD will get new strength. They will rise up with wings like eagles. They will run and not get tired. They will walk and not become weak. @Isaiah 40:31*

Sometimes we lag behind God. Like Jonah. Like Lot's wife. Like myself when God told me to go to seminary.

Follow Him.

> *Then He (Jesus) said to another, "Follow Me."*
> *"Lord," he said, "first let me go bury my father."*
> *But He told him, "Let the dead bury their own dead, but you go and spread the news of the kingdom of God."*

Another also said, "I will follow You, Lord, but first let me go and say good-bye to those at my house."

But Jesus said to him, "No one who puts his hand to the plow and looks back is fit for the kingdom of God." @Luke 9:59–62

Don't get ahead of God. Don't get behind Him. Just follow Him. Follow Him, and you'll get to *know* Him. Follow Him, and you'll learn to *be* like Him. Follow Him, and you'll *do* what He does.

HOW TO DISCERN GOD'S WILL

God wants you to know His will more than you yourself want to know it.

Remember, your heart is deceptive.

God, however, is receptive. He wants you to connect with Him and His plan for your life. He's revealed Him*self* plainly, and He reveals His *will* plainly, too. Although He doesn't hide His will, it does have to be discovered. Just like the New World wasn't hidden, but it had to be discovered by Europeans.

*So that you may **discern** what is the good, pleasing, and perfect will of God. @Romans 12:2*

The word *discern* in this verse is also rightly rendered *to prove* or *to test* by some translations. The idea is that at first you may not be certain what God's will is. So you run some tests on it, get some more data, so that you formulate the right conclusion. It's a process, and the process is really about getting to *know* Him so well, you'll know His will, too. Here are three diagnostic tests you can run to make sure you're correctly discerning God's will.

GOD'S WORD

"Just step out in blind faith," I've heard many well-meaning but misguided Christians say. They totally misunderstand what true faith is. True faith is always triggered by a word from God. Peter didn't just step out of the boat and start walking on the water. First, came a simple word from the

Lord: "Come." Then and only then did Peter climb out of the boat and walk on the water.

True faith is our obedience in response to God's Word. It's not us acting and Him reacting. It's Him acting and us reacting by following Him. He doesn't "have our back." Because if we're following Him, He's in front, not on our backside.

True faith also isn't blind. It's well lit by the lamp of God's Word.

Your word is a lamp for my feet and a light on my path. @Psalm 119:105

> **True faith is always triggered by a word from God. God's Word and God's will are like headlamps on a car. On a dark night, they shine just far enough down the road for us to navigate the way in the present.**

God's Word and God's will are like headlamps on a car. On a dark night, they shine just far enough down the road for us to navigate the way in the present. We don't need to see farther than they shine. We just follow as the rolling light illuminates the path. When we get to the end of where we can see right now, the light will have revealed the next section of road.

Taking the metaphor a mile further, you can't steer a car that's not moving. So keep moving forward, following Him the best you know. If you make a wrong turn, your Co-Pilot can take over the wheel. But if you stop moving, He seldom gets out and pushes the car!

So, as soon as God says, "Come," step on the gas. The key, of course, is to be so consistently immersed in God's Word that He has ample opportunity to give you directions and you have abundant occasions to hear Him. Some Christians get one 20-minute sermonette a week, and then wonder why they can't discover God's will for their lives.

The vast majority of God's will for your life is laying right on the surface of the Bible. Worship. Pray. Witness. Serve. Focus on first things first. "Put the big rocks in the jar first," and everything else—the gravel, the sand, the water, will fill in the gaps.

In Chapter 20, I'll discuss in more depth the Know Be Do Bible Study method. But for now, remember that in order to test and prove God's perfect will, you must *know* God. And the best way to know God is through His Word.

GOD'S SPIRIT

When unsure about a certain move in my life, I've been known to say, "God, I trust. It's me, I don't." That's really just another way to confess that I don't *know* God well enough.

I earnestly believe God is willing to show me His will. I believe that He is *able* to show me. Sometimes I just doubt my ability to perceive it. I know how deceptive my heart is. I might be following my own self-deceived will. I might be misinterpreting what He's trying to tell me. I might just be in outright rebellion.

That's why God gave us His Spirit. God lives right inside of us. He speaks to us. The problem is, there are usually so many competing voices inside us that it's hard to discern which one is His.

Here's how I've learned to recognize God's Spirit.

I calm myself and get somewhere quiet and distraction free. Then I stop and listen to the quietest, most still voice among all the many voices that I may hear.

I learned it from Elijah.

> *Then He (God) said, "Go out and stand on the mountain in the LORD's presence."*
>
> *At that moment, the LORD passed by. A great and mighty wind was tearing at the mountains and was shattering cliffs before the LORD, but the LORD was not in the wind. After the wind there was an earthquake, but the LORD was not in the earthquake. After the earthquake there was a fire, but the LORD was not in the fire. And after the fire there was a voice, a soft whisper. @1 Kings 19:11–12*

God's voice wasn't in the mountain-shattering winds. It wasn't in the earthquake. It wasn't in the fire.

God's voice was after all that subsided. It was a soft whisper. "A still, small voice." Quiet. Gentle. Soft.

It came through loud and clear. It cuts through the clutter and clamor. It's a clarion call. Clear. Concise. Calm.

It brings comfort, even if it brings hardship. It brings peace, even if it means tribulation.

God's Spirit is the Comforter. He brings peace. And that peace is how we know His voice.

Want to know God's will? Get to know God's voice. His Spirit. Listen for the still, small voice. Tune out the wind, the earthquakes, the fire all around you. And wait for His peace. Once you know His peace, you know you've heard from Him. *Know* His voice. *Be* at peace. *Do* His will.

GOD'S PEOPLE

When I first believed that God might be calling me into full-time Christian service, I made a list of 12 godly men with whom I wanted to meet.

> *Plans fail when there is no counsel, but with many advisers they succeed. @Proverbs 15:22*

One by one, I meet with each one. I didn't pick ones that would tickle my ear. I wanted an honest, objective response to what I thought God was doing in my life. And I wanted sage wisdom that would help me traverse new territory.

I got a wealth of both. I was leaning towards missions work. One man asked me if I was *being* a missionary now. It was embarrassing to admit I really wasn't. That motivated me to do more, and gave me pause to consider that missions might not be the direction God was leading. Another man loved me enough to point out that I was not a gifted speaker. That stung, but helped confirm that a pastorate was probably not in my future.

Of course, God can equip us to overcome any deficiency. He did it for Moses. He did it for Paul. But God's people can sometimes be the mouthpiece that gets across His message, when we might otherwise miss it due to blind spots, deceptive hearts, and bad motivations.

God is well-connected. He wants us to use the community that He forms to steer us. Connect with His people, and you will connect with His will.

DO WHATEVER YOU DESIRE

Want the simple answer for how to *do* God's will? Two words:

Know. Be.

Then *do* whatever you want.

That's it. *Know* God intimately. *Be* filled with God's Spirit. And then *do* whatever you yearn to do. No magic formulas. No complicated steps. Simply *know. Be.* Then *do* whatever your heart desires. Because when you truly know God and know who you are in Him, your desires will be His desires.

> Take delight in the LORD, and He will give you your heart's desires.
> @Psalm 37:4

Try to discern God's will without *knowing* Him and *being* in Him, and you're just shooting in the dark. But to the degree that you are filled with the Spirit, His will and your will operate in complete unity and integrity.

This side of Heaven, however, how can we ever be sure that we are 100% filled with the Spirit? So our "desire" compass might be a little off. And that could take us off course. What to do?

Trust but verify.

Ronald Reagan famously used the phrase "Trust but verify" when dealing with the Russians. He wanted to let them know that while he believed they would comply with the peace treaties, he would require extensive verification.

When it comes to discerning God's will, "trust but verify." Verify not because God is not trustworthy. Verify because our hearts are not always trustworthy. Trust the God that you know. Trust your desires when you are living in Him. But verify to make sure self-deception doesn't lead you astray.

There's a small harbor in Italy that can be reached only by sailing through a narrow channel. The thin throat of the harbor is lined with treacherous rocks—and wreckage from careless ships. Even the most experienced captains won't attempt to enter the port unaided. Three lights have been erected in the harbor in a perfect line. The captain maneuvers his ship until all three lights line up and become one. Then it's a straight shot to safety.

God's Word, God's Spirit, and God's people are the three lights that help us verify that we're lined up with God's will. Be wary of circumstances that may line up; sometimes they're on shifting sand.

Trust and verify. *Know* God. Be keenly aware of His presence and follow His voice. Then *be* in Him. Abide in Him and Him in you. Then let His Spirit fill the sails of your desires. Keep a verifying eye on the three lights to make sure you stay on course. And get ready for the adventure of your life.

Chapter 16

OVERCOMING STUBBORN SIN

Ever wondered if it's possible for us to sin in Heaven?

Scary thought.

Lucifer did. He was cast out of Heaven and will burn forever, Satan and the rest of his minions.

But he wasn't a human being. Satan is an entirely different order than man. So our situation is unique.

Certainly, there will be no sin in Heaven. Revelation 21:27 makes that clear: "Nothing evil will be permitted in it—no one immoral or dishonest—but only those whose names are written in the Lamb's Book of Life."

But could we sin and fall from Heaven? That's a terrifying thought.

The answer, I submit, is "No. Will not happen. Could not happen."

Why not?

It's not merely because Heaven will be a perfect environment, free from the influences of Satan, the world, and the flesh. Adam and Eve had a perfect environment, yet sinned.

It's not because we won't have a free will. A free will is mandatory in order for love to be possible. And certainly we will love God freely and lavishly in Heaven.

It's not because we'll be angels or some kind of different type of being that's not human. We will still be who we are today, but in a glorified state.

I believe the reason we won't sin in Heaven is simple:

Because in Heaven we will *know* God fully.

> *For now we see in a mirror dimly, but then face to face; now I know in part, but then I will know fully just as I also have been fully known.* @1 Corinthians 13:12

All three occurrences of *know* in this verse are forms of *ginosko* knowing. A knowing so intimate that it's also used for sexual intimacy in the Bible, as in the virgin Mary who did not *know* a man.

Here on earth, we know God only dimly. Like the reflection in a crude, first-century mirror.

But in Heaven, how well will we *know* God? As well as *He knows us*. "Then I will know fully *just as I also have been known*." That's full, well *knowing*.

God knows us fully. He created us. He knows our innermost thoughts. He knows our heart deceptions. He knows our motives. He knows how many hairs are on our head and how many hairs we've turned gray on our loved ones. He knows (*ginosko*) us more intimately than we know ourselves.

In Heaven, we will know God fully. We'll know His holiness fully. We'll know His power fully. We'll know His love fully. We'll know His grief over sin fully. We'll know His wrath over sin fully. We'll know His purpose fully. We'll know His forgiveness fully.

We'll be so full of the knowledge of God that there won't be any room for sin.

MEANWHILE, BACK ON EARTH

I can't wait to see Jesus face to face. What a glorious moment that will be!

But in the meantime, we must settle for dull-mirror glimpses of God. But the more we polish our mirrors and keep our eyes fixed His reflection, the more we'll *know* Him. This whole book is simply about polishing your mirror.

The more we *know* Him, the less we'll sin. And the less we sin, the more we'll enjoy abundant, eternal life now. As mentioned before, sin is self-destruction. God's rules are meant not just for His glory, but for our good. Every time we sin, we give ourselves a black eye. That makes the view in our mirror even more dim. Which makes it easier to sin next time. It's a downward spiral.

Every time we obey, however, God comes into focus a little better. Which makes it easier to obey next time. It's an upward spiral.

Let's see if we can do a little mirror polishing here. Most people I know have one major weakness that accounts for a large portion of their sin. Some people call it "the besetting sin," alluding to Hebrews 12:1: "Wherefore seeing we also are compassed about with so great a cloud of witnesses, let us lay aside every weight, and the sin which doth so easily beset us, and let us run with patience the race that is set before us."

"Beset" in the original here suggests the picture of a runner whose feet are entwined in thick vines, wholly encircling, ensnaring, and entangling his feet. The word also connotes that it happens *easily*. You don't have to work hard to get tripped up.

Even ministers struggle with it. Four of them went on a retreat, and sitting around the fireplace, one suggested, "Let's confess our besetting sins. I'll go first. My besetting sin is that I let curse words slip out sometimes when I'm not around church folks."

The second minister sheepishly confessed, "My besetting sin is that I steal toilet paper from the church and take it home in my briefcase."

The third minister coyly admitted, "My besetting sin is that I constantly tell little lies about my achievements to make myself look better."

The fourth minister clammed up, but the others insisted he reveal his besetting sin. Finally, he relented. "OK, my besetting sin is gossip, and I can't wait to get back home!"

As these ministers unwittingly discovered, the first step in overcoming a besetting sin—or any sin—is naming it, confessing it. Just make sure you don't confess to a gossip! God already knows about it. He wants to make sure that you know about it, and that you know that He knows about it.

Exposing it helps you operate on it, like a surgeon who must cut surrounding tissue to get to the problem area. It hurts. But once it's out in the open, it looks uglier, and that makes it easier to reject. It's no longer hiding under lies, masquerading as something good.

So let's get it out on the table. What's your besetting sin? What sin seems to get control of you no matter how hard you try to tame it? I'm thinking of mine. I've climbed into the ring with it about a hundred million times, and it's bludgeoned me in the first round nearly every time I've tangled with it. I've tried managing it. I've tried avoiding it. I've tried everything that I've read to do about it. But my feet are still tangled up.

My besetting sin is lust. There, I just confessed it to all seven billion people on earth.

Now, what's yours? You *know* what it is. Say it out loud.

OK, let's start cutting those vines away from our feet.

THE FUNDAMENTAL ERROR

I've been entangled in many sins in my life, and I praise God that He's cut me loose from a number of them. My besetting sin, however, is another story. It's been a lifelong process, but God has helped me to understand what works and what doesn't. Here it is in a nutshell:

Sin is ultimately not a defect in what we *do*. It's a deficiency in Who/what we *know* and in who we are (*be*). A lot of advice about how to have "victory over sin" focuses on the behavior itself—the *doing* or *not doing*. That's like fixing a broken down car by hooking it up to a tow truck. The car will start moving again, but you haven't fixed the problem. The solution begins with *knowing*—God and His truth.

> Sin is ultimately not a defect in what we *do*. It's a deficiency in Who/what we *know* and in who we are (*be*). Every sin is a product of not fully *knowing* (*ginosko* knowing) Who God is and who we *are* in Him.

You will know the truth, and the truth will set you free. @John 8:32

Every sin is a product of not fully *knowing* (*ginosko* knowing) Who God is and who we *are* in Him. It might be caused by incomplete knowledge. It might be distorted knowledge. It might be total ignorance. In my experience, it's often a case of volitional ignorance.

I freely *choose* to *ignore* God, voluntarily making myself ignorant. I push Him, His Word, His Spirit to the back of my mind—quenching the Spirit (1 Thessalonians 5:19)—so that I can do what I want to do. Yet even choosing to ignore Him is ultimately a result of not truly, fully *ginosko* knowing God.

If we fully *knew* God, like we will one day in Heaven, we would not commit sin. So every sin is the result of a deficiency in *knowing* God. To the extent that you know, agree with, and trust God and His truth, you won't believe the lies, and sin will lose its attractiveness.

Let's take a look at the very first sin. In the beginning, God told Adam and Eve everything they needed to *know* about Him and His creation. But then the serpent came and cast a doubt on some of that knowledge (@Genesis 2:15–3:7).

> *He said to the woman, "Did God actually say, 'You shall not eat of any tree in the garden'?"*

Right off, the serpent muddies the water. Actually, God had said, "You are free to eat from any tree of the garden" with one exception. Period.

Satan twisted it, insinuating, "Can God be trusted?" Satan turned God's period into a twisted question mark.

It confused Eve to the point that she started misquoting God, too, saying that not only should they not eat from the forbidden tree, but that they shouldn't *touch* it either.

Then the serpent got really low, moving from doubt to distortion to outright denial: "You will not surely die." Then he presented his own interpretation—an outright lie about God.

The world was turning upside down. Suddenly, in Adam and Eve's new distorted "knowledge," God wasn't trustworthy, but Satan was. God was withholding good things, and Satan was offering it freely. What God had said was off limits now appeared "good for food," "a delight to the eyes," and "desired to make one wise." The age-old, three-fold nature of sin:

> *For all that is in the world—(1) the desires of the flesh and (2) the desires of the eyes and (3) pride of life—is not from the Father but is from the world. @1 John 2:16*

The upside-down world—not from God the Father, but the Father of lies: Satan.

Let's take Know Be Do and apply it to Adam and Eve's situation. First, you two, stop focusing on the "do" and "don't do." Instead, focus on what you *know* about God. He created you and everything in the world. Gave you a perfect companion. Provided a wonderful garden where you could freely eat anything, save the fruit from one tree. Offered instructions to keep you safe, to ensure that you would live forever.

So, this you *know*. And yet you're going to listen to a beast of the field that God made, let him question your Creator's motives, and then follow his suggestions? The question mark should be on the creature not the Creator.

If you *know* the Creator is trustworthy, then believe His Word, abide in His Word, and *be* who God made you to *be*. In the case of Adam, he was to *be* the husbandman of the garden. *Be* a trustworthy worker, and *do*, then, will take care of itself. Simply do what He made you and enables you to do.

EXCHANGING TRUTH FOR A LIE

It's easy to pile on Adam and Eve for trusting a sneaky snake and eating from the one tree God warned them against. Maybe I could have made it through Genesis 3:17: "The tree of the knowledge of good and evil you shall not eat." Maybe not. But before I get too proud, I'm reminded by my besetting sin that I probably wouldn't have made it seven verses further. Genesis 3:24: "A man shall leave his father and his mother and hold fast to his wife, and they shall become one flesh."

That's where I fall.

Here's the truth: Lust isn't "holding fast to your wife." Lust isn't "becoming one flesh" with her. Lust is trusting the sneaky snake instead of my Creator. Lust isn't being a trustworthy husband. Lust is "naked and ashamed."

Let's break this down. Sin takes God knowledge and exchanges it for Satan's lies. I'm using the example of lust, but you can do the same thing with your besetting sin. Go ahead. Try it. Make a chart. List everything you know about God and His truth as it relates to your sin.

GOD KNOWLEDGE	SATAN'S LIES
Man and wife bond and become one flesh for life.	I would find more enjoyment going from woman to woman.
Marriage is a reflection of the Gospel and a picture of Christ and the church.	Marriage is just another human/legal convention which can be dissolved.
Women are made to worship God, not be worshipped.	Women are sex objects, existing for my sexual pleasure.
My eyes were created by God for His glory.	My eyes are sex orbs, existing for my sexual fulfilment.
God knows our thoughts and when we commit adultery in our hearts.	I can hide my lust.
Lust destroys my relationship with God and my wife.	I can control my lust and still appear to be a good Christian and husband.
Marriage is for my sanctification and holiness.	Sex brings satisfaction and happiness.
Lust detracts from your sex life.	Lust enhances my sex life.
Married sex as God intended it is the most ultimately satisfying.	Forbidden sex is more gratifying.
Sin enslaves and kills.	I'm in control of my sin.
God forgives and cleanses.	God will never forgive you. Give up. You'll never be clean.

It's another classic case of "Did God actually say?..." And we buy it time after time.

They exchanged the truth about God for a lie and worshiped and served the creature rather than the Creator. @Romans 1:25

Oh, wretched man that I am!

Romans 1:18–32 paints a hideous picture of the unrighteous. Yet I see a lot of myself there. It's not that I don't *know* God well, it's that I suppress what I know. In my brief paraphrase below, note how the Bible connects the dots between ignoring the *knowledge* of God and *doing* sin.

The unrighteous <u>suppress the truth</u> in spite of <u>God showing us what can be plainly known about Him</u>. His invisible attributes—His power and divinity—are <u>clearly perceived</u>. Yet <u>knowing God</u>, we don't honor Him. We don't see fit to <u>acknowledge Him</u>. We <u>know</u> His righteous decrees, yet we practice all manner of unrighteousness.

In my lust, I'm tempted to replace God's truth with a lie. I must instead replace lies with God's truth. Knowing God more intimately is simple *replacement*. I must simply *be* more obsessed, more infatuated, more enamored by His Spirit than a woman's flesh. Yes, she may be lovely. But truly, His mercy is infinitely more beautiful. His grace is so wonderful, so pure, so sure, so abundant, so accessible, so rich, so free, so redeeming, so hopeful, so compelling. She can't hold a candle to Him. Once I see how His majesty eclipses worldly beauty, I no longer need to focus on *doing*—defeating lust. I simply focus on *knowing*—captivated by the matchless beauty of His presence.

Want to live righteous? *Know* God.

Want to live unrighteous? Ignore what you know about God.

Once you ignore God's truth, Satan's lies rush in to fill the vacuum.

Fill yourself with the *ginosko* knowledge of God. It's the key to overcoming stubborn sin.

> **Once you ignore God's truth, Satan's lies rush in to fill the vacuum.**

How do you keep yourself filled with God knowledge? Here are three practical pointers.

FOCUS ON KNOWING HIS PERSPECTIVE

Nobody wants to get that call.

My daughter had not been driving long. She'd already had a minor mishap or two, but only at slow speeds in parking areas. No big deal. But she was an inexperienced driver—and frankly, not a real good one yet. We'd done everything we could. We logged dozens of hours behind the wheel. We stressed the responsibilities and dangers of being behind the wheel. Our prayer life had improved considerably. Yet, being of little faith, just to be safe, we bought a vehicle that provided as much steel as possible surrounding her priceless, fragile, 105-pound body—a big ol' ½-ton Chevy Suburban.

And every time she left the house, she heard the same words: "Be careful!"

Her response was usually sarcastic, obligatory for a 16-year-old. "Not this time, Dad." Or "OK, but only this once." Or "No, I'm going to be *wreckless!*"

Deep down, I knew, and she knew "Be careful" was simply code for "I love you."

Today was no different. "Be careful," I said as she hopped into the Suburban.

A few minutes later, we got that call.

To be honest, I don't even remember who called us. I think it was the police. It might have been a witness or the other driver. My mind recalls only one thing: sprinting from the phone to the car and driving as fast as I could to the scene of the accident.

There sat the crippled, white Suburban in the middle of the intersection, shards of debris sprinkled on the road around its sagging right side.

Then I saw her. She was standing on the corner—on her own two feet! She was OK. Shaken up. But not injured. The Suburban had done its job. Actually, God had answered our prayers.

I've learned a lot about God by being a father. Knowing how my heart feels about my children has given me perspective on *knowing* my Heavenly Father. It's made me closer to God. It's helped me understand how He feels about me and about my sin.

Every command, every warning against temptation, every admonition to live rightly is simply our Heavenly Father saying, "Be careful. Don't hurt yourself. I love you."

When I'm in the heat of a temptation to sin, it usually does little good to recall "driving lessons." It's not the "rules of the road" that inspire me. It's not remembering to "leave myself an escape route." Those things can help. But what usually gets to me is remembering that "Be careful" means "I love you."

God's perspective is not that of a cosmic killjoy. He's a Father Who loves His children and doesn't want any harm to come to them. He wants us to drive through life and enjoy all the good things He's given us. He wants to go with us, so that we can enjoy the best thing of all: His presence. He gives us only enough rules to keep us from making our lives a wreck.

When we "wreck the Suburban," is He angry? Plenty. Wrathful, to be sure. I certainly was when my daughter had her wreck—after I found out she was OK.

Does He grieve when we get hurt? Absolutely. Knowing that our sin provokes Him to anger and causes Him to grieve is also a powerful perspective that can motivate us to "be careful," to avoid sin. *Knowing* Him in this fatherly way leads to *doing* things the right way.

One of my favorite verses is an apparent paradox:

> *But with you there is forgiveness, that you may be feared.* @Psalm 130:4

Forgiveness and fear don't seem to go together. Once I'm forgiven, I have nothing to fear, right? Wrong.

Make no mistake. "Fear" here isn't merely reverence and honor. That's part of it. But this is real fear. This same word is used elsewhere in the Bible when men were in danger and feared for their life.

So how can forgiveness produce fear? The same way freedom can produce obedience. The same way trust can produce loyalty. The same way joy can produce tears. When we grasp just

> **The fact that He holds the power to zap me and my sin into oblivion produces sheer terror. But *knowing* that He has an even higher power—the power to forgive—produces a blend of fear, reverence, and awe that truly motivates me to trust and then obey.**

how much God loves us and wants only good for us, it aligns our hearts with Him. His fatherly love, grace, mercy, and forgiveness motivate me to avoid sin in ways that obligation, guilt, shame, and duty never will. The fact that He holds the power to zap me and my sin into oblivion produces sheer terror. But *knowing* that He has an even higher power—the power to forgive—produces a blend of fear, reverence, and awe that truly motivates me to trust and then obey.

Next time your besetting sin comes calling, don't focus on what you should *do* or *don't do*. Focus on the Father's perspective. His love for His children. His wrath and grief over sin, yes. But His grace, mercy, and forgiveness for the sinner. *Know* the Father. *Be* His child. And be careful. He loves you.

FOCUS ON KNOWING HIS PRESENCE

Say you invite your pastor over for dinner. You enjoy a nice meal, great conversation, and then you pull out the computer, say, "Wait till you see this," and start showing porn videos.

Unthinkable.

Or what if your favorite Christian author or speaker invited you to lunch, and you monopolize the entire conversation, talking about yourself and all the things you own and all the stuff you're going to buy.

Inappropriate.

Or say the most godly, kind, elderly woman comes up to you after church to say hello, and you light into her with nothing but angry insults aimed at her along with complaints about your job, your spouse, and your home.

You've got issues!

We'd never dream of showing a porn video to our pastor. But that's precisely what we do to the Holy Spirit every time we have a sexual fantasy. We'd never bore a Christian leader with so much talk about ourselves. But that's often how we pray as we obsess over materialism. We'd never chew out a sweet old lady, but that's often how we approach God when we harbor anger or bitterness.

Lust. Materialism. Anger. You know what your besetting sin is. It's dark. It's disgusting. It's disturbing. It's polluting your life—and if you're a believer, it's destroying the home you've invited God to live in. He lives in you, and you in Him.

> *He is the Spirit of truth. The world is unable to receive Him because it doesn't see Him or know Him. But you do know Him, because He remains with you and will be in you.* @John 14:17

Yet, out of sight, out of mind. That's how we treat God.

But His presence is more real than if we could touch Him. A continual awareness of His constant presence can inspire us to overcome our besetting sin.

First, apply His purity. Imagine His holiness in contrast to the dark, dank dirt of your sin. Let His purity wash over you instead of your pollution flooding His abode.

> *What partnership is there between righteousness and lawlessness? Or what fellowship does light have with darkness?* @2 Corinthians 6:14

I've found that simply meditating on the supreme holiness of God is enough to make impure thoughts evaporate. Holy, holy, holy is the Lord God Almighty. *Know* His holiness. *Be* holy.

> *Be holy, because I am holy.* @1 Peter 1:16

Second, access His power. His presence within you can be tapped with a simple prayer, "God, help!" He's with you in the battle. He's already won it. Call on Him to help.

> *Since the weapons of our warfare are not worldly, but are powerful through God for the demolition of strongholds.* @2 Corinthians 10:4

Besetting sins are sometimes called "strongholds." Because where we are weak, Satan is strong. He exploits weakness, like any enemy does. But don't despair, because where we are weak, the Spirit is God-strong. Why let Satan exploit a weakness when we can let God explode it?

Third, acknowledge His perseverance. God is relentlessly persistent in His pursuit of you. He's no fair-weather friend. He is the "Friend Who stays closer than a brother" @Proverbs 18:24. He never leaves you. And you *can't* leave Him. Nothing will separate you. Not even yourself.

Sometimes I'll hear a backslidden Christian say that he's "running away from God." He must think He can run pretty fast. But he's not gaining much of a lead. Because God is sticky. And I'm so thankful.

When I feel a million miles away from God, all I have to do is remember He's still right there. That melts my heart. When we wreck our lives, He's at the scene of the accident in a split second. He might take the car away. But He walks home with us.

FOCUS ON KNOWING HIS PROMISES

We've got the Two Greatest Commandments, basically: Love God and love people. We've got the Ten Commandments. We've got Jewish law scholars who tell us there are 613 commandments in the Pentateuch. Plus, someone counted 1,050 commands in the New Testament.

Whew! It's not surprising that a lot of people define Christianity by the dos and don'ts.

That's a lot of occasions to miss the mark. To sin.

Or, positively, you could say it's a lot of opportunities to obey. To make God smile.

But here's something to make you smile. By at least one count, there are 3,573 promises in the Bible—more than twice as many promises as commands.

> Spend twice as much time getting to know God and His Word, and you'll spend half as much time struggling with sin.

I'll leave it to someone else to verify these numbers, but here's my point: Spend twice as much time getting to know God and His Word, and you'll spend half as much time struggling with sin.

God's Word is filled with indicatives and imperatives. The indicatives are statements of fact, often promises.

The imperatives are commands. You'll find indicatives-imperatives all throughout Scripture.

> *But seek first the kingdom of God and His righteousness, and all these things will be provided for you.* @Matthew 6:33

Imperative: Seek first God's Kingdom and righteousness.
Indicative: All these things will be provided.

> *As the Lord has forgiven you, so you also must forgive.* @Colossians 3:13

Imperative: Forgive.
Indicative: The Lord forgives you.

> *I am the LORD your God, who brought you out of Egypt, out of the land of slavery. You shall have no other gods before me.* @Exodus 20:2–3

Imperative: Have no other gods before Him.
Indicative: He is the Lord your God, Who brought you out of slavery.

> *Do not fear, for I am with you; do not be afraid, for I am your God.* @Isaiah 41:10

Imperative: Do not be afraid.
Indicative: I am with you. I am your God.

> *Think of all the hostility he endured from sinful people; then you won't become weary and give up.* @Hebrews 12:3

Imperative: Think about Christ's persecution.
Indicative: You won't grow weary and give up.

He doesn't ask us to do what He Himself hasn't already done. What He commands you to do, He pledges the resources to do it. And what He tells you not to do, He promises a way out.

> *The temptations in your life are no different from what others experience. And God is faithful. He will not allow the temptation to be more than you can stand. When you are tempted, he will show you a way out so that you can endure. @1 Corinthians 10:13*

What a contrast from the promises of sin. Sin makes a promise that it can never deliver. It's just a lie. Lust? It never lives up to the fantasy. Materialism? It never fulfills. Anger? It never gains you more than you lose.

What's your besetting sin? Satan promises it will make your life better—but you're on your own. Christ promises it will hurt you, but He will help you overcome it.

Focus on the sin, and you may give in. Focus on the Savior, and you'll have His perspective, His presence, His promises to get you through. Confess your sin, yes. But don't obsess over it. Obsess over the Savior.

He's already saved us from the penalty of sin. He's in the process of saving us from the power of sin. And one day when we get to Heaven, we'll be saved from the very presence of sin. Because then we will fully *know* *His* presence. For now, we'll have to settle for dim glimpses in a dingy mirror. And that's enough. But thank Heaven, we have the promise of a bright eternity.

Chapter 17

ANSWERING LIFE'S DOUBTS WITH FAITH

"Was there one thing in particular that caused you to lose your faith in God?" he asked.

"It was a photograph in *Life* magazine," the old man answered. "It was a picture of a black woman in Northern Africa. They were experiencing a devastating drought. And she was holding her dead baby in her arms and looking up to Heaven with the most forlorn expression. I looked at it, and I thought, 'Is it possible to believe that there is a loving or caring Creator when all this woman needed was *rain*?'"

This poignant exchange was part of an interview by Lee Strobel, a former atheist turned Christian, interviewing a former Christian evangelist turned agnostic named Charles. The interview, recorded in Strobel's book *The Case for Faith,* was conducted near the end of Charles' life.

But the story begins decades before.

Charles was an evangelistic visionary at a young age, and by age 30 the bright young preacher had helped to found Youth for Christ International. In 1945, he hired another budding young preacher three years his junior as its first full-time evangelist: William Franklin Graham, Jr. Better known as Billy.

Charles, then known as Chuck Templeton, and Billy Graham toured together in the 1940s, holding evangelistic crusades around the globe. Many thought that the talented Charles had the best chance of becoming America's next great evangelist.

Charles was well on his way in the 1950s, hosting a weekly religious TV show on CBS. Then, however, came a long, dark season of doubts, culminating in an announcement in 1957 that stunned the evangelical community. Templeton declared he was now an agnostic. Questions such as the problem of evil and suffering had caused him to reject the Christian faith. He went on to write a book with one of the saddest titles I have ever heard: *Farewell to God.*

Billy? What many don't know is that he had his own crisis of faith, well into his career as an evangelist. The surprising story is told in *Billy Graham: God's Ambassador*:

> In the late 1940s, Billy attended a conference in California only weeks before his largest crusade to date was to start. Some young theologians were also there, who were expressing their doubts about the authority of the Bible. "Suddenly, I wondered if the Bible could be trusted completely."
>
> Billy began to study the subject intensively, turning to the Scriptures themselves for guidance. "The Apostle Paul," Billy said, "had written to Timothy saying, 'All Scripture is given by inspiration of God.' Jesus Himself had said, 'Heaven and earth shall pass away but my Word shall not pass away.' I thought also of Christ's own attitude. He loved the Scriptures, quoted from them constantly, and never once intimated that they might be false."
>
> Billy then recalled the moment that changed him forever. "That night, I walked out in the moonlight, my heart heavy and burdened. I dropped to my knees and opened my Bible on a tree stump. If the issue were not settled soon, I knew I could not go on. 'Oh God,' I prayed, 'there are many things in this Book I do not understand. But God, I am going to accept this Book as Your Word

by faith. I'm going to allow my faith to go beyond my intellect and believe that this is Your Inspired Word.' From that moment on I have never doubted God's Word. When I quote the Bible, I believe I am quoting the very Word of God and there's an extra power in it. One month later, we began the Los Angeles crusade."

The 1949 Los Angeles revival meetings became a turning point in Billy's ministry. Billy preached with new confidence and fervor. Planned for three weeks, the city-wide meetings in L.A. continued night after night for *eight* weeks and catapulted Billy into the national spotlight.

A CRISIS OF FAITH

Christian history is replete with such stories of a crisis of faith. Augustine was prompted by a voice to "take up and read," and as he opened a Bible that fell open to Romans, he was gloriously transformed, converted.

Questioning his faith at age 34, John Wesley felt his heart "strangely warmed," and he trusted Christ.

My own Mother, daughter of a Baptist preacher, lifelong church attender, and one of the most selfless and Christ-like people I have ever known, had a crisis of faith. In her mid 60s, she called me out of the blue one evening to let me know she had just been saved. Hallelujah!

Did these crises come *at* the point of salvation or *after* salvation? It makes little difference in the end. The important part is the condition of the soul after the crisis. For Graham, Augustine, Wesley, and my Mother, they emerged strong in the faith.

They began to really *know* God with a true *ginosko* knowing.

I remember going through such a crisis of faith in my own life a number of years after I believe I was saved. I recall telling myself, "I've got to decide if I really believe this or not." I had read the Bible. I knew what was in there. I knew it contained "far-fetched" stories like ax heads floating and dead men rising. I had to determine once and for all whether or not I believed this. I took inventory of the informants:

Human reason was little help. I knew my mind was finite. If there's a God Who created all this, His mind goes *way* beyond mine. I'm never going to wrap my finite brain around an infinite being. Human reason is an inadequate resource for understanding God because it is not an *authority*. If I want to know how to spell a word, I go to the authority—the dictionary. Uninformed by God, human reason has no authority. It *seems* like it's good enough. But that's because its source is *itself*. It's like a teen who thinks he knows it all. He doesn't *know* enough to *know* he doesn't *know*!

Science was of limited help. It has definite limits. Science depends on the observable; it cannot prove or disprove historic events. It also cannot prove or disprove anything in the spiritual realm which is invisible and outside the perception of the senses. Science relies on information perceived by the five senses. They're great as far as they go, but not capable of fully perceiving God.

So, the determination of whether or not I believed in God and the Bible had to be informed by something else—a sixth sense.

Faith.

SIXTH SENSE

Faith is our sixth sense. It's a unique sense that can perceive things within the spiritual realm in a supremely real way. Man is a tri-part being, made in the image of the Triune God. We are physical-mental-spiritual. There are senses informing each dimension—six total. We cannot fully interact with the universe/God by ignoring any one of these six senses. It takes *all six* senses to fully experience the universe—to fully *know* God.

Trying to say science is superior to faith or that faith is superior to science is pointless. It's like arguing that hearing is superior to sight. Or that sight is superior to taste. Or that touch is superior to smell. It depends on what attribute you're experiencing at the moment. If I'm in a dark room, sight does me little good, but I definitely want touch and hearing. If I'm in a fine restaurant, I definitely want taste and smell. If I'm in church, I want faith and hearing. If I'm watching a sunrise, I want sight and faith. In reality, you can employ all six senses to fully experience and enjoy any given moment.

It's so silly and sad for science and religion to be at odds with each other. All science, *properly interpreted*, **supports** the Bible. Science and religion are not in competition or contradiction; they are simply different perspectives for experiencing the universe. Science experiences it through the five physical/mental senses. Religion experiences it through a sixth, spiritual sense: faith. *All six* senses point to God.…

> *For since the creation of the world His invisible attributes, His eternal power and divine nature, have been clearly seen, being understood through what has been made, so that they are without excuse. @Romans 1:20*

> *For by Him all things were created, both in the heavens and on earth, visible and invisible, whether thrones or dominions or rulers or authorities—all things have been created through Him and for Him. @Colossians 1:16*

On my computer desktop is a photo of a pole with another kind of serpent on top of it. It's part of a 19th century grave monument in the beautiful Lexington Cemetery. You'll also often see the snake on a pole used as a symbol in medicine for healing. But the snake on the pole has a very special meaning to me.

You may recall the story (@Numbers 21:4–9) where the hungry, thirsty Israelites were wandering around in the wilderness whining to Moses about how much better they had it as slaves in Egypt. That's the five senses for you! Basically, the Israelites were losing faith in God's ability to get them to the Promised Land. The Lord disciplined them by sending venomous snakes that bit them, and many died. Then they turned back to God and asked Moses to pray for them. He did, and God told him to make a bronze snake and put it on a pole. "Then when anyone was bitten by a snake and looked at the bronze snake, they lived" @Numbers 21:9.

This story was instrumental in my salvation by helping me finally understand how simple faith is. I had been making it far too complicated. Faith is not something you must muster up within yourself. Faith is as simple as sight. It's simply another sense.

> *Now **faith** is the **reality** of what is hoped for, the **proof** of what is not seen. @Hebrews 11:1*

When it comes to spiritual matters, faith is the only sense we have.

*For we walk by **faith**, not by **sight**. @2 Corinthians 5:7*

*While we look not at the things which are **seen**, but at the things which are **not seen**; for the things which are **seen** are temporal, but the things which are **not seen** are eternal. @2 Corinthians 4:18*

ESP

Faith.

The Bible says it's so simple, even a child can have it—just like sight, hearing, touch, smell, and taste. And yet faith is so far-sighted, it can see into the future. It's the original and true "ESP"—extrasensory perception. It can see the invisible. It can see in the dark. Faith is like night-vision goggles. And it can help you read the Bible—and see God—in a whole new light. It's the primary sense for truly *knowing* God. It's the highest form of *ginosko* knowing. It goes beyond knowing Him in the physical realms. Beyond knowing Him mentally and emotionally. Faith experiences God *spiritually*—our spirit and His Spirit intimately interacting, perceiving, and trusting. Faith is *knowing* God in the highest order.

> Yet faith is so far-sighted, it can see into the future. It's the original and true "ESP"—extrasensory perception. It can see the invisible. It can see in the dark. Faith sees the object of obedience instead of the obstacles.

Faith also impacts our *being.* It helps us accept who we are in Christ. Faith sees us as forgiven when we don't feel forgiven. Faith feels His power even when we feel powerless. Faith hears God expressing His love and our value to Him when all others are shouting otherwise.

Finally, faith inspires our *doing.* Faith sees the object of obedience instead of the obstacles. Faith acts on

His authority when all the forces of this world are against us. Faith applies the will of God to override our own feeble will.

They say losing *one* sense makes the other senses more acute. For example, a blind man may have extra sensitive hearing or sense of touch. Perhaps that's because there are fewer senses competing.

I believe that in the spiritual world it helps sometimes to block out the five senses. Maybe that's why we close our eyes and find a quiet place to pray. Sometimes, we have to block out our senses to perceive God, to *know* Him more closely. We might have to ignore the raging sea under our feet to focus on God. We might have to hold our nose when a man dead three days comes out of the grave. We might have to ignore our trembling knees when we hear God speaking from a burning bush.

And sometimes we simply believe—to "faith" (faith is a verb in the original language of the New Testament)—what we can't experience through the five senses. We have to "faith" that God can part a sea—though we've never seen it happen. That a universe can come into existence when God speaks—though we've never heard Him. And that His hand still bears a nail scar—though we've never touched it.

To some, seeing *is believing*. To me, believing *is* seeing. Sometimes it takes a blind man to see that. "One thing I *do know*: I was blind, and now I can *see!*" @John 9:25. Crisis over. Oh, faith. Faith! What a beautiful sight!

DIFFICULT QUESTIONS

But what about Charles Templeton's question as he looked at that photo in *Life* magazine?

"How could a loving God *do this* to that woman?" Templeton continued in the interview. "Who else but a fiend could destroy a baby and virtually kill its mother with agony—when all that was needed was *rain?*"

Questions.

They often teach us more about God—and about ourselves—than the answers.

The quick—and true—answer to Templeton's questions? Simple.

Suffering is a product of man's sin.

Our God is loving—but holy. His justice means sin has consequences. But His love provides an ultimate remedy to sin: His Son Jesus Christ.

Christ's heavenly reign relieves more suffering than earthly rain any day.

He's more than fair. None of us gets worse than we deserve, which is eternal suffering for our sins. Those who believe get much better than they deserve. Eternal life.

But those easy answers often don't teach us as much about God as the questions.

In the last chapter, we looked at how imperatives and indicatives are often paired in the Bible to help us *know* God and overcome sin (*do*). In this chapter, we'll look at how the interrogatives of Scripture help us to better *know* God and understand who we are (*be*).

Here are the basics:

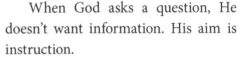

> When God asks a question, He doesn't want information. His aim is instruction. When Satan asks a question, he doesn't want clarity. His aim is confusion.

When God asks a question, He doesn't want information. His aim is instruction.

When Satan asks a question, he doesn't want clarity. His aim is confusion.

When man asks a question, he usually doesn't want answers. Often, his aim is to avoid accountability. When a wise man asks a question, however, he aims to *know* God better.

Let's see how we can better get to *know* God—and ourselves—from questions. Distorted questions. Discovery questions. Difficult questions.

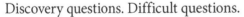

DISTORTED QUESTIONS—"HATH GOD SAID?"

The very first question ever recorded in history came from the serpent.

"Did God really say?...."

And just like that, distortion, darkness, doubt, defiance, delusion, disturbance, discontentment, disdain—and every other demonic disgrace the devil could dream up—entered the world. (Have you ever noticed how many negative words begin with "d"?)

Everything had been plugging along just fine with no questions. An entire universe had been engineered. Man had been formed. Adam had named every living creature. Even a companion had been tailor made for him.

No questions asked.

God had given only one imperative: Don't eat of the tree of the knowledge of good and evil. Period. Simple. Clear cut.

If there was any need for clarification, Adam and Eve could have asked God. God's Word would have been a lot more reliable than getting into a hermeneutical discussion with a twisted serpent.

We'd do well to remember that principle: God's Word > Better than Satan's misleading questions.

Did God really say...sin kills?

> *"For the wages of sin is death." @Romans 6:23*

Did God really say...salvation is by grace not works?

> *"For you are saved by grace through faith, and this is not from yourselves." @Ephesians 2:8*

Did God really say...unbelievers will go to hell and believers to Heaven?

> *"Then He will also say to those on the left, 'Depart from Me, you who are cursed, into the eternal fire prepared for the Devil and his angels!...And they will go away into eternal punishment, but the righteous into eternal life." @Matthew 25:41, 46*

God gave us His written Word so we'd have it in black and white. We're much better off than Eve who had to rely on her memory of what God had said (which she misquoted, by the way).

Satan always tries to take what God said in black and white, mix it up, and turn it gray.

Not even God Himself is immune from the distorted questioning of Satan. Look at how he tempted Jesus in the desert (@Matthew 4:3, 6):

"*If* you are the Son of God..."

If...? Really, Satan? Even you know better than that. Jesus responded simply by quoting God's Word.

Look at how Satan responded to God's invitation to consider His faithful servant Job (@Job 1:6–12). Another insinuating question: "Does Job fear God for nothing?" God's answer was dramatic and emphatic: the Book of Job. It answers why bad things happen to good people—and why good things happen to bad people. Job cries out to God in despair, "If only there were someone to mediate between us, someone to bring us together" @Job 9:33. God's ultimate answer? Jesus. The one Mediator between God and man.

Know this about God: He always has an answer. You may not like it. You may not want to hear it. You may not understand it. But God's definitive answers bring clarity. Satan's distorted questions bring confusion.

In the dark? Doubtful? Discontent? Don't let Satan deceive you. You don't have to know all the answers. All you have to *know* is God.

DISCOVERY QUESTIONS—"WHERE ARE YOU?"

The very first question God ever asked comes just eight verses after Satan's fake fact-checker. In Genesis 3:9, God asks Adam:

"Where are you?"

As I mentioned, God's questions are not for His benefit. They're for ours.

Adam's answer wasn't bad. It showed he was already learning something about God and himself:

"I heard You in the garden, and I was afraid because I was naked, so I hid."

Already Adam had learned several truths: God is holy. I am not. God is to be feared. My sin is shameful.

God still uses that question on us: "Where are you?"

> God still uses that question on us: "Where are you?" And it's still quite effective. He asks it not when He can't see us, because He always sees. He asks it when we can't see Him.

And it's still quite effective. He asks it not when He can't see us, because He always sees. He asks it when we can't see Him. Like a small child who hides under a blanket thinking that because he can't see you, you can't see him.

The question shocks us back into an awareness of God's presence. We should respond as Adam did: Be reminded how holy He is. How unholy we are in our sin.

Jesus was the Master at asking discovery questions. He knew that a principle discovered by the student has a great, more lasting impact than one presented by the teacher directly.

> *He asked His disciples, "Who do people say that the Son of Man is?...But you," He asked them, "who do you say that I am?"*
> *@Matthew 16:13, 15*

Peter's appropriate reply, "the Messiah, the Son of the living God!" showed Jesus' effectiveness as a teacher.

My favorite is the way He confounded the Pharisees with discovery questions. He often answered their questions with another question, using paradoxes or "double binds":

> *Where did John's baptism come from? From heaven or from men?*
> *@Matthew 21:25*

Trapped, they replied, "We don't know." His point exactly.
In the next chapter, He flusters them again:

> *"If David calls Him 'Lord,' how then can the Messiah be his Son?"*
> *No one was able to answer Him at all, and from that day no one*
> *dared to question Him anymore.*

To those *hiding* from the truth, like Adam or the Pharisees, God's questions highlight their sin. To those *seeking* truth, God's questions focus the truth. Either way, His questions are designed for our benefit. They help us *know* God better. And they help us see ourselves as God sees us (*be*).

DIFFICULT QUESTIONS—"WHERE IS HE?"

The very first question asked by man in the New Testament comes from the wise men (@Matthew 2:2):

"Where is He?"

That's the root question behind all man's difficult questions: Where is God?

Wise men seeking God ask that question, and He guides them to Himself with His light. Then they worship Him.

Draw near to God, and He will draw near to you. @James 4:8

Foolish men ask the same question, but they are really seeking to hide from God. They ignore Him because they've pulled a blanket of rebellion over their eyes. To them He answers with a question of His own:

"How will we escape if we neglect such a great salvation?" @Hebrews 2:3

For thousands of years, all kinds of people have been asking difficult questions in a number of ways, but it all boils down to the same question: "Where is God?"

Where is God when starving children need rain?

Where is God when evil seems to be overpowering virtue?

Where is God when people go to hell?

Where is God when I pray and nothing seems to happen?

Where is God when science and the supernatural seem to conflict?

Where is God when bad things happen to good people?

Where is God when billions of people have never heard of Jesus?

Where is God when religion teaches good works are the way to Heaven?

Where is God when Christians act like hypocrites?

Where is God when life gets overwhelming?

Where is God when I can't see Him?

Where is God?

The wise men followed the light, and found Him. Follow the light, and where will you find Him?

Holding an innocent child in His arms as she marvels at the glories of Heaven.

Shedding a tear of compassion as man rebels and sins.

Dying on the cross to pay our death penalty.

Interceding on our behalf as we pray.

Performing miracles that magnify His majesty.

Watching as His children get stronger through adversity.

Displaying the handiwork of His creation so that all are pointed to the light.

Illuminating His Word so that we are trained in righteousness.

Disciplining believers so that they stand stronger next time.

Walking with us through life's storms, not just around them.

Opening our eyes of faith in the blackest darkness.

He is there.

He *is*.

Never doubt Him. Discover Him. Use your faith eyes to see Him and *know* that He is God. *Know* that all that God allows is ultimately for His glory and our good. *Know* that He withholds no good gifts from His children. *Know* that He will never leave nor forsake us. *Know* that He is always good on His Word.

Even when you don't like it. Even when may not want to hear it. Even when you may not understand it. And especially when you can't see it. Faith sees and *knows* that God is good, and God is great. No doubt about it.

Chapter 18

KNOW BE DO AND YOUR SPIRITUAL LIFE

Four days after the Boston Marathon bombing, suspect Dzhokhar Tsarnaev was still on the lam. An unprecedented manhunt was underway, however, and police were closing in on him. They narrowed the search down to a 20-block area, and one resident discovered Tsarnaev hiding in a boat in his backyard. SWAT Teams moved in for the capture, and in an effort to take him alive, they used a device of which many Americans had never heard. It was called a "flash bang." Police tossed the flash bang into the boat in which Tsarnaev was hiding. It went off, and the fugitive was in custody within seconds.

A flash bang or stun grenade is a "non-lethal explosive" that overwhelms the subject's senses temporarily, giving law enforcement time to move in and capture the bad guy. A bright flash of light blinds the vision. A loud blast deafens the hearing and causes a loss of balance. It's sensory overload in the extreme. And it's highly effective.

I see a lot of Christians stumbling around like a flash bang just went off. Sometimes the stun grenade is tossed into their lives by the world. We're bombarded with media from the moment our smartphone starts chirping in the morning until we switch off the late show at night. Our ears endure mind-numbing amounts of information. We're thrown off balance by bad news, stressful jobs, and a culture that keeps demanding more, more, more.

Sometimes the flash bang gets tossed by our own churches and the demands of spiritual disciplines. Sunday is a marathon with Sunday school, morning worship, meetings, choir practice, discipleship training, and evening worship. Then there's the Monday men's group, Tuesday women's ministry, Wednesday prayer meeting, Thursday visitation, Friday students events, and Saturday missions opportunities. Oh, and don't forget the church softball game and the yard sale fundraiser. We stay busy six ways from Sunday for the Lord.

Flash. Bang.

Our senses are so overloaded with all the world or the church is throwing at them, we're in blind stupor, hardly aware that God is waiting to have a relationship with us.

Be still and *know* that I am God.

I wonder sometimes what everyday life was like for the great men and women of the Bible. Paul seemed pretty busy with his missionary travels and all. But he stayed and made tents for a while in Corinth, and I'm sure he had a lot of time with God on all those boat rides.

Abraham was a man of great faith, but I imagine a big chunk of his time was spent managing his thriving livestock business. I don't think he was up at the church every night of the week. Moses probably had a lot of "unproductive downtime" in all his wanderings. Isaiah, Jeremiah, Ezekiel each had their moments and wrote a major book, but we don't get a lot of information about what they did the rest of their lives. And what about Obadiah. He wrote only one book of the Bible, and only one chapter at that. What was he *doing* with his life?

What these spiritual giants did is walk with God, and—first things first—that's mostly about *knowing* Him, not fetching things for Him.

Do might be how 21st century American Christianity defines spiritual success, but it's not necessarily how God defines it.

When it comes to God, I believe *do* is highly overrated.

So let's back off the flash-bang, overstimulated spiritual life for a moment, and look at your spiritual walk through the lens of Know Be Do.

WHAT'S YOUR THORNBUSH?

Two to three hundred years after Christ, a well-meaning movement began gaining steam in which some believers strived to live a higher spiritual life by renouncing all attachments to the world. They abstained from "worldly pleasures." Sex. Food. Possessions. They denied themselves any comforts, and many took it one step further, intentionally inflicting pain on themselves to ensure that they were not enjoying any pleasure from this world. They were called ascetics. Some practiced rituals such as flinging themselves on thornbushes in an effort to show God how dedicated they were to emulating the self-denying lifestyles of John the Baptist, the Apostle Paul, and Jesus Christ Himself.

All this effort was designed to unclutter their life and make more space to meditate on Scripture and pursue inner peace. Monasteries were created where the really committed ones could better escape the externals and embrace the internals.

I believe many of these believers were sincere and well-intentioned. The problem is self-denial became an external itself. And the inward focus turned their salt and light in on itself instead of out on the world that needed it.

So what's your thornbush? What external *do* are you conspicuously flinging yourself into so that you can show God—and your social media friends—how committed you are?

Now don't get me wrong. Not everyone who shows up for the 6:00 a.m. men's prayer group, or volunteers for the nursery, or signs up for the 2:00 a.m. slot in the prayer chain is throwing themselves on a thornbush. But my point is this: *Doing* things for God won't necessarily make your spiritual walk more healthy. It could have the reverse effect.

First things first: *Know.* Then *be.* Then *do.*

WORSHIP

Let's start with worship. It's not something you *do.*

> God is spirit, and those who worship Him must worship in spirit and truth. @John 4:24

A spirit is something you *know*. A truth is something you *know*. Neither is something you can *do*.

Aaron's sons Nadab and Abihu learned this the hard way. The whole community was watching. Moses told Aaron to go make the various sacrifices. He did everything just as the LORD had commanded. They came out to the people, blessed them, and then…

> *"The glory of the LORD appeared to all the people. Fire came from the LORD and consumed the burnt offering and the fat portions on the altar. And when all the people saw it, they shouted and fell facedown on the ground." @Leviticus 9:23–24*

Wow! Nadab and Abihu thought, "We can do that!" Emphasis on *do*.

So they "each took his own firepan, put fire in it, placed incense on it, and presented unauthorized fire before the LORD, which He had not commanded them to do. Then fire came from the LORD and burned them to death before the LORD."

Unauthorized fire. Some translations call it strange fire. Foreign fire. Illegitimate fire. Unholy fire.

They got so wrapped up in *doing* something for the Lord they forgot all about Who they were doing it for. God is holy, and He had conscribed precise methods for making the sacrifices so that they pictured His holiness in all its glory. Nadab and Abihu didn't know or didn't care to know. Either way, they neglected *know* in favor or *do*. God responded with a "flash bang" of His own, and this one was lethal. Nadab and Abihu perished.

How do *we* bring "strange fire" into our worship? By focusing more on what we *do* in worship than Who He is (*know*).

Nadab and Abihu offered something profane, something not sanctified, not holy, not consecrated. They attempted to worship God the way they willed, not the way God willed. Instead of taking fire from the altar that had just come down from the Lord (as God had commanded @Exodus 30:9), they manufactured their own fire. It was self-effort, self-generated worship.

On the surface, it might seem like this story is concerned with maintaining a precise method of worship. But the lesson is not so much about method as it is mindset. Nadab and Abihu's error isn't that they followed the wrong method. That was just the result. The root cause is that they began with the wrong mindset. They were focused on what they wanted to *do* instead of Who God is and what He had just done.

God had just held one of the greatest tent meetings of all time. The glory of the Lord appeared. Fire came down. And the people shouted and fell facedown on the ground. I'm pretty sure this worship service beat any other worship event with light show and fog machine that's ever been attempted. The proper response was to "be still and know that He is God." To worship Him in spirit and in truth.

Instead, Nadab and Abihu wanted to get in on the act. Maybe they wanted to bring attention to themselves. Maybe they thought they could impress God. Either way, their focus was on doing something instead of appropriately worshipping Someone—God.

Want to worship God the right way? First, forget about yourself. Self-conscious worship is an affront to God. Lose yourself in an awareness of Him. He's plenty big enough for that.

Second, focus on *knowing* God more intimately. Worship Him simply for Who He is. Holy. Eternal. Wise. Powerful. Kind. Worship Him for what He has done. Stand in awe of the fire that's come down.

If you have the right mindset—one focused on more intimately knowing God—then the methods are not important. The worship wars— the battle over various styles of worship and music—are nothing more than Nadab and Abihu arguing about whose firepan they're going to use. Forget the firepan. Focus on the Fire. The Glory of God.

Why is it so important to approach worship with a mindset of getting to know God more intimately? Because whatever we worship is what we become more like. If you worship gold idols, you become more like gold— cold, hard, dumb. If you worship famous people, you become more like them. If you worship yourself, you magnify your pride.

The more you worship God, the more you *become* like Him (*be*). So it helps to *know* what He's like. It all comes back to knowing God. Knowing God informs your worship of Him. Worshipping Him inspires you to mirror Him, to *be* who you are in Him. That in turn empowers you to *do* what He does. Know. Be. Do.

CORPORATE AND PERSONAL WORSHIP

Focusing on knowing and not doing is part of what makes corporate worship such a challenge. I confess that when I'm standing in a church worship service, I'm often all too wrapped up in myself, the people around me, and what's going on up on the stage. Too often, it feels more like *doing* worship than *knowing* the One Who we are there to worship. The harder I try to focus, the more it feels like doing. If someone installed a "True Worship Meter," I'm ashamed to say that some Sundays I might not clock 60 seconds total of absolute, God-absorbed worship. What would *your* meter read?

While corporate worship challenges me, personal worship changes me. When I'm alone with God, no longer distracted and inhibited by other people, I'm free to worship God in all the spirit and truth I can handle. My daily quiet time is a conversation. First, He speaks, and I listen. Then I speak, and He listens.

He speaks to me through His Word, through His Holy Spirit, and through praise music. I listen and respond. I stand and lift my hands. I prostrate myself on the floor. I record His insights in my prayer journal. Sometimes I pace. Sometimes I sit still and just *know* that He is God.

I encourage you to read the Word out loud when you're reading Scripture. There's something about *hearing* the Word—not merely reading it—that brings it to life—yours. The Bible itself often tells of Scripture being read aloud. God is a real person, and hearing His Word makes it more personal. After all, the Bible is not just God's Word, it's His *voice*.

I speak to Him through prayer. I confess sin. I pray for needs, a different set for each day of the week. I pray for people who need to be saved. I pray for special current needs. I thank Him. And the final thing I do is bow before Him and profess that He is my God and King, and I pledge my allegiance to Him anew.

In Chapter 20, I outline a specific Know Be Do Bible Study method that has helped me and I pray will help you in your personal worship time. I also discuss prayer in more depth at the end of this chapter.

You cannot worship one whom you do not know. Get to *know* God intimately through Bible study (Him speaking to you) and prayer (you speaking to Him)—two-way communication. It will set your worship on fire!

FELLOWSHIP

I'm Fine with God, It's Christians I Can't Stand.

That's a book title that I think I could have written. People. Equal. Problems.

Problem one: If you have problems with people, it may be *you* who has the problem. You can't be fine with God if you're not OK with His bride. You can't rise in your vertical relationship with God past your lowest horizontal relationship with your brothers and sisters.

> # You can't rise in your vertical relationship with God past your lowest horizontal relationship with your brothers and sisters.

But if you don't forgive, neither will your Father in heaven forgive your wrongdoing. @Mark 11:26

Problem two: Many Christians are simply not very loveable or likeable. I don't even like myself about half the time. We're hypocritical. Ignorant. Backwards. Obnoxious. Paranoid. Self-righteous. Too pushy. Or too timid. We know what we believe—and we're mad about it. Or we don't have a clue what we believe. Our churches feel like secret lodges to outsiders. We seem to have the same bad habits and hang-ups as the world. We're known more for what we're against than what we're for. And we make uber-cheesy, cringe-worthy movies.

Problem three: We're going to spend all eternity with these people.

Of course, we won't be sinners in Heaven, so it should be a lot easier. But how about now? What about...

If possible, on your part, live at peace with everyone. @Romans 12:18

That's Paul writing. The one who used to be a terrorist to Christians. Now he's got an even scarier job: ministering to them. Big chunks of his letters were written to keep them from choking one another. Thankfully, he provides two disclaimers: One, "If possible…" Of course, Jesus told us "With God all things are possible." Two, "…on your part…" So again, not much wiggle room there: God lives in your part.

So how can we get past all the dysfunction of Christian relationships and enjoy genuine Christian fellowship the way God intended? Again, it all comes back to *knowing* God. Don't attempt to *do* Christian fellowship until you've grown in *Christ* fellowship. There's a reason why Paul gave us 11 chapters of solid theology—our vertical relationship with God—before he turns the corner to horizontal, human relationships in Romans 12.

And what have we learned about God in those first 11 chapters of Romans that will help us survive being thrown to the lions, er, Christians? (Which is worse?)

For openers, Romans 1:7 says "Grace to you and peace from God our Father and the Lord Jesus Christ." Don't miss that. The source of grace and peace? God, not people. If you're looking to people to bring that kind of fulfillment, you'll never live in peace. That flows from God through you to people. Not the other way around.

Romans chapter 2: There's no partiality with God (@Romans 2:11). So *be* like Him. Treat everyone equally. Be careful not to judge hypocritically or by appearances.

Romans chapter 3: God loves the unlovable sinner. Are we better than God that we can afford to despise people and harbor bitterness?

Space doesn't allow us here to consider all the attributes of God that promote Christian fellowship. But keep in mind that the purpose of Paul's entire letter is to explore how man is reconciled to God in order to exist in eternal harmony. Certainly, our relationship with God introduces us to a harmonious fellowship with our fellow man.

In Chapter 9 of this book, we considered how God is a God of connectivity. As a Trinity, He exists as a union in perfect unity. He designed us to live in unity and community. He gave us the family as the inner circle of our closest relations. And he gave us the church as the home of our Christian community. These gifts are a slice of Heaven on earth. May we ever cherish them. Even if we do make dreadful movies.

WITNESS

"I see dead people. They walk around like regular people. They don't see each other. They only see what they want to see. They don't know they're dead."

This eerie line from the psychological thriller film *The Sixth Sense* is spoken by 9-year-old Cole, a troubled boy who is haunted by dead people only he can see. An equally disturbed child psychologist played by Bruce Willis tries to help the boy, (SPOILER ALERT) but fails, until one day he has an epiphany. He tells young Cole that the dead people need his help; that's why they come to him. If only he will lay aside his fears, see what they need, and help them, then he will no longer be afraid. He'll be helping the dead and the ones they loved.

I don't believe the film was created to be a spiritual metaphor, but as my friend and teacher Dr. Lindell Ormsbee points out, there's a lot of application for believers in our call to witness, to share our faith with unbelievers. Sharing our faith comes back to *knowing* God, seeing the world as He sees it. When God looks at people, He sees two kinds: dead people and living people. We don't tend to view the world as He does. We just see people. We divide them into groups, like… Good people. Bad people. Attractive people. Unattractive people. Rich people. Poor people. But most of the time, we're not really sensitive to whether they are spiritually dead or alive. Of course, only God knows for sure. But we have His Spirit. It resonates with other believers. And senses the vital signs of those around us. If only we could see people as God sees them, sharing our faith would be supernaturally natural.

Sharing one's faith is probably the number one command that most Christians dread. That's because most believers are starting with *do*. They know witnessing is something they should *do*. But most people would rather attend an all-night prayer meeting than share the Gospel with people. It takes a massive amount of guilt, self-will, or training to get most Christians to share. They just don't want to *do* it.

We give all kinds or reasons and excuses. "They don't want to hear.... What if they ask a question I can't answer?...I don't know how....I don't have time....I'm not a people person....I'm scared." Just like little Cole. But the bottom line is we're simply approaching it backwards, from a *do* perspective instead of a God-*know*-how perspective. God's perspective:

> *You were dead in your trespasses and sins in which you previously walked according to this worldly age... But God, who is rich in mercy, because of His great love that He had for us, made us alive with the Messiah even though we were dead in trespasses. @Ephesians 2:1–2, 4–5*

Hallelujah! We're wanted: dead or alive. All we need to do is see the world with God's eyes. *See* the dead ones. Don't be afraid of them. God isn't. Don't reject them because they're dead. God doesn't. Let the mercy and love that God has for dead people flow through you, and then simply *be* a witness. A witness just tells what he's seen and heard (@1 John 1:1–3). *Be* a witness. Tell the dead what's it's like to be alive. You can help them, just like Cole. It's really quite simple.

You might think that if you could ever hold a focus group in hell (long distance, of course!), you might get some good strategies for witnessing to dead people. Not so. It's already been tried. Remember the story Jesus told of the rich man in hell? He begged Abraham to send Lazarus, the recently deceased beggar who now was enjoying Paradise, to travel from Heaven to Hell. His only request? For Lazarus to dip the tip of his finger in water and cool the rich man's agonizing tongue.

When the request was denied, the rich man suddenly becomes vitally interested in evangelism! He develops his own evangelism program: Send the deceased Lazarus to his five brothers with a warning to avoid this place of torment. It was literally the evangelism program from hell.

> *"But Abraham said, 'They have Moses and the prophets; they should listen to them.'*
>
> *"'No, father Abraham,' (the rich man) said. 'But if someone from the dead goes to them, they will repent.'*

"But he told him, 'If they don't listen to Moses and the prophets, they will not be persuaded if someone rises from the dead.'" @Luke 16:29–31

The rich man's strategy was dead on arrival. That's because the earth is already full of former dead people sharing the Gospel. Moses. The prophets. Me. You, if you're a believer. Even the resurrected Christ Himself. We *are* the former walking dead—now alive and living forever. God doesn't need to shuttle people from Heaven. There are plenty of us to take the message of eternal life to the spiritually dead. But we must see the dying world through the eyes of God. We must *know* His great love and mercy, and not be afraid of the dead.

SERVE

"Don't go to Brazil to fall in love with the Brazilian people. Go to Brazil and fall more in love with Jesus."

That's the best piece of advice I've ever heard for going on a missions trip. It was given by our project lay leader and missions trip veteran, Eric Brand.

Plug any act of service into that sage advice:

Don't volunteer in the nursery to fall in love with the babies. Serve and fall more in love with Jesus.

Don't visit the nursing homes to fall in love with the seniors. Serve and fall more in love with Jesus.

There's a corollary for less enjoyable tasks:

Don't show up on campus work day to make improvements to the church. Serve to become more like Jesus.

If ever there was a "spiritual discipline" that has "do" written all over it, it's serving. Especially for us task-oriented people; just give us the church to-do list, and get out of our way. There are a lot of ministry needs out there, and we're just not quite sure what God would do without us. To us, serving is all about *doing*.

And eventually failing.

Statistics say that 1,700 pastors leave the ministry every month. I've known a few of them. Their reasons are varied. Disappointment. Failure.

Loneliness. Pressures. Sin. Burnout. But I believe that the root problem is usually the same. The focus was on *doing* ministry, instead of *knowing* God.

For volunteer ministry, the problems are just as staggering. The classic statistic is that 20 percent of the people do 80 percent of the work. Burnout and dropout rates are high among volunteers as well.

Serving that's focused on doing instead of knowing God leads to quitting. Jonah got swallowed by in that blunder.

> **Serving that's focused on doing instead of knowing God leads to quitting.**

> *The word of the LORD came to Jonah son of Amittai: "Get up! Go to the great city of Nineveh and preach against it, because their wickedness has confronted Me." However, Jonah got up to flee to Tarshish from the LORD's presence. @Jonah 1:1-3*

Notice Jonah's failure. It wasn't because he wasn't equipped. It wasn't because the call wasn't clear. He had a Word from God. It wasn't because the need wasn't valid. The wickedness was great.

Jonah fled from the Lord's *presence*. He didn't want to be near God. He didn't want to commune with God. He didn't want to listen to God. He didn't want to have any part of *ginosko* knowing God.

Why? The answer comes in the last chapter.

> *That's why I fled toward Tarshish in the first place. I knew that You are a merciful and compassionate God, slow to become angry, rich in faithful love, and One who relents from sending disaster. @Jonah 4:2*

Jonah knew facts about God. His mercy, His compassion, His love. But it wasn't *ginosko* knowing. Jonah didn't connect with God to the point that God's attributes flowed into his being and became his attributes. And he became a ministry dropout statistic.

Being who we are in God is the proof that we have truly known God. If we don't connect the dots between Who He is and Who we are, then *doing* will be a chore. It will be an obligation. God's ways will anger us like they did Jonah. And we will run from His presence.

Serving people will motivate us only so far. We'll gravitate to the lovable people, the people who give us positive feedback, the people who give back.

Serving *people* is merely *doing.*

> *For am I now seeking the approval of man, or of God? Or am I trying to please man? If I were still trying to please man, I would not be a servant of Christ. @Galatians 1:10*

Serving God is *knowing* and *being.* To *know* Him is to serve Him. To *be* Christ to those we serve. He flows through us to give us the will to do it and the way to do it.

> *Serve with a good attitude, as to the Lord and not to men. @Ephesians 6:7*

Job didn't go on his mission trip to Nineveh and fall more in love with Ninevites. He didn't fall in more love with God either. And the trip probably did nothing for his appetite for seafood. Don't wait until you're inside the belly of a fish to get inside God's thoughts. Let the waves of His mercy, compassion, and love wash over you. Let the humility that washes a brother's dirty feet spill over onto you. Then *be* the servant that He is. *Do* it for the Father's glory. Do it for the Lord. Do it to serve the One Who came to serve. Do it and fall more in love with Jesus.

PRAY

I've heard a lot of answers to this question, but I'll never forget this one.

Two fellow church members and I were making EE (Evangelism Explosion) visits one summer evening in a modest neighborhood. We'd been invited into a home, and now it was my turn to pop the two EE questions: "Do you know for certain you're going to Heaven?" I posed to the young man in his 20s.

"Yes," he replied.

"Great," I continued. Question two: "If you were to die today, and God said, 'Why should I let you into My Heaven, what would you say?'"

"Well, me and God are tight, and the reason I know is that one time I had a goldfish who got sick, and I prayed to God, and God made my goldfish better, and he got well."

Talk about your fish tales! I choked down my laughter, and acting as if that was a perfectly reasonable response, I plunged into the Gospel. I explained that Christ's righteousness, not our answered prayers, are the basis of our salvation. By the end, he understood that God makes dead men alive, not just sick goldfish well.

Though the young man's theology of salvation was more than fishy, his understanding of prayer was actually pretty insightful. Prayer says a lot about how tight you are with God.

The tighter you are with God, the more you pray. And the more you pray, the tighter you are with God.

Likewise, drift from God, and you'll drift from prayer. Drift from prayer, and you'll drift from God.

Like the other topics in this chapter, prayer needs an entire book to explain how to pray through the lens of Know Be Do. Praying is the epitome of *ginosko* knowing God. But prayer is also *being*. And prayer is *doing*.

Too often, we begin with the *doing*. We pray backwards. Viewing prayer as a task, we quickly hand our "to-do" list to the Lord. Prayer becomes more of a consumer time than a communion time.

Slow down. Even when the prayer is urgent, there's always time to acknowledge the Lord. Take the shortest prayer in Bible. Peter gets out of the boat, and facing the wind and the waves, gets that sinking feeling and cries out: "Lord, save me." Just three simple words. But he begins with an acknowledgement of the Lord. He confesses his allegiance to and reliance on the Lord. He begins with the relationship—Lord—not the request. Then and only then does he state what he needs God to do: Save me.

Prayer is simple. Way more simple than we tend to make it. In fact, Anne Lamott distills it down to the three essential prayers:

Wow.

Thanks.

Help.

Each of these centers on a different aspect of Know Be Do, although they are all interconnected. "Wow" centers on an acknowledgement of His attributes (*know*). "Thanks" centers on a grateful acceptance of our position in Christ (*be*). "Help" centers on the application of His power (*do*).

Richard Foster in his book *Prayer* slices and dices up prayer into 21 different varieties, seven each under three different divisions. Again, I see an alignment between Foster's divisions and Know Be Do:

- Moving Upward: Seeking the Intimacy We Need (*know*)
- Moving Inward: Seeking the Transformation We Need (*be*)
- Moving Outward: Seeking the Ministry We Need (*do*)

Fully-orbed, well-rounded prayer touches on all three aspects of Know Be Do. You'll see these aspects reflected in prayers throughout the Bible (more about this in Chapter 20).

> **When prayer seems like a chore, it's because I'm too focused on *doing*— me doing prayer and God doing answers. Want to bring the joy back to your prayer life? Focus first on *knowing* God.**

Sometimes prayer comes easy. Sometimes prayer is just plain ol' hard work. I mean bear-down, ditch-diggin', keep-your-nose-to-the-grindstone hard work! It's simple, but hard. But I've noticed that when prayer seems like a chore, it's because I'm too focused on *doing*—me doing prayer and God doing answers.

Want to bring the joy back to your prayer life? Focus first on *knowing* God. Slow down, sit at His feet, and just bask in the radiance of His holiness. It will make confessing your sins and praying for power over them easier. Meditate on

His kindness. It will make your heart tender and prayer for your enemies more genuine. Marvel at His wisdom and power. It will open the flow of knowledge and strength to your life. Observe the unity and community of the Trinity. It will bond you with your fellow man. Take notes on the suffering servant. It will remind you of your humble position as His willing slave and your brother's servant.

This world will always keep tossing flash bangs into your life that will overwhelm your senses and distract you from worship, fellowship, witnessing, serving, and praying. Keep tuned into your sixth sense— faith—and stay constantly aware of God's presence.

Be still and *know* that I am God.

Chapter 19

KNOW BE DO AND YOUR EARTHLY LIFE

One day, out of the blue, my wife said to me, "I'm really happy with you right now."

I said, "What made you say that? What did I *do*?" I wanted to file this away for future reference. I do plenty of dumb stuff that provokes the opposite feedback: "I'm really *not* happy with you right now." So I was vitally interested in making notes on how I could make deposits in her love account.

"Nothing you *did*," she replied. "Just bein'."

It's perhaps the highest compliment she's ever paid me.

Just bein'. When it comes to everyday, ordinary life, the key to abundant living is "just bein'."

Don't get me wrong. You cannot compartmentalize life. It's not that there's a spiritual part of your life that revolves around the Son, and the key to it is *know*—knowing God. And then there's the earthly part of your life that revolves around the sun, and the key to it is *be*—being who we are in Christ. That's not how it works at all.

Knowing God is the foundation of all of life. Period. We should live every moment in a constant awareness of His presence. Praying without ceasing. Rejoicing in the Lord always. Doing everything as unto the Lord.

This God-consciousness is especially critical as we worship, fellowship, witness, serve, and pray. And in a very real sense, *everything* we do is an expression of our relationship with God. Our work can be worship. We serve our families for Christ's sake. We witness in everything we say and do.

But when it comes to everyday life, the secret of success is connecting the dots between *knowing* God and simply *doing* what we do with our 24 hours each day. And the key to connecting those dots is *being*.

Forget "Just do it" for now.

Just *be*.

BRANDING

Are you Apple or PC?

Are you Chevy, Ford, Dodge, Toyota, or Jaguar?

Are you Walmart or Macy's?

Are you Coke or Pepsi?

Are you Nike or Converse?

Are you McDonald's or Panera Bread?

Branding no longer merely defines our products. It defines our personalities. Using data mining, marketers can ask a dozen strategic questions about what brands you use, and make predictions about who you are with amazing accuracy. Your income. Your education. Your age. Your gender. Your lifestyle. Even your political preferences.

Likewise, give a marketer a little demographic information about yourself, and they can also predict which brands, products, and entertainment you probably prefer.

That's because individuals have brands just like products do—and the two have a tendency to find each other.

So what's your Christian brand?

I'm not asking if you are a Baptist or Presbyterian or Methodist or Episcopal or Catholic or Charismatic. I'm not asking if you're a conservative or moderate or liberal. When it comes to Christianity, there's only one brand: a disciple of Christ. What I'm really asking is, are you the genuine article?

That doesn't mean every Christian is identical. Levi's makes hundreds of different types of jeans. At last count, there are 15 different styles of men's jeans alone. Each style comes in a variety of colors. And each style and color comes in a variety of sizes. Then there are jeans for women and for kids. Plus a plethora of other attire and accessories. But they all are Levi's. The genuine article.

Christians come in all kinds of glorious variety. They make up the body of Christ. But if you're going to wear the red tag that says "Christian," you need to *be* the real thing. Yes, that all begins with *knowing* God. But what the world will primarily see is who you *are* (*be*).

The Christian brand—any brand—is comprised of three parts:

Your **image** = Who people think you are (perception)—external

Your **identity** = Who you really are (reality)—internal

Your **ideal** = Who you want to be (aspiration)—eternal

The goal of being who you are in Christ is to bring all three into alignment. It's a two-step process:

1. Bring your **identity**—who you really are—into alignment with your **ideal**—who you want to be (the biblical ideal).
2. Then bring your **image** into alignment with your new, consistent **identity/ideal**.

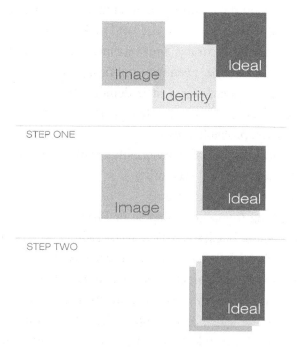

Step 1 takes a lifetime, and you never fully get there. But to the degree that you grow in your *ginosko* knowledge of God, that movement *will* gradually take place. The Bible calls it sanctification.

Sadly, many Christians are most concerned with bringing their **image**—not their **identity**—into alignment with the **ideal**. The Bible calls this hypocrisy. They're usually focused on *do* because do is what gets noticed.

Jesus blistered these religious hypocrites with some hellfire preaching:

> "Don't do what they do, because they don't practice what they teach....They do everything to be observed by others....But woe to you, scribes and Pharisees, hypocrites! You lock up the kingdom of heaven from people. For you don't go in, and you don't allow those entering to go in.... You travel over land and sea to make one proselyte, and when he becomes one, you make him twice as fit for hell as you are!... You clean the outside of the cup and dish, but inside they are full of greed and self-indulgence! Blind Pharisee! First clean the inside of the cup, so the outside of it may also become clean. Woe to you, scribes and Pharisees, hypocrites! You are like whitewashed tombs, which appear beautiful on the outside, but inside are full of dead men's bones and every impurity. In the same way, on the outside you seem righteous to people, but inside you are full of hypocrisy and lawlessness." @Matthew 23:3, 5, 13, 15, 25–28

Modern translation: Woe to you, 21st Century Christians! You post verses on Facebook, and then look at things on the Internet that are not for your eyes. You put an ichthus fish on your car, then drive selfishly and flip off others who cut you off. You go on missions trips across the ocean but won't walk across the street to invite your neighbor to church. You wear Christian T-shirts, but ogle girls with short shorts. You give little to the offering, and then begrudge the pastor if he drives a nicer car than you. You clean up for Sunday morning, but spend Saturday partying all night long. You spend four hours a day with the TV or Internet, and maybe four minutes a day reading My Word.

Ouch!

Are you living up to your brand? Are you truly more concerned with bringing your **identity**—who you really are—into alignment with the **ideal** than you are your **image**?

How you live the Christian life on earth makes a world of difference in eternity. Yours and those you know and love. Let's look at five spheres of your earthly life: Career, Stewardship, Leisure, Citizenship, and Relationships. Let's connect the dots between *know* and *be* and *do*. And let's strive for true **integrity: image = identity = ideal**.

CAREER

Quick, which job is more important in the Kingdom of God: a gardener or a missionary?

If you said missionary, re-read Genesis 2:15—the very first job description:

> *The LORD God took the man and placed him in the garden of Eden to work it and watch over it.*

The very first "help wanted" ad in God's brand spanking new universe was for a gardener. It was job one—a noble and important task to God. And He employed Adam. He was *perfect* for the position—literally.

We have a lot of misconceptions about work. Some view it as part of God's curse that resulted from man's sin. Not true. God gave man work to do—tend and keep the Garden of Eden—*before* sin ever entered the picture. Far from being a curse, God calls work a gift:

God has also given riches and wealth to every man, and He has allowed him to enjoy them, take his reward, and rejoice in his labor. This is a gift of God. @Ecclesiastes 5:10

God did curse the ground, making work more difficult (@Genesis 3:17–19), but work itself is a blessing.

Another faulty view of work is that spiritual/eternal work has more value than physical/temporal work. A related myth is that sacred work, "full-time Christian service," is higher than secular work, which only has real purpose as a platform for evangelism. All these wrong ways of thinking about work are exposed in the excellent book *Your Work Matters to God* by Doug Sherman and William Hendricks.

If you don't *know* how God views work, you'll never *be* the kind of worker you can be. It's not about what you do, but how you do it, why you do it, and most importantly, for Whom you do it. Bob Reccord tells a story about a man who got it:

Nothing was going right at the construction site. The weather was hot. The boss was frustrated. The crew was grouchy. And the site's port-a-john was *long* overdue for service. It reeked. Suddenly, a truck slid up, music blaring, and out popped a big burly guy with tattoos, flashing a contagious grin. He declared he would be the new port-a-john maintenance man, and he ducked into the broiling, odiferous 4 x 4 catastrophe. Thuds and thumps emanated from inside, and the crew wondered if he was wrestling with a tiger in there. Eventually, however, the stench dissipated, and after what seemed like an eternity, the man finally emerged, big smile still intact.

"From here on out," the man declared, "I guarantee this will be the best it can possibly be, because I'm here to serve you." With that he hopped back in his truck and began backing out, music still blaring, which the crew recognized as a Christian radio station.

One of the crew called out to the mysterious maintenance man, "How can you do that? More important, why do you do that?"

"Oh, it's simple," he replied. "You see, I work for the Lord. And I do every task as though I were doing it for Him. See you next week!"

Whatever you do, do it enthusiastically, as something done for the Lord and not for men. @Colossians 3:23

Your job may not seem like a gift from God. It may really stink—quite literally even. But once you *know* that God values your work, that's He's your Boss, and that you're ultimately working for a perfect Boss, then *be* the best employee you can *be* for God & Son Unlimited. *Be* an employee of integrity. Enjoy working for God, and before long, you'll be enjoying more what you do.

Don't start with yourself, with what you do. Start with what you *know*, with *Whom* you know. Tend and keep the work that God's assigned to you. Enjoy God's gift; enjoy honoring Him. Then *do* will take care of itself. And you'll soon find the stench is fading.

What's more, Know Be Do is not just a spiritual principle; it's a business principle, too. Want to succeed in your career? Know. Be. Do. *Know* your business, your customers, your boss, and your coworkers thoroughly. *Be* a conscientious worker who's a bargain to your company and your customers. Then *doing* your work will naturally flow into a win-win proposition for everyone involved. Know. Be. Do. That's true success.

STEWARDSHIP

We are born with nothing, and we leave this earth with nothing.

But in between those two nothings the average American earns and spends about $1–2 million and lives about 700,000 hours. That's a lot of resources entrusted to us. Time and money. Two valuable gifts from God.

Jack Benny, a comedian on radio and during the early days of television, had a famous skit where he was accosted on the street by a robber. The crook demanded, "Don't make a move, this is a stickup. Now, come on. Your money or your life." Benny just chuckled. Irritated, the robber repeated his demand, "Look, bud! I said your money or your life!"

Benny, known by his audience for being a tightwad, snapped back, "I'm thinking it over!"

Your money or your life. Satan makes that demand, and so many people willingly give him both. Often, they don't spend much time thinking it over.

Your money *and* your life. That's God's demand. And many people give Him neither.

Why? Because most people start with a focus on *doing* instead of *knowing* God.

How can knowing God make you a better steward of the time and money God entrusts with you?

Doing focuses on what I own and what I need and want.

Knowing acknowledges the fact that God is the Owner and simply appointed us as stewards of what belongs to Him.

Doing focuses on how much I should give.

Knowing God is thankful for how much He allows us to keep.

Doing fixates on how hard we work to earn what we make.

Knowing God recognizes that without Him we can do nothing.

Doing is obsessed with protecting our possessions and our time.

Knowing God confesses that He is free to take what He gave us at any time.

Doing views the giving of time and money as a wild favor to God.

Knowing God understands that He doesn't need us; He *wants* us.

Doing looks at our self as our greatest resource.

Knowing God perceives God as our ultimate resource, the Source of all we have and are.

Doing thinks we are in control.

Knowing appreciates that He is in control.

Doing approaches the future with dread and uncertainty.

Knowing God sees the past with gratefulness and the future with hope.

Doing gives if there's anything left over.

Knowing God cheerfully gives the first and the best gift, worthy of His love and sacrifice.

Doing strives to win favor with God by what we give.

Knowing God rests in the awareness that God gave everything for us.

> *He did not even spare His own Son but offered Him up for us all; how will He not also with Him grant us everything?* @Romans 8:32

His money and His life.

He gave us both. You can trust Someone like that.

Be a good steward. *Be* wise in how you spend the money God entrusts to you. *Be* faithful in how you spend the time God grants you. And related to that, *be* healthful, so that you don't cut short the time God wants to give you. *Be* a good steward of your body.

Take your $1-2 million and your 700,000 hours and invest it all in Heavenly Treasures Unlimited. You won't lose a penny or a second. Because if money really could talk, it would say, "In God we trust."

LEISURE

Never has there been a time when people worked so hard at playing. Our whole reason for working seems to be to enjoy the weekend or an early retirement. Sports. Recreation. Hobbies. Interests. Entertainment. Vacations. Amusements. Passions. It's what we do with our free time. Are we being good stewards of our time? *Knowing* God, His answer may surprise you.

God rested. That's still one of the most mind-blowing statements in the Bible to me. God worked six days, then He rested the seventh day. Rest is built into the rhythm of life. God designed man in such a way that he requires sleep for nearly a third of his life. God ordained festivals and celebrations that punctuated the routine of everyday life. He equipped man to create beautiful works of art and music to enjoy. His Word talks about running races (a precursor, no doubt, to the ultimate sport: basketball). He tells us there is a time to laugh and dance. Jesus attended weddings, dinners, and feasts. He took mountain retreats. He observed the Sabbath.

Spend more time getting to know God, and you'll know what He wants you to do with your free time. Certainly, it won't include filling your mind with questionable music, movies, and other media. It won't include becoming more passionate about a hobby than more important matters, like family, church, and ministry. It won't include being a poor steward of money to pursue extravagant vacations or hobbies. I don't believe it will include "retirement," if that is defined by doing no work, which as we know, is a gift from God. And it certainly will not involve rooting for the Duke Blue Devils.

But God wants us to rest. Recharge. Celebrate. Experience the wonders of His creation. Listen to beautiful music. Be entertained by athletic competition. Enjoy a hobby or interest. You don't have to "spiritualize" everything. Every vacation doesn't have to be a missions trip. Every hobby doesn't have to connect directly to ministry. Whatever you do, do it enthusiastically, as something done for the Lord and not for men (@Colossians 3:23). If you can't do it enthusiastically as to the Lord, don't do it.

It's easy to get leisure out of balance. To become more passionate about what you do in your free time than about your walk with God. Leisure can become an idol. The key once again is *knowing* God. Don't look at your Christian walk as just another activity you *do*. Don't get your life upside down so that you're taking a break from your life to spend a day with God. Give Him first place and let your leisure have the leftovers. Not vice versa.

> *Seek first the kingdom of God and His righteousness, and all these things will be provided for you.* @Matthew 6:33

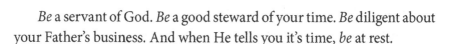

Give Him first place and let your leisure have the leftovers. Not vice versa.

Be a servant of God. *Be* a good steward of your time. *Be* diligent about your Father's business. And when He tells you it's time, *be* at rest.

CITIZENSHIP

God created and ordained three great institutions. First, the family. Then, government. And finally, the church. *Knowing* God helps us make the most of our role in all three. We've touched on the church and family in several sections, and the next section will focus specifically on relationships. Here, let's talk about God and government.

For starters, God believes in separation of church and state. He wants church and state to remain distinct. He formed two separate institutions.

Jesus said to them, "Render to Caesar the things that are Caesar's, and to God the things that are God's." And they marveled at him. @Mark 12:17

Though separation of church and state is biblical, that doesn't mean separation of God and government. God instituted government. He authorizes it. He empowers it. He's intimately involved in it.

Everyone must submit to the governing authorities, for there is no authority except from God, and those that exist are instituted by God. @Romans 13:1

He removes kings and establishes kings. @Daniel 2:21

How does knowing God's mind on government affect our role and our responsibilities?

It's been said that the best form of government is actually a benevolent dictator. A powerful autocrat that always has the people's best interest at heart. No elections, no politics, no corruption. Problem is, there's only one qualified candidate: God. Everyone else is a sinner and, to one degree or another, malevolent—not benevolent. God *tried* to set up a theocracy. But the people demanded a monarchy. So God accommodated them. He gave them a human king (@1 Samuel 8). Three thousand years later, about the best we've been able to do is a semi-benevolent monarchy or a democracy. Yet, above it all God is still ultimately King.

What has our true King empowered government to do?

Government's primary function is to restrain evil. That involves defense and security—"bearing the sword," as Paul puts it in Romans 13:4—which comprise the military and law enforcement. It also involves the judicial and justice department—"bring punishment on the wrongdoer" (Romans 13:4).

Government's other main function is stewardship of common property. The Bible is full of examples of how God blessed men involved in public service as they rebuilt city walls (Nehemiah) or built city infrastructures. Government should be in the business of building common roads, sewer systems, and other infrastructure that we share. I think this principle can be extended to intellectual property as well, such as establishing trademarks and copyrights and establishing manufacturing standards and regulating radio waves and specs for other common property (real and intellectual)—stuff like making sure that you can plug in your TV in Kentucky or in Oregon, and it works.

So what is a Christian's role in government? *Be* a model citizen, but remember that your ultimate citizenship is under King Jesus in Heaven. Pay your taxes. Defend your country. Vote your biblical values. Pray for your leaders. Support your communities. Take an active role, but always remember that God has authorized the family and the church to be the primary vehicle for welfare and education. If the families and churches will only live up the standard God has set, government will be more free and better funded to do what God has ordained it to do. It's funny how things just work better when you do them God's way. He invented everything after all. Get to *know* the Inventor and His Owner's Manual. *Be* active in the role He created you to be. And let's get back to *being* one nation under God.

> It's funny how things just work better when you do them God's way. He invented everything after all. Get to *know* the Inventor and His Owner's Manual.

RELATIONSHIPS

You'll encounter four types of people in this world:

1. Lost and unlovable
2. Lost and lovable.
3. Saved and unlovable.
4. Saved and lovable.

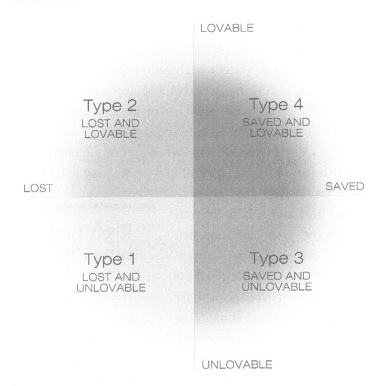

You can probably think of at least one person you know in each of these categories.

Most believers have no problem being around type 4 people. The only challenge they present is to be more like them. I know quite a few of these people, and I thank God for putting them in my life. Let's focus on the other three.

Type 3 people are the hardest to deal with. Jesus reserved His harshest words, not for the prostitutes and other sinners, but for the "religious" who offended God with their lives. Not that the Pharisees and their ilk were true believers, but a believer who knows better and yet consistently makes choices that dishonor God is a real challenge to Christian charity.

Type 1 and 2 people are lost, so I tend to be more understanding about their behavior. They're blind, so it's no wonder they keep falling into sin. Still, however, I find myself getting steamed when a type 1 person acts like a type 1 person. I think that makes me type 3.

I've been all four types at one point or another in my life (although type 4 is up for debate!). And here's my point:

God never stopped loving me.

Not for a second. Not when I'm a self-righteous Christian jerk. Not when I spent years in a quest to find satisfaction outside God. Not when I was a lovable Sunday school boy yet still lost in his sin.

God loves the lost. God loves the unlovable.

In an effort to manipulate people to be lovable as we define it, we withhold favor from those we deem unworthy of our love. How unlike God.

He loves unconditionally. He commands us to love without exception.

> *"Love the Lord your God with all your heart, with all your soul, with all your mind, and with all your strength. The second is: Love your neighbor as yourself." @Mark 12:30–31*

Our problem is we think we can keep the second commandment without first keeping the first.

First things first.

Love God with your *all*.

Love God with all your heart, soul, and mind. In other words, your inner man (mind, will, emotions). He also said love God with your strength—your body. The only part of your tri-part being that's not mentioned is your spirit. That's the part that's made alive by God Himself living in you. So it goes without saying that your spirit loves God.

But in order to love God—soul, body, and spirit—you must *know* God. You can't love someone you don't know.

And you can love your neighbor until you love God. It all comes back to *know*.

Want to have better relationships with the people around you?

Cultivate your relationship with God. The more you *ginosko* know Him, the more you will love Him. The more you love Him, the more you will love others.

Don't try it backwards. Don't try to go further in your horizontal relationships than you are in your vertical relationship with God. Just ask Jonah. Try it on your own, and you'll tend to view everyone else as Type 1 or Type 3. When in reality, that's exactly what you will be. First Corinthians 13 was written for these types.

They come off as clanging cymbals. They move mountains, but amount to nothing. They do good deeds, but gain only boasting. They keep account of offenses but rejoice when others suffer wrong. They eventually lose faith, hope, and love.

The more you *know* God, the more you will love Him and *be* like Him. You'll be patient and kind. You'll be faithful and hopeful. *Know* the God Who is the source of unconditional love, and you'll never lack for love under any conditions.

Christ Himself provided the supreme example. His great love for you and for me drove Him to the Cross. But it was His even greater love for the Father that came first:

> *"My Father, if it be possible, let this cup pass from me; nevertheless, not as I will, but as you will." @Matthew 26:39*

His loving relationship with His Father fueled His love for the human race. Even as He endured great suffering at the hands of His executioners, He knew His Father's love was even greater:

> *"Father, forgive them, because they do not know what they are doing." @Luke 23:34*

Think of those Type 1, 2, and 3 people in your life. The lost. The unlovable. Don't try to muster up love for them in your own strength. *Be* like Christ. Focus on the Father's love. *Be* like Jesus, the God-man Who let His love for His Father flow into His love for man.

Christ's relationships with people are perfect because His relationship with His Father is perfect. His relationship with His Father is perfect because He is one with the Father. *Know* God intimately. *Be* one with Him. And you, too, will love the lost and unlovable.

Chapter 20

KNOW BE DO BIBLE STUDY METHOD

I was smitten.

I went to a friend, the only person who knew her, and implored, "Tell me everything you know about her. I want to know everything."

She was the New Girl at church, and I wanted to know where she'd been all my life. I wanted to know her name. I wanted to know where she lived. I wanted to know what she liked. I wanted to know if she was dating anyone (not that it would have deterred me). I wanted to know where she came from. I wanted to know if my friend thought I stood a chance (he didn't, but again, it didn't deter me). Most of all, I wanted to know how I could get to know her better.

If you've ever had a teenage crush, you've experienced just a taste of what the Psalmist felt when he wrote:

> *Just like a deer that craves streams of water, my whole being craves you, God. @Psalm 42:1*

To crave. Pant after. Reach out to. Long for. Cry out for. Thirst for.

I never got to know the New Girl very well, and my infatuation lasted only about as long as it took for the next New Girl to come along.

But God is different.

When you get a true taste of God, it satisfies. And yet, it leaves you wanting more.

You might say that about a NY Strip steak. Eventually, however, you get your fill.

But with God, you never finish getting your fill. And you never fully plumb His depths. He's the only thing in the world that's like that.

Oceanographers map the ocean floor. Astronomers map the surface of the moon or the far reaches of the known universe. It takes a scientist, however, to really explore those worlds.

But with God, a young child can know Him. And a triple Ph.D. can overlook Him. He's the only thing in the world that's like that.

You may read a biography about an interesting person who lived long ago. You may become an expert on that individual. You may know more about him than any other person on earth. He is dead, however, and the books are dead. You cannot have a relationship with Him.

But with God, He's alive, and His Word—His autobiography—is alive. He interacts with you. He relates to you. He changes you. He's the only One in the world that's like that. The Bible is the only book that's like that.

> *For the word of God is living and effective and sharper than any double-edged sword, penetrating as far as the separation of soul and spirit, joints and marrow. It is able to judge the ideas and thoughts of the heart. @Hebrews 4:12*

God's Word is as alive as God Himself. It's the best, surest way we have to get to *know* God.

Suppose a magnificent, glowing angel landed in front of you right now, circled by a legion of cherubim, and heralded a glorious pronouncement. Fact-check it against the Word of God before you believe one word of it.

> *But even if we or an angel from heaven should preach to you a gospel other than what we have preached to you, a curse be on him! @Galatians 1:8*

The Word of God is sure. The Word of God is living. The Word of God is how we get to *know* God. It's how we get to understand who we *are* in Him. And it's how we learn what He wants us to do. Not even God the Spirit contradicts the Word of God. After all, He helped write it.

Do you thirst to *know* God? Do you long to commune with Him? Do you want to really get to *ginosko* know God in a way that will leave you craving more? Look no further than His Word.

DISCOVERING HIS WORD THROUGH THE LENS OF KNOW BE DO

3-D glasses for movies have come a long way since the red and blue cellophane lenses I wore as a kid. They really make the flat screen come alive. Objects fly off the screen and career right towards you. Creatures reach out and seem to grab you. It's like you're in the movie instead of just watching it.

Reading the Word of God through the lens of Know Be Do can make the Bible come alive for you in ways you may never have experienced. Bible reading shouldn't be boring. There are no boring passages in the Bible—only bored persons reading the Bible. Using Know Be Do to study your Bible keeps you engaged and interacting with the Author. New truths jump out at you. Characters and events grab your attention like never before. And you feel like you're in God's "movie," not just watching it.

> Reading the Word of God through the lens of Know Be Do can make the Bible come alive for you in ways you may never have experienced.

When I was a new believer, someone recommended a book to me entitled *How to Study the Bible for Yourself* by Tim LaHaye. In it, he recommended keeping a daily spiritual diary or journal. He included a suggested format and even a sample diary page that you could copy and then fill out each day of the week. I used that simple method for years, and it watered and fertilized my spiritual growth in a way that got me solidly rooted in my relationship with God. A Bible study method is a tool. It's a key that helps unlock the door to a closer relationship with God.

The Know Be Do Bible Study method grew out of my gradual, life-long discovery that life begins with knowing Him, not with me. If you start with yourself and try to work back to God, you'll be looking at things—God, yourself, the world—from the wrong perspective. Upside down. Begin with yourself, and you'll be like *that* guy, the one who goes out on a date and spends the whole time talking about himself. Start with yourself, and you'll miss out on seeing the majesty of God. You'll miss out on your true God-value. You'll misunderstand why He asks you to do certain things. And you'll miss living the joyful, courageous, adventurous, peaceful Christian life that God has in store for you.

Start with first things first. And the first thing is to focus on Him.

> *You will keep in perfect peace all who trust in you, all whose thoughts are fixed on you! @Isaiah 26:3*

BENEFITS

Your view of God will grow bigger, stronger. We visited the Statue of Liberty a few years ago, and I was blown away by how big it was up close. I'd seen plenty of photos of it, of course, even shots of people standing in her crown looking out. But until I got up close and personal, I didn't realize how massive she was.

God is the same way. Hearing and reading others talk about God is one thing. But when you begin to get closer to Him, getting to know Him by studying the Words that He Himself wrote, He'll grow on you. The bigger He gets, the smaller your problems seem. The closer we get to God, the further away we get from Satan.

> *Resist the Devil, and he will flee from you. Draw near to God, and He will draw near to you. @James 4:7–8*

Your self-image will get sharper and right-sized. "We sing 'Onward Christian soldiers, marching as to war,'" Billy Graham writes. "But so often when Satan mounts an attack against us we behave as if we are prisoners of war, or worse, conscientious objectors!" That's because we forget who we are in Christ. Our self-image should be shaped by God's image. We're made in His image. So as His image comes into sharper focus, our self-image does, too.

It can work in both directions. Sometimes, our pride artificially inflates our image. We need a dose of Christ's humility. Sometimes, Satan makes us feel like his slave. We're children of the King! Once we grasp His hand of grace with our hand of faith, we gain God's right perspective of ourselves:

> *For by the grace given to me, I tell everyone among you not to think of himself more highly than he should think. Instead, think sensibly, as God has distributed a measure of faith to each one. @Romans 12:3*

God says not to think *too* highly of ourselves. But it's equally wrong to underestimate our worth in Christ. We are so valuable, He let His Son die in our place. Think sensibly. Once we comprehend our right standing in His eyes, our self-image will be right-sized and ready to *do* whatever God wants us to accomplish.

You'll have more power in life and prayer. Once you know God, you know yourself. Most of the heavy lifting is done then. *Doing* will spring out of the overflow. You'll have more victory over sin. You'll have assurance of your salvation. You'll supernaturally experience lasting joy and peace. You'll be able to discover the will of God. You'll witness to non-believers faithfully and fearlessly. Your prayer life will be informed and energized by your close relationship with God. The benefits go on and on. It all begins with *knowing* Him.

BASICS

A definite time and place. I've enjoyed getting to know a new friend during the past few years. I've learned a lot about him just doing ordinary life things together. But about a year ago we formed a book club with another friend. Having a standing time and place to meet has really accelerated our friendship. Having a definite time and place to meet with God daily is the number one way to enhance your relationship with God. Walk with Him every step of every day. But sit down and meet with Him at least once a day.

> *Early in the morning Abraham went to the place where he had stood before the LORD.* @Genesis 19:27

> In the morning, O LORD, *You will hear my voice. In the morning I will lay my prayers before You and will look up.* @Psalm 5:3

> *In the morning the word of the LORD came to me:* @Ezekiel 12:8

> *Early in the morning, well before sunrise, Jesus rose and went to a deserted place where he could be alone in prayer.* @Mark 1:35

See the pattern? I believe the morning is the best time to meet with God. It orients your outlook and gives you your marching orders for the day. Doing it any other time is kind of like an orchestra tuning up during or after the concert. At the start of your day, your mind will be fresh, not preoccupied with the day's events. And you'll be less likely to miss it because your schedule didn't go as planned. I make it a habit not to do anything—except my workout and shower, just to wake me up—until I've met with God. Give Him the first and best fruits of your day. Not the leftovers. Make a commitment and stick with it. What counts, costs.

> I believe the morning is the best time to meet with God. Doing it any other time is kind of like an orchestra tuning up during or after the concert.

A good Bible and tools. Find a good Bible and make it your friend. Have trouble understanding the King James Version? Use one of the many modern translations that are highly readable and reliable. I like the Holman Christian

Standard Bible (HCSB), New International Version (NIV), New American Standard (NAS), and the English Standard Version (ESV). No version is perfect, and each has its own strengths and weaknesses. So it's helpful to use a variety of versions when studying a passage. The many new online tools make it easy and affordable.

It's also helpful to use resources such as Bible commentaries and other reference resources. Make sure, however, the author or publisher is solid and actually believes the Bible. Not all do. Also, consult those *after* you've done your own study. You want to get to know God personally, not just read about someone else's conversation with God.

A personal devotion journal. If my house ever caught on fire, my personal devotion journals would be among the few possessions I would risk my life to save. What an inspiration they are to go back and re-read a year, five years, 20 years later. Seeing how God has answered prayers and drawn me to Himself reinforces my faith and reminds me of how faithful He is.

Writing down insights that God shows you helps you stay focused and solidifies thoughts in your mind. In Appendix A, you'll find a sample **Know Be Do Bible Study Journal** page that you're free to copy and use.

BEFORE BEGINNING

If you received an invitation to the White House to meet with the President, you'd probably spend some time getting your body and mind prepared before you went in. How much more so should you be prepared before a meeting with the King of the Universe? Prepare your body, mind, and spirit before you begin.

When my daughters were a part of a student ministry, they repeated a confessional before each Bible study time. It went like this:

> *This is my Bible. I am what it says I am. I have what it says I have. I can do what it says I can do. Today, I will be taught the Word of God. I boldly confess my mind is alert, my heart is receptive. I will never be the same. I am about to receive the incorruptible, indestructible, ever-living seed of the Word of God. I will never be*

the same. Never, never, never. I will never be the same, in Jesus' name. Amen.

Start with a sense of expectancy before you open the Word. You don't have to use this confessional. In fact, be careful about using any kind of prayer that's repeated too often. The point is to pray first. Ask God to guide you into all wisdom and truth. And prepare your body, soul, and spirit to meet your maker—and live!—abundantly, eternally, for the glory of God.

So, we're ready to get started. Put on your 3-D Know Be Do glasses, look into the Word of God, and discover...

Know—Discover Who God is and what He does (attributes and actions).

Be—Discover Who I am in Christ and how God interacts with me.

Do—Discover God's plans for me and specifically what He wants to do through me.

HOW TO USE THE KNOW BE DO BIBLE STUDY METHOD

First, let me say that we're not really studying the *Bible*. We're studying *God*. Our goal is not to get to know the Bible *per se*, but to get to *know* God, and not just study Him. It's not merely to read His Word, but hear His voice. The point is to grow in our relationship with Him. To commune with Him. To become best friends with Him. To let the fire that's in His heart light the fire in ours. To fall more deeply in love with Him. The best way we have of doing that is to study God's autobiography.

So, we're going to take a section of the Bible and explore it in depth to

> We're not really studying the Bible. We're studying God. Our goal is not to get to know the Bible *per se*, but to get to *know* God, and not just study Him.

discover all you can about knowing God, being a Christian, and doing His will. It's exciting and invigorating.

PICK A PASSAGE

How do you get started? 31,102 verses. 1,189 chapters. 66 books. Where do you begin? Anywhere really. You'll find Know Be Do all through the Bible. It's embedded in the very DNA of Scripture. It's fine to start with Genesis if you like. But if you start at the beginning, you may be bogged down by the time you get to Leviticus. If you've never done much Bible study, I suggest you start with the book of John. The apostle John is the "know" author of the Bible. It's the perfect place to begin. In fact, John starts off just like Genesis, "In the beginning..."

There are actually a number of ways to pick a passage to explore:

- By book of the Bible, one book at a time
- By names of God
- By prayers from the Bible
- By promises in the Bible
- By narratives
- By chronology
- By topic
- By Person of the Trinity (God the Father, God the Son, God the Spirit)
- By genre (law, history, wisdom, poetry, prophecy, epistles, Gospels, parables, apocalyptic)

Far and away my favorite way is by book of the Bible. Each book is a free-standing unit, yet a perfectly unified portion of the whole. Exploring the Bible book by book until you've covered all 66 books gives you a comprehensive, methodical way of getting to know God. If you do too much picking and choosing randomly or by your own preferences, there's a good chance you could get a lopsided view of God.

One method I don't recommend: the "lucky dip" method. That means just letting the Bible fall open. Sure, God can guide that. But He also guides your brain, and there are more sure ways to cover the entire biblical waterfront than the "lucky dip." Pick your passages prayerfully and thoughtfully. God will direct you.

KNOW

Read straight through your passage once to get the general meaning. Then read through it again slowly and list everything it says about God. The object is to get to *know* God. Here are some things to look for:

- What He thinks.
- Who He is (attributes and character traits).
- What He does.
- How He interacts with people.
- What His will is.
- Where He goes and dwells.
- What His emotions are and what causes these emotions.
- What He sees, hears, and touches.
- What He loves.
- What He hates.
- What He commands.
- What He promises.
- What He blesses.
- What He curses.
- What He owns.
- What positions He has.
- What powers He possesses.
- What He values.
- What He gives.
- What work He does.
- What lessons and wisdom He teaches.

Several other important notes:

- God has many names in the Bible: God, LORD, Lord, Father, Son, Spirit, Jesus Christ, King, Master, Holy One, the Word, Creator, I AM, Alpha and Omega. Some lists contain more than 600 names for God. When you come across a name, write it down and star it. Names are key, and you may want to do additional study on His names.

- Try this: When you read a verse, emphasize a different word in each phrase. For example, @John 14:27b: "My peace I give to you."
    a. *My* peace I give to you—Jesus is the owner and source of peace.
    b. My *peace* I give to you—Since it's from Jesus, it is perfect, lasting peace.
    c. My peace *I give* to you—His peace is a gift from Jesus, free and priceless.
    d. My peace I give *to you*—Jesus gives it to me, so I am the new owner of His peace. I possess it just like He possesses it.

- Whether you're writing notes in your **Know Be Do Bible Study Journal** or directly in your Bible, you might want to mark *Know* Scriptures with the △ symbol.

- Again, remember, the object is not to study the Bible or even to study God. It is to get to *know* Him so that you can commune with Him and enhance your relationship with Him.

BE

Next, read through the passage again slowly and list everything it says about *you*. The object here is to create a list of truths from the Bible about who you are as a child of God, in Christ.

Note: There are two categories of persons in the Bible: non-believers and believers. The context usually makes it clear to which category of persons it is referring. Believers are sometimes called God's children or the people of God. When the Bible is actually referring to *you*, the passage might be talking about another believer or child of God, so be alert to that. In some passages, you might want to make two lists: one for what the Bible says about non-believers and another for what the Bible says about believers.

So again, here are some things to look for:

- Who you are in Christ /as a child of God (character traits and attributes).
- Whose you are.
- What standing you have before God.
- What relationship you have with God.
- What your emotions are and what causes these emotions.
- What you are promised.
- What brings you blessing.
- What brings you discipline.
- What you possess as a child of God.
- What positions you have.
- What power you possess.
- What freedoms you have.
- What values you have.
- What knowledge you have.
- What you receive from God.
- What work you do.
- What inheritance you have.
- Who fellow members of the family of God are.
- What roles God has for you in His family.
- What roles God has for you in *your* family.
- What attributes you as an image bearer share with God.

Several other important notes:

- Key words to look for in the passage include "being" verbs, such as: am, are, is, be, being, become. Also, look for words that convey your position or possessions, such as: have, has, in Christ, in Him.
- Focus on who you *are* as a child of God, in Christ, not what you should be *doing*. That will be covered in the next list: *Do*.
- Again, try emphasizing a different word or phrase in each verse. For example, @Ephesians 1:7a: "In him we have redemption through his blood, the forgiveness of our trespasses."
  a. ***In him*** we have redemption through his blood, the forgiveness of our trespasses —I am *in* Christ.

b. In him ***we have redemption*** through his blood, the forgiveness of our trespasses —I am redeemed—present tense, which means now and on-going.

c. In him we have redemption ***through his blood***, the forgiveness of our trespasses —I am considered valuable enough for Him to shed His precious blood for *me*.

d. In him we have redemption through his blood, the ***forgiveness*** of our trespasses—I am forgiven.

e. In him we have redemption through his blood, the forgiveness of ***our trespasses***—I am a trespasser, yet still redeemed and forgiven, thanks to His blood.

- In your **Know Be Do Bible Study Journal** or in your Bible, you might want to mark *Be* Scriptures with the □ symbol.

- Keep in mind that you are made in the image of God, and through Christ, many of the attributes are passed down to you. "I can do all things through Christ who strengthens me." @Philippians 4:13. That certainly doesn't mean we become mini-Gods. Some of God's attributes are non-communicable, such as His omnipotence. But in some respects, such as righteousness, in Christ, we are just as righteous as God's own Son (@2 Corinthians 5:21). Hallelujah! Let that sink in!

DO

Finally, read through the passage once more and list everything it says about what God wants you to *do*. Many of these appear as imperative statements—commands. But some will be more subtle, as the Bible describes genuine godly living in narrative/story-telling sections.

- Commands relating to our interaction with God.
- Commands relating to our interaction with non-believers.
- Commands relating to our interaction with believers.
- God's will for you in your family.
- God's will for you in your church.
- God's will for you in your community.

258 KNOW BE DO

- God's will for you as a worker.
- What to do with your money.
- What to do with your time.
- How to pray.
- How to worship.
- How to serve.
- How to fellowship.
- How to witness.
- How to forgive.
- How to love.
- How to live in peace.
- How to have hope.
- How to rejoice.
- What to do when trials and tribulations come.
- What to do to gain eternal life.

Several other important notes:

- The Old Testament contains a large number of commands that are part of the Law. There are three types: civil laws, ceremonial laws, and moral laws. A full discussion of this is beyond the scope of this book. But here are a few basics. Civil laws were the governmental laws of Israel. Ceremonial laws detailed the Old Testament sacrificial system which Christ came to fulfill. Moral laws, such as the Ten Commandments are still in force today.

  We don't live under the civil and ceremonial laws any longer and are not obligated to keep them. *Behind* every civil and ceremonial law, however, lies a *principle* that *is* still valid today. For example, Deuteronomy 22:11 forbids wearing clothes of wool and linen woven together. What's that all about? One explanation is that in Old Testament culture, *pagan* priests wore special garments made of wool and linen. So God warned His people to stay away from the appearance of evil. Discovering the principle behind an Old Testament Law can require some digging, and that's where study resources come in handy. Many of the Old Testament Laws, however, are beautiful pictures of Christ's work on the Cross and well worth exploring.

- Not everything *described* in the Bible is *prescribed*. Abraham and other patriarchs had multiple wives, but polygamy is clearly not taught in the Scriptures. Bible characters lie, cheat, betray, lack faith, argue, get legalistic, and otherwise act like sinners just like us. Don't make the mistake of imitating what they do when the rest of God's Word clearly teaches otherwise.

- In many passages, you'll encounter things "not to do," as well as things to do. (That goes for *be*, as well.) Write down these negatives, but also make a note of its positive counterpart. For example, if the Bible says, "Don't be deceived," then the converse is "Seek truth and believe it."

- In your **Know Be Do Bible Study Journal** or in your Bible, you might want to mark *Do* Scriptures with the ○ symbol.

- Remember, our ultimate goal here is not to create Christian "to-do" and "to-don't-do" lists. The goal is to cultivate our relationship with God so deeply that we naturally—and supernaturally—do what He desires and has empowered us to do.

CONNECTING THE DOTS

Here's where the Know Be Do method all comes together. Even though the Bible consists of thousands of verses, 66 books, at least 40 authors with various backgrounds, is written over 1,600 years, in 13 countries, and in three languages...there is one Author.

So everything connects.

Everything agrees.

Everything supports.

The goal of Know Be Do Bible study is to make these connections. Often, when you write down something about God under Know, it will illuminate something for you to *be*, and in turn, to *do*. Follow the Spirit's guidance on making these connections. Write them down in your journal.

When it's connected, truth inspires, liberates, and empowers. Disconnected, truth can confuse, enslave, and discourage. Example: We are commanded to go and make disciples. In isolation, that truth can seem overwhelmingly burdensome. It's why so few are doing it. But back up and let's connect what we *know* about God and about ourselves (*be*). In fact, it's all right there in the same passage. Jesus says, "Go, make disciples" @Matthew 28:19. The Great Commission. That's the *Do*.

But look what He says about *Know* and *Be* in the oft-overlooked verses before and after:

- He came near (Know)
- All authority has been given to Him... (Know)
- ...In Heaven and on earth (Know)
- He is with us... (Know and Be)
- ...Always (Know and Be)
- He is with us and has authority, therefore *we* have authority (Be).

Connect all these truths—Know Be Do—and sharing our faith no longer feels like an intimidating solo act. He is with us, authorizing us, empowering us, never leaving us. The apostles actually believed this. No wonder they took the world by storm in the Book of Acts. Our relationship with the Authority can be just as powerful.

Take Know Be Do and write your own Book of Acts.

But before you take off, get a Word from God, just like the Apostles. You'll find a blank Know Be Do Bible Study journal page in Appendix A, followed by three simple, sample studies, demonstrating how to use the Know Be Do method with different genres of Scripture:

- A Psalm (poetry)
- Gospel (narrative)
- Epistle (instruction)

So put your 3D glasses on, and get ready to write the story of your life. *Know. Be. Do.*

EPILOGUE

The speaker was a good friend of ours.

So there was *no-oooo* way I was getting out of going to this marriage seminar. Especially since *we* were the ones who invited him to come!

We and the 20 or so other couples crowded into the hotel meeting room for the weekend. My wife and I were there to make a good marriage better. Several couples were there hoping to get their marriage off life support.

With 25 years of marriage under my belt, I wasn't expecting to learn a lot about my wife or about marriage.

I was wrong.

I left the seminar that weekend with one of the most valuable things my wife has ever given me: seven words that prescribed what she needed from me. She needed to be...

1. Loved
2. Adored
3. Desired
4. Fulfilling (to me)
5. Admired
6. Needed
7. Touched

LADFANT. I even made an acrostic so I could remember them.

It was like the Book of First Tina, Chapter 1 for me. A word from her—seven actually—written just to me so that I could *know* her better, *be* a better husband, and *do* the things she wanted.

It was kind of like a love letter—only better. Because it said, "I love you, and here's what I love about how you love me."

Her seven words helped me better understand how to relate to her, how to love her, how to value her as she should be valued. I didn't view it as a "to-do" list but as a "*know*-her" list. It also didn't go unnoticed that her seven words related mostly to who she *is* rather than what she *does*.

How much more so can we use God's Words to *know* Him?

As deserving as my wife is, how much more so is God worthy of our highest devotion to Him?

My wife's seven words and countless more apply to how we can relate to God. He wants us to love Him. To adore Him. To desire Him. To be fulfilled by Him. To admire Him. To need Him. To touch Him—now in Spirit and one day in eternity. In a word, to *ginosko know* Him.

> *This is eternal life: that they may know You, the only true God, and the One You have sent—Jesus Christ. @John 17:3*

As we draw close to Him, He draws close to us. He is the consummate Bridegroom, and we, His imperfect bride. He knows us perfectly. And He waits patiently as we move closer, then away, from Him. Yet He never strays. He draws us. He pursues us. He divinely romances us. He never minds going to a "marriage seminar" with us.

I once did a study on what makes God "smile." I looked up every verse I could find about God and what brings Him pleasure and delight. It was enlightening—and somewhat surprising. I expected that He would mostly delight in us keeping His commands, things we *do*. That is certainly part of it, but a major way that we make Him smile is when we commune with Him, depend on Him, honor Him, walk with Him, *be* like Him. *Know* Him.

Quit practicing churchianity and start following Christianity.

Let go of the idea that a relationship with God is all about His "to-do" list. Quit practicing churchianity and start following Christianity. Stop trying to *do* holy things, and focus on *knowing* the Holy One Who will help you *be* holy. Holiness is not the way to Christ. Christ is the way to holiness.

Let's get to know Him in all His glory. Let's discover what "makes Him smile." Let's sit in His lap and look through His "Scrapbook." Let's read His Words and find out how He wants us to love Him. Let's turn our lives in Christ right side up. Not Do-Be-Know.

Know. Be. Do.

> *"I pray that He may grant you, according to the riches of His glory, to be strengthened with power in the inner man through His Spirit, and that the Messiah may dwell in your hearts through faith. I pray that you, being rooted and firmly established in love, may be able to comprehend with all the saints what is the length and width, height and depth of God's love, and to know the Messiah's love that surpasses knowledge, so you may be filled with all the fullness of God. Now to Him who is able to do above and beyond all that we ask or think according to the power that works in us—to Him be glory in the church and in Christ Jesus to all generations, forever and ever. Amen." @Ephesians 3:16–21*

APPENDIX A

Know Be Do Bible Study Journal Page

Reading the Bible is no less God speaking to you than were He sitting face to face with you. Listen and let Him speak. Sometimes He'll talk about Himself (*know*). Sometimes He'll talk about you (*be*). Sometimes He'll talk about what He wants you to do or not do (*do*). Each passage you read won't necessarily have an equal number of points under *Know*, *Be*, and *Do*. But often there's more there than appears on the surface, if you let the Holy Spirit illuminate it for you. Pray and ask Him for clarity. Use commentaries and other tools only when you're stumped or need a catalyst to get your thoughts flowing. The more time and effort you invest, the more dividends you'll receive. Every minute, every passage will help you cultivate your relationship with Him. Nothing you do the rest of the day will be as important as the time you spend with Him.

A letter-size version of the Know Be Do Bible Study Journal page is available to download free at **LarryAlanThompson.com/ KnowBeDoJournalpage**. You are free to make unlimited copies.

PASSAGE

▲ KNOW   ■ BE   ● DO

CONNECTING THE DOTS

APPENDIX B

The following three Bible studies provide simple samples of how to apply the Know Be Do Bible Study method to different kinds of Bible passages. This first example is a Psalm, part of the poetry or wisdom literature of the Bible, rich with insights about the character of God. Many of the Psalms, including this one, are prayers or contain prayers. Prayer petitions can be often viewed as commands from God expressed as requests by man. So you'll notice that many of the direct requests in the prayer are listed under the *Do* section.

PASSAGE: PSALM 86

A Davidic prayer.
[1] Listen, LORD, and answer me,
for I am poor and needy.
[2] Protect my life, for I am faithful.
You are my God; save Your servant who trusts in You.
[3] Be gracious to me, Lord,
for I call to You all day long.
[4] Bring joy to Your servant's life,
because I turn to You, Lord.
[5] For You, Lord, are kind and ready to forgive,
rich in faithful love to all who call on You.
[6] LORD, hear my prayer;
listen to my plea for mercy.
[7] I call on You in the day of my distress,
for You will answer me.
[8] Lord, there is no one like You among the gods,

and there are no works like Yours.
⁹ All the nations You have made
will come and bow down before You, Lord,
and will honor Your name.
¹⁰ For You are great and perform wonders;
You alone are God.
¹¹ Teach me Your way, Yahweh,
and I will live by Your truth.
Give me an undivided mind to fear Your name.
¹² I will praise You with all my heart, Lord my God,
and will honor Your name forever.
¹³ For Your faithful love for me is great,
and You deliver my life from the depths of Sheol.
¹⁴ God, arrogant people have attacked me;
a gang of ruthless men seeks my life.
They have no regard for You.
¹⁵ But You, Lord, are a compassionate and gracious God,
slow to anger and rich in faithful love and truth.
¹⁶ Turn to me and be gracious to me.
Give Your strength to Your servant;
save the son of Your female servant.
¹⁷ Show me a sign of Your goodness;
my enemies will see and be put to shame
because You, LORD, have helped and comforted me.

KNOW

You are Lord. @1
You listen and answer. @1
You protect life. @2
You are my God. @2
You are gracious. @3
You offer joy. @4
You are kind. @5
You are ready to forgive. @5
You are rich in faithful love. @5

You hear me. @6
You listen to my plea for mercy. @6
You answer distress calls. @7
You are a one-of-a-kind God. @8
No one duplicates Your works. @8
All the nations bow before You, honor You. @9
You are great. @10
You perform wonders. @10
You alone are God. @10
Your truth is life. @11
Your name is to be feared. @11
You are praise-worthy. @12
Your love for me is faithful and great. @12, 15
You are compassionate. @15
You are gracious. @15, 16
You are slow to anger. @15
You are rich in truth. @15
You give me strength. @16
You are good. @17
You help me. @17
You comfort me. @17

BE

I am poor. @1
I am needy. @1
I am faithful. @2
I am Your servant. @2, 4
I have Your joy. @4
I am forgiven. @5
I am loved faithfully. @5, 13
I am heard by God. @6
I live by your truth. @11
I am delivered from Sheol. @13
I am attacked by arrogant, ruthless, godless men. @14
I am strong in You. @16

I am comforted. @17

DO

Pray. @Psalm 86
Be faithful to God. @2
Trust in You. @2
Call to You constantly. @3, 4
Seek joy. @4
Turn to You. @4
Seek forgiveness. @5
Plea for mercy. @6
Call on You when distressed. @7
Bow before You. @9
Honor Your name forever. @9, 12
Seek Your way. @11
Live by Your truth. @11
Seek Him for an undivided mind. @11
Fear You. @11
Praise You with all my heart. @12
Seek You for strength. @16

CONNECTING THE DOTS

Lord, what a contrast I see between You and me. I see how high and lifted up You are. You alone are God, worthy of honor and praise. The nations bow to You, and You perform great wonders. Your attributes and actions are amazing. On the other hand, I am poor and needy, distressed and weak. Ruthless people attack me. Yet, You are not too big to care about me, to comfort me, to forgive me, to love me faithfully. Help me to lean on You constantly for strength, joy, grace, mercy, deliverance, truth. I praise You for listening to my needy prayers and helping me when I call on Your mighty resources.

APPENDIX C

This Bible study is an example from a Gospel and also of narrative. Narratives or stories are abundant in the Bible, especially in the Old Testament. When reading narratives, you find a richness of Know Be Do insights, but you'll often need to observe them from actions rather than by direct teaching, such as you find in Psalms or epistles. Stories are one of God's favorite ways to teach us about Himself, and Jesus was a Master at teaching through storytelling. Think about the details of the story. Why were certain elements included? Who are the characters and what do they represent? What is the story teaching? Put yourself in the story. Let the Spirit guide you into all truth and draw you into a closer relationship with God.

PASSAGE: JOHN 11:17–44

[17] When Jesus arrived, He found that Lazarus had already been in the tomb four days. [18] Bethany was near Jerusalem (about two miles away). [19] Many of the Jews had come to Martha and Mary to comfort them about their brother. [20] As soon as Martha heard that Jesus was coming, she went to meet Him. But Mary remained seated in the house.

[21] Then Martha said to Jesus, "Lord, if You had been here, my brother wouldn't have died. [22] Yet even now I know that whatever You ask from God, God will give You."

[23] "Your brother will rise again," Jesus told her.

²⁴ Martha said, "I know that he will rise again in the resurrection at the last day."

²⁵ Jesus said to her, "I am the resurrection and the life. The one who believes in Me, even if he dies, will live. ²⁶ Everyone who lives and believes in Me will never die—ever. Do you believe this?"

²⁷ "Yes, Lord," she told Him, "I believe You are the Messiah, the Son of God, who comes into the world."

Jesus Shares the Sorrow of Death

²⁸ Having said this, she went back and called her sister Mary, saying in private, "The Teacher is here and is calling for you."

²⁹ As soon as she heard this, she got up quickly and went to Him. ³⁰ Jesus had not yet come into the village but was still in the place where Martha had met Him. ³¹ The Jews who were with her in the house consoling her saw that Mary got up quickly and went out. So they followed her, supposing that she was going to the tomb to cry there.

³² When Mary came to where Jesus was and saw Him, she fell at His feet and told Him, "Lord, if You had been here, my brother would not have died!"

³³ When Jesus saw her crying, and the Jews who had come with her crying, He was angry in His spirit and deeply moved. ³⁴ "Where have you put him?" He asked.

"Lord," they told Him, "come and see."

³⁵ Jesus wept.

³⁶ So the Jews said, "See how He loved him!" ³⁷ But some of them said, "Couldn't He who opened the blind man's eyes also have kept this man from dying?"

The Seventh Sign: Raising Lazarus from the Dead

³⁸ Then Jesus, angry in Himself again, came to the tomb. It was a cave, and a stone was lying against it. ³⁹ "Remove the stone," Jesus said.

Martha, the dead man's sister, told Him, "Lord, he's already decaying. It's been four days."

⁴⁰ Jesus said to her, "Didn't I tell you that if you believed you would see the glory of God?"

⁴¹ So they removed the stone. Then Jesus raised His eyes and said, "Father, I thank You that You heard Me. ⁴² I know that You always hear Me, but

because of the crowd standing here I said this, so they may believe You sent Me." [43] After He said this, He shouted with a loud voice, "Lazarus, come out!" [44] The dead man came out bound hand and foot with linen strips and with his face wrapped in a cloth. Jesus said to them, "Loose him and let him go."

KNOW

Jesus is never late. When He arrives, He's always right on time. @17

Jesus is Lord. @21, 32, 33

Whatever Jesus asks of His Father is granted—complete unity in the Trinity. @22

Jesus knows our future. @23

Jesus has power over life and death. @23

Jesus is the resurrection. @25

Jesus is the life. @25

Jesus gives life to those who believe in Him. @25, 26

Jesus wants us to believe. @26

Jesus is the Messiah. @27

Jesus is the Son of God, who comes into the world. @27

Jesus is the Teacher. @28

Jesus calls for us in our time of need. @28

Jesus is deeply moved and troubled by sin and sorrow. @33, 38

Jesus wept. @35

Jesus opened the blind man's eyes. @36

Jesus keeps His promises. @40

Jesus displays the glory of God to those who believe. @40

Jesus prays to His Father, and His Father hears. @41

Jesus is thankful to His Father. @41

The Father always hears Jesus' prayer. @42

Jesus performs miracles for our benefit, so that we might believe. @42

The Father sent His Son. @42

Jesus commands the dead. @43, 44

Jesus looses from grave clothes. @44

BE

We are comforted by Jesus. @19
We will be resurrected. @24
We live and never die—ever. @25, 26
We are loved by Jesus. @36
We see the glory of God in Christ. @40
We are believers. @42
We have been loosed by Christ. @44

DO

Wait on the Lord when troubles come. @17–22
Believe that His presence and power will change things. @27
Go to Him as soon as He calls. @29
Fall at His feet. @32
Tell Him your troubles. @32–34
Don't be a skeptic or second-guesser. @37
When Jesus tells you to do something, do it without arguing. @39–40
When Jesus calls, obey. @43–44

CONNECTING THE DOTS

Jesus, I see your amazing humanity and divinity in this story. As a Man, You are moved to tears by our sorrow. You relate to our heartbreak. As God, You are troubled, angered by the sin that ultimately results in this sorrow. As a Man, You come to comfort us. But as God, You have the power to not only comfort, but to correct the situation. You bring life where there was death. You bring help and healing where there was no hope. You are never late. You are always right on time. I thank You for always being there when we need You, for speaking to the Father on our behalf. I praise You for being the Resurrection and the Life in my life.

APPENDIX D

This Bible study is an example from a direct teaching passage and an epistle. This passage is so rich an entire volume could be written about it—and has—so this simple sample study is just an overview of the unfathomable truths it contains. Meditate on each verse, each phrase, each word. You'll discover enough Know Be Do principles here to chew on for days. Let it feed your spirit continually as you go deep into a *ginosko* relationship with God.

PASSAGE: ROMANS 6:1–14

[1] What should we say then? Should we continue in sin so that grace may multiply? [2] Absolutely not! How can we who died to sin still live in it? [3] Or are you unaware that all of us who were baptized into Christ Jesus were baptized into His death? [4] Therefore we were buried with Him by baptism into death, in order that, just as Christ was raised from the dead by the glory of the Father, so we too may walk in a new way of life. [5] For if we have been joined with Him in the likeness of His death, we will certainly also be in the likeness of His resurrection. [6] For we know that our old self was crucified with Him in order that sin's dominion over the body may be abolished, so that we may no longer be enslaved to sin, [7] since a person who has died is freed from sin's claims. [8] Now if we died with Christ, we believe that we will also live with Him, [9] because we know that Christ, having been raised from the dead, will not die again. Death no longer rules over Him. [10] For in light of the fact that He died, He died to sin once for all; but

in light of the fact that He lives, He lives to God. [11] So, you too consider yourselves dead to sin but alive to God in Christ Jesus. [12] Therefore do not let sin reign in your mortal body, so that you obey its desires. [13] And do not offer any parts of it to sin as weapons for unrighteousness. But as those who are alive from the dead, offer yourselves to God, and all the parts of yourselves to God as weapons for righteousness. [14] For sin will not rule over you, because you are not under law but under grace.

KNOW

God's grace is not to be presumed upon. @1–2
Christ died. @3, 5, 8, 10
Christ was buried. @4
Christ was resurrected by the glory of the Father. @4, 5, 9
Christ was crucified. @6
Christ lives; He lives to God. @8, 10
Christ will not die again; death does not rule over Him. @9
God wants us to offer ourselves to Him. @13

BE

I have died to sin. @2, 8
I have been baptized into His death. @3
I have been buried with Him by baptism. @3
I have been resurrected to walk in a new way of life. @4
I am joined with Christ in His death and resurrection. @5
My old self was crucified with Him. @6
Sin's dominion is abolished. @6
I am no longer enslaved to sin. @6
I am freed from sin's claims. @7
I died with Christ and now live with Christ. @8
I am dead to sin, but alive to God in Christ Jesus. @11, 13
I have weapons for righteousness. @13
I am not under law. @14
I am under grace. @14

DO

Do not continue in sin that grace may multiply. @1–2

Die to sin; don't live in it. @2

Be baptized into Christ's death, burial, and resurrection. @3–4

Walk in a new way of life. @4

Be joined with Him. @5

Be freed from sin and its claims. @6–7

Live with Him. @8

Consider myself dead to sin, but alive to God in Christ Jesus. @11

Do not let sin reign in your body. @12, 14

Do not obey its desires. @12

Do not offer any parts of your body as weapons of unrighteousness. @13

Offer all the parts of myself to God as weapons of righteousness. @13

CONNECTING THE DOTS

Jesus, when You were crucified, died, buried, and resurrected, I went through that same process because I am in You. Now, I also am dead to sin and alive in You. Sin has no claim on me unless I submit myself to it. I want to offer myself to You, not to sin. I want to be used as a weapon of righteousness, not unrighteousness. Lord, help me to see that not only has Your grace wiped away my sins, but Your death, burial, and resurrection have also abolished my old sinful being. I am a new being. Help me walk in a new way of life with You reigning in me and me joined in You. May I *know* Your life in me, *be* alive in You, and *do* life through You.

The perfect companion for your Know Be Do personal study or small group.

Enhance your study of Know Be Do with the 13-session
Know Be Do Bible Study Resource booklet.

Perfect for small groups or your own in-depth personal study, this Bible Study Resource guides you through the *Know Be Do* book with 13 sessions filled with insightful questions for discussion and discovery as you Read, Respond, and Reflect. It's an interactive and inspiring complement to *Know Be Do* that really brings its truths to life—yours.

Available in print and for download at
LarryAlanThompson.com